What the Experts Are
Look Who's Ta

"Laura's book is wonderful. It should be included with the owner's manual as each child is born."
—Edward Chapman, CCC-SLP, http://edchapman.tripod.com/ParentLinks.html

"This book provides comprehensive information and entertaining, easy-to-use activities to enhance early communication and language development with young children from birth through the elementary years. Laura's suggestions are easily applied to gifted children, children adopted from other countries, as well as children with special needs. It's a must-have resource for all parents, teachers, and caregivers!"
—Debbie Lesser, CI & CT, Little Signers, Inc.

"*Look Who's Talking!* is filled with great advice for any parents adapting to their first newborn. This book is a must-read."
—Frank E. Fogg, Frank Fogg Reviews, www.fogg.cc

"A user-friendly guide describing normal language development in children. This book is a tremendous reference manual for new parents and healthcare providers alike."
—Sarah Berry, MD

"*Look Who's Talking!* provides parents with a practical way to enhance their children's language abilities. She addresses many normal development milestones as well as special needs situations including daycare, chronic ear infections, bilingual households, and many more. It's a great reference for any parent wanting to improve communications with his or her child."
—Lisa Young, MD

"*Look Who's Talking!* is a comprehensive, well-researched, but readable resource for parents. I will be recommending it to the parents with whom I work."
—Diane Bahr, speech-language pathologist and author of *Oral-Motor Assessment and Treatment: Ages and Stages*

"Thank you, Laura, for 'speaking up' so eloquently on the art of language."
—Rita Brenke, Director of Education Clearinghouse & Education Explorations

Look Who's Talking!

How to Enhance Your Child's Language Development, Starting at Birth

by

Laura Dyer, MCD, CCC-SLP
Certified Speech-Language Pathologist

Meadowbrook Press
Distributed by Simon & Schuster
New York

Library of Congress Cataloging-in-Publication Data

Dyer. Laura.
 Look who's talking! : how to enhance your child's language devel[o]pment, starting at birth / Laura Dyer.
  p. cm.
 Includes bibliographical references and index.
 ISBN 0-88166-465-0 (Meadowbrook), 0-684-02069-6 (Simon & Schuster)
  1. Language acquisition--Parent participation. I. Title.

P118.5.D94 2003
401'.93--dc21

2003046426

Editorial Director: Christine Zuchora-Walske
Editors: Megan McGinnis and Joseph Gredler
Proofreader: Angela Wiechmann
Production Manager: Paul Woods
Graphic Design Manager: Tamara Peterson
Illustrations: Susan Spellman
Cover Photograph: Thomas Schweizer/Corbis

© 2004 by Laura Dyer

All rights reserved. No part of this book may be reproduced or transmitted in any form or by any means, electronic or mechanical, including photocopying, recording, or using any information storage and retrieval system, without written permission from the publisher, except in the case of brief quotations embodied in critical articles and reviews.

Published by Meadowbrook Press, 5451 Smetana Drive, Minnetonka, Minnesota 55343

www.meadowbrookpress.com

BOOK TRADE DISTRIBUTION by Simon and Schuster, a division of Simon and Schuster, Inc., 1230 Avenue of the Americas, New York, NY 10020

09 08 07 06 05 04   10 9 8 7 6 5 4 3 2 1

Printed in the United States of America

Dedication

To Mark, Brent, and Phillip—who have taught me the most about having speech full of grace and seasoned with salt.

Contents

Acknowledgments vi
Introduction 1

Chapter 1: General Ways to Enhance Language Development 5
    The Basics 5
    How to Be a Good Language Model 6
    Child-Directed Speech 10
    How Do Babies Communicate before Using Words? 13
    Techniques to Help Your Baby Want to Communicate 21
    Good Verbal Techniques to Help Your Child's Language Development ...24
    When Are Speech Sounds Learned? 26

Chapter 2: Significant Influences on Language Development 31
    Gender 31
    Birth Order 32
    Multiple Births 33
    Parents 34
    Childcare 36
    TV 41
    Computers 44

Chapter 3: Common Concerns about Language Development 47
    Ear Infections 47
    Hearing Impairment 49
    Auditory Processing Problems 52
    Pacifiers 54
    Sippy Cups 55
    Oral Motor Development 56
    Tongue-Tie 58
    Common Speech Problems 60
    Why Children Experience Language Delays 67
    Developmental Delays 71
    Seeking Professional Help 72

Chapter 4: Language Development Facts and Warning Signs 75
    Birth to Age 2 Months 76
    Age 3 to 4 Months 77
    Age 5 to 6 Months 78
    Age 7 to 8 Months 79
    Age 9 to 10 Months 80
    Age 11 to 12 Months 81
    Age 13 to 14 Months 83
    Age 15 to 18 Months 84
    Age 19 to 24 Months 86
    Age Two to Three Years 88
    Age Three to Four Years 90
    Age Four to Five Years 92
    Age Five to Six Years 93
    Age Six to Seven Years 95
    One Last Thought on Normal Language Development 97

Chapter 5: Enhancing Your Child's Language Skills at Each Stage 99
    Birth to Age 2 Months 99
    Age 3 to 4 Months 101
    Age 5 to 6 Months 103
    Age 7 to 8 Months 105

Age 9 to 10 Months 106
Age 11 to 12 Months 110
Age 13 to 14 Months 112
Age 15 to 18 Months 114
Age 19 to 24 Months 116
Age Two to Three Years 118
Age Three to Four Years 120
Age Four to Five Years 123
Age Five to Six Years 126
Age Six to Seven Years 128

Chapter 6: Nurturing Pre-literacy Skills 131
Beyond the ABCs 131
The Parent's Role 131
Developing Pre-literacy Skills 133
Building Overall Sound Awareness (Phonological Awareness)................141
When Is My Child Ready to Read? 143
Tips for Successful Early Reading Attempts 146
An Overview of Whole Language Methods versus Phonics...................147
Literacy Performance Levels 148
What to Do If You Suspect Your Child Has a Reading Problem..............152
A Few Words on Writing and Spelling Skills 153
One Last Word on Language and Literacy 155

Chapter 7: Gestural Communication (Sign Language) 157
Why Sign with My Child Who Hears Perfectly Well? 157
Will Sign Language Delay Spoken Language? 158
Where Do You Start? 160
Steps for Successful Signing 161
Go with the Flow...164
Transition to Verbal Communication 165
One Last Word on Signing 167

Chapter 8: Bilingualism and Second-Language Learning 169
Why Should My Child Learn a Second Language?................................169
How Do Children Become Bilingual? 171
Introducing a Second Language 174
Providing Rich Bilingual Experiences 175
Trilingualism 178
When Your Child Is Adopted Internationally...180
ESL and Bilingual Education 191
How Varying Cultures Affect Language...195
Bilingual Testing and Intervention for Speech and Language Delays 196
One Last Word on Bilingualism and Second-Language Learning....................197

**Chapter 9: Using Musical Activities and Imaginary Play to Enhance
Language Skills..199**
What's the Magic behind Music and Learning? 199
Music, Babies, and Development...200
Singing, Music Play, and Musical Instruments for Toddlers and Preschoolers 203
Music's Role in Reading Readiness..205
The Importance of Imaginary Play 207
One Last Word on Musical Activities and Imaginary Play 210

Afterword 211
Appendix A: *Little Language* **Song Lyrics** 213
Appendix B: Organizations and Associations for Additional Information....228
Appendix C: Recommended Materials, Books, and On-line Resources....231
Notes...235
Index..257

Acknowledgments

Special thanks to Bruce Lansky, Joseph Gredler, Megan McGinnis, Christine Zuchora-Walske, Susan Spellman, Tom Steinmann, Tonya Clarkson, Joseph Garcia, Jean Feldman, William Haynes, Rita Brenke, Patricia Shuster, Lisa Hoover, Rachel Sumner, Edward Chapman, Leatha Ogden, Peggy Daniels, Candy Carlile, Jill Chafitz, Ashley Driggs, Ann Smit, Diane Bahr, Ying-Chiao Tsao, Debbie Lesser, Lora Heller, Adele Marshall, Rebecca Lovell, Irene Helen Zundel, Frank Fogg, Laura Dwight, Tina Garrett, Jennifer Gilliam, Marsha Camp, Monique Trotter, Liya Lev Oertel, Katherine Hankin, Sarah Grissom, Wendy Tate, Barbara VanHooser, Sara Chandler, Carolyn Chandler, Lisa Young, David Dyer, Angie Dyer, Jay Berry, Sarah Berry, Mark Dyer, and all the researchers who have dedicated their lives to furthering our knowledge in these areas.

Introduction

If you're a new parent, congratulations! You'll soon be exploring your child's incredible potential to communicate. Do you know that your child communicates with you from day one? Long before she utters her first word, she soaks up information and learns to filter what she sees and hears. She finds many ways to communicate her needs to you.

While working with researchers at Florida State University, I studied the early detection of communication problems in infants. I helped record babies' communicative acts to better define what actions were typical for different ages. This research taught me a lot about how babies communicate with gestures, eye contact, and vocalizations. Although learning to communicate happens naturally, you can make a real difference in *how* your baby learns to communicate.

If your child has already begun to talk, you may wonder whether she's developing language correctly and at a normal rate. While working as a speech-language pathologist for nine years, I provided information and advice to parents of children with speech and language problems. After my husband and I started our family, a number of parents in my community asked me questions about speech and language development. Many wondered if their children were on track: "Is my child supposed to leave the ends off her words?" "Why can't she say the *r* sound?" These concerns relate to typical development, and by knowing what to expect with normal language development, parents will know what problems they can solve and when they should refer to a professional for help.

I wrote *Look Who's Talking!* because I believe parents want and need a reliable, comprehensive resource about typical speech and language development. I encourage parents to start thinking about these issues long before their children utter first words or show signs of a problem. I want to help reduce the anxiety some parents may feel about their children's speech and language development, and I want to help them be the best language role models they can. I've used the latest research to provide you with the most comprehensive, up-to-date information available. Chapter 1 provides essential information about language acquisition and the ways parents can facilitate their children's language development. Chapter 2 discusses the outside influences that affect a child's language development. Chapter 3 covers common concerns and questions that parents raise during their children's formative years. Chapter 4 explains the various stages of development and shows what a typical child's skills are at each stage. Chapter 5 suggests ways to enhance your child's speech and language skills, from birth to age seven, by stimulating all areas of communication.

Chapters 6 through 8 provide key information on literacy, signing, bilingualism, second-language learning, and language issues pertaining to international adoptions. Because I believe musical activities teach and reinforce some language skills easily, Chapter 9 explains how to use music with infants, toddlers, and preschoolers to promote language development. In Appendix A, you'll find song lyrics my husband and I wrote that incorporate specific speech and language goals into fun musical activities.

While this book provides ways that you can interact with your child to create a rich communicative environment, please remember that no matter how much time you spend reading, talking, and playing with your child, she may still have a speech and/or language delay. In the United States, 8 to 12 percent of preschoolers have some form of language delay, and 10 percent of children entering the first grade have moderate to severe speech disorders.[1] A child's difficulty acquiring speech is rarely a parent's fault, and nothing in this book is meant to suggest otherwise.

This book shouldn't take the place of professional evaluation and therapeutic services. If your child shows some of the warning signs listed in this book, seek professional help. You may be surprised to discover a number of early intervention services in your community. After you've developed a treatment plan with a certified and licensed professional, you may find that some of the information in this book augments the services your child is receiving.

As a professional, I hope this book will be a resource that you'll use continuously throughout your child's early years. And as a parent, my wish is for you to know the joy of every precious moment you've been given with your child.

Laura Dyer, **MCD, CCC-SLP**

P.S. To avoid any perception of gender bias, the use of masculine and feminine pronouns alternates with each chapter.

Chapter 1

General Ways to Enhance Language Development

The Basics

Your child is born with an amazing ability to learn. Starting at birth and peaking at around age two, your child's brain forms millions of connections when stimulated by interactions with the outside world.[1] These experiences enhance his physical, cognitive, language, and social-emotional development and increase his ability to learn. Although children develop language innately, parents and caregivers who talk and play often with babies influence and enhance the children's language and cognitive development.

At first, your baby communicates by crying, and his cries are reflexive rather than intentional. He cries to tell you he's hungry, wet, gassy, or overstimulated. While crying is effective (because you respond to it), it's not efficient, because you often must guess *why* your baby is crying. As his communication skills develop and become more intentional, he uses eye contact, facial expressions, body language, gestures, vocalizations, and eventually speech—the most efficient way to communicate.

Speech and language are two skills measured separately and considered together to reflect a child's overall verbal ability. Speech consists of the sounds people make with their mouths to convey a message; it's a medium used for communication. It's measured by comparing the specific sounds and sound combinations a child uses with the norms for his age group. Speech also involves voice quality, pitch, rate, and intonation.

Language is a much broader concept than speech. It's a symbolic system used to represent a person's thoughts. It refers to the vocabulary, grammar, and social conditions that govern the way we communicate through mediums like speech, signing, and writing. Language gives meaning to all the speech sounds we make. To understand the difference between speech and language, consider this example: If you went to a country where you didn't know the language, you'd hear speech sounds, but they would mean nothing to you. Language can be broken down into two categories:

- *Expressive language*: formulating and conveying a message to another person using a specific medium like speech, signing, or writing
- *Receptive language*: understanding a message from another person

Verbal stimulation is important to a child's language acquisition, especially his vocabulary and grammar skills. For the first several years of life, there's a big gap between the number of words your child can understand and the number of words he can say. Children learn and understand language long before they can speak it. Research shows that a child's language competence is linked to the amount of stimulation he receives before he speaks his first words.[2] One study found that infants whose mothers spoke often to them knew 131 more words at age 20 months than babies whose mothers were less verbal with them.[3] These results show that it's never too early to be a good language model and begin talking and reading to your baby.

How to Be a Good Language Model

You are your child's first and most important language model. What you say to your child and how you interact with him affects his language development. To be a good language model, remember: *If you always anticipate your child's needs without letting him try to communicate first, you teach him that he doesn't need to use language to get what he wants.*

Imagine a three-year-old boy who's not yet talking. You might think his silence makes things difficult for him, but he actually functions quite well. He rarely has to ask for anything, because his parents make sure he has everything he needs. At noon, his mother puts sandwiches and chips on the table. At three o'clock, she turns on the TV because she knows his favorite show is coming on. His parents figure he's shy, and they're confident he'll talk someday. Sometimes his mother asks him to say a word, or she invites him to imitate her. He watches with fascination and amusement, but he doesn't respond.

It wasn't always this way. Early on, his mother tried to get him to say *milk* by telling him he couldn't have a drink unless he tried to say the word. He threw a temper tantrum, and she realized this strategy didn't encourage him to communicate. Over time, she tried other ways to help him talk, but nothing worked. His refusal to communicate discouraged her. One day she learned the local public school would be providing a preschool program for three- to five-year-olds with disabilities, including speech and language delays. She was elated that someone was finally going to do something about her little boy's problem.[*]

Language delays can occur despite one's best intentions. According to the American Speech-Language-Hearing Association, speech, language, and related disorders affect about fourteen million Americans. In 1999, about 8 to 12 percent of children ages three to five had some kind of language impairment or delay.[4] Many of these disorders involve the inability to say specific sounds.

It's important that parents and caregivers understand how language acquisition works because their involvement is crucial to enhancing normal development and identifying potential problems. One of the best ways to promote normal development is to provide an environment in which a child *needs to communicate* without being forced to do so. Here are some techniques you can use.[†]

- **Encourage and respond to your child's attempts to communicate.** Whenever possible, talk to your child about what's going on. For example, if you're doing laundry or filling the dishwasher with your child nearby, talk to him about what's happening. Answer his communicative

---

[*] Adapted from W. Haynes and others, *Communication Disorders in the Classroom: An Introduction for Professionals in School Settings*, 3rd ed. (Dubuque, IA: Kendall/Hunt Publishing, 1999), 81. Used with permission.
[†] Ibid., 99–101. Used with permission.

General Ways to Enhance Language Development

attempts (cooing, babbling, eye contact, and so on) with similar responses.

- **Follow your child's lead.** Instead of always talking to your child about things *you're* interested in, talk to him about things *he's* interested in at the moment. Take advantage of his already-focused attention.
- **Talk about objects that can be readily seen and events that are currently taking place.** Your child understands you better when you focus on what's in front of him. Avoid talking about things that are in another room, that have occurred in the past, or that will happen in the future.
- **Shorten your sentences.** Your sentence length should be only one or two steps ahead of your child's ability. If your child is preverbal, you should use one- to three-word sentences. If your child can say one or two words, you should use three- to five-word sentences.
- **Simplify your sentences.** Whenever possible, avoid connecting two thoughts together, and stay away from long strings of modifiers in the early stages of language development. For example, avoid sentences such as, "Let's get you dressed and ready to go to the park that has the pretty, round water fountain."
- **Repeat and restate.** Repeat your sentences a few times when talking to your child, and occasionally say the same thing a few different ways. For example, if you think your child wants a cookie, say, "Want a cookie? Want one? Does Johnny want a cookie? Want it?"
- **Exaggerate your intonation and stress important words.** Emphasize words you want your child to focus on. For example, if you're teaching your child about size, say, "This is a *big* ball."
- **Use simple, concrete vocabulary.** Avoid big words and abstract concepts. For example, use *car* instead of *Chevrolet*.
- **Use words with broad applications.** Choose words that can be used over and over for many objects and events. For example, *go* can be used to describe driving, walking, running, swinging, and so on.

- **Talk at eye level with your child.** Kneel or sit on the floor or across the table from your child to capture his attention. Seeing your facial expression and eyes helps him understand what you're saying.
- **Be enthusiastic.** Let your facial expression and tone of voice show your child that what you're doing is interesting and fun.
- **Involve your child in activities.** Encourage your child to participate in activities that are naturally conducive to communication. Play with toys together, read together, take walks around your home and neighborhood, have your child observe you doing chores, and so on. Language is best learned by *doing*.
- **Slow down and pause.** Reduce how fast you speak so your child can learn to differentiate the sounds and words. Also, exaggerate the natural pauses between phrases and clauses to highlight these structural units.
- **Create communicative opportunities.** Create situations so your child needs to communicate to get something he wants. One way is to let him make a choice. For example, instead of placing all the toys in the bathtub automatically at bath time, ask him if he wants to play with the duck or the boat. If he gestures without saying the word, repeat the word often while he's in the tub.
- **Avoid using baby talk.** Whenever possible, encourage your child to use adult forms of speech. Use Child-Directed Speech (see page 10) to emphasize correct speech and language forms. Avoid imitating and modeling your child's immature verbalizations. For example, if your toddler says, "More ju-ju?" you should say, "Sure, here's more juice," instead of, "Here's your ju-ju."
- **Don't dominate the "conversation."** Try to avoid overwhelming your child with too much verbal stimulation. Pauses are natural parts of conversation, and the silence gives your child the opportunity to respond to what you've said and to initiate utterances.
- **Avoid too many questions and commands.** Model good language skills, but *don't command them*. Avoid telling

your child what to say or asking him too many direct questions such as, "What's this?" Some children find direct questions intimidating and withdraw from them.
- **Demonstrate your expectations.** Show your child that you expect him to communicate. For example, after saying something to him, maintain eye contact and look at him expectantly. This attentive pause shows him that you expect a response.

Child-Directed Speech

People often change how they speak when talking to babies. You may recall the scene in the movie *Three Men and a Baby* in which Tom Selleck's character reads a sports magazine to a baby. He uses a higher-pitched voice, exaggerates his facial expressions, makes frequent eye contact, and holds the baby close. The words he uses aren't as important as the *way* he says them. Knowingly or not, he speaks this way for a good reason: Babies respond to the melody of speech long before they respond to the words.[5]

The formal term for this language style is Child-Directed Speech (CDS). It's also known as Parentese, and it exists in many cultures.[6] During your baby's first 18 months, CDS not only helps your baby's language development, but he actually prefers it![7] CDS speakers use a higher-pitched voice and vary their pitch more often than usual.[8] Talking melodiously holds a baby's attention and eye contact for longer time periods.

CDS speakers also use the baby's name frequently, and they often use rising intonation at the ends of their sentences.[9] For example, a parent might say, "Look who's *up*! Is Joshua *awake*? Joshua is such a sw-e-e-e-t *b-a-by*! Here is Joshua's *bear*! Bear says, 'Good morning, Joshua!'" Emphasis within sentences differs among cultures.[10] For example, CDS speakers in some cultures use falling intonation.

Other characteristics of CDS include slower rates of speech and simpler forms of language.[11] Simpler forms of words (like *doggy, kitty, sissy,* and *choo-choo*) are fine to repeat during the early stages of language development because they're easier for a child to say. A child should begin phasing out these forms by age two and a half. Parents should begin modeling the correct forms of words (*dog, cat, sister, train*) when their children are around age 18 months.

Notice that each of the previous examples contains correct speech sounds. That is, none of them contains a sound that's inappropriate for the word. If your baby shows you a duck, for example, it'd be appropriate for you to say, "Duck," or "There's your duck." On the other hand, if your baby shows you a duck and says, "Dudi," it'd be inappropriate for you to say, "There's your dudi."

Although these incorrect forms are cute to hear and fun to record in baby books, reinforcing them won't encourage your child to use correct forms of speech and language. I loved hearing my son sing "Baa Baa Black Sheep" before he acquired the *l* sound: "And one for the wittuh boy who wives down the wane." Such forms are normal in developing speech. A parent, however, should avoid reinforcing these forms by repeating them to the child. In my son's case, it would have been wrong of me to ask him if he wanted "a wittuh more juice in his cup." A parent should model the correct forms *without correcting or instructing the child.*

CDS speakers pay close attention to infants' vowel sounds, coos, and babbling, and they use CDS to encourage their children's production of speech sounds.[12] CDS speakers also tend to use short, grammatically simple sentences. They tend to lengthen the final syllable of a sentence as well as the pauses between clauses and sentences.[13] For example, a father might say, "Look at the doggie, Phiiilip! [pause] See the doggieee?" These pauses help the baby hear the beginnings and ends of clauses and sentences.[14] They also allow the speaker to look expectantly at the child, invite a response, and show how turns are taken during conversation.

Combining CDS with other types of stimulation might help your baby expand his vocabulary.[15] For example, touching an object while naming it or talking about an object that your baby is holding gives your child redundant information.[16] In this case, redundancy is good because it helps your baby learn. This technique is especially helpful for infants age 5 to 8 months, and it carries over to the ages when children begin to say their first words (around age 12 to 14 months). Redundant information, however, becomes less necessary as children learn to talk about objects without visual clues.[17]

Despite the benefits of CDS, some parents hesitate to use it, or they ask others not to use it with their children. I've heard parents express concern that their children won't develop good speech skills if they hear this type of "baby talk." CDS is *not* baby talk. Unlike baby talk, CDS doesn't reinforce the use of incorrect speech sounds. For example, if a young child points to a neighbor's pet and says, "See dok," a CDS speaker says, "Yes, I see the dog," while someone speaking baby talk says, "Yes, I see dok."

The only time it's okay to use baby talk is when a baby just begins to vocalize and his vocalizations most likely don't represent specific words. Repeating these earliest vocalizations reinforces your baby's attempts at communication and encourages him to continue. For example, while a parent plays with her 7-month-old baby, you might hear the following exchange:

    Baby: "Oooooo."
    Parent: "Ooooo. Look at the *ball!*"
    Baby: "Ahheee."
    Parent: "Ahheee. Here it comes!"
    Baby: "Uh, uh, uh."
    Parent: Uh, uh, uh. Oh, you want it back?"
    Baby: "Ahheee!"
    Parent: "Ahheee! This is fun!"

Many parents refer to these early interactions as their first "conversations" (or proto-conversations) with their children.

In short, CDS encourages your child to listen and begin to learn the way sounds are formed. It teaches babies about pitch, stress, intonation, rhythm, loudness, pauses, and turn taking—the features that make language come alive.[18] It also captures your child's attention and encourages him to respond to you, if with only a smile.

How Do Babies Communicate before Using Words?

During the first 8 months, babies use various ways to communicate, including crying, eye gaze, facial expressions, and body movements. Until babies reach age 9 months, they can't communicate with the *intention* of reaching a specific goal. Adult interaction, however, can enhance a baby's awareness of how his behavior affects others. When parents interpret and respond to their babies' communicative attempts during the first 8 months, they help their babies develop intentional communication.[19]

The Communicative Act

When a typically developing child begins to communicate intentionally, he continues to use methods already familiar to him, but now he uses them purposefully to control his environment.[20]

- *Eye gaze*: looking at you and/or an object. Starting at around age 9 months, a baby can follow an adult's eye gaze and pick out an object as long as it's in his visual field. Starting at around age 12 months, a baby can use eye gaze to draw someone's attention to an interesting object.
- *Gestures*: picking up an object, showing it to you, reaching for it, holding it tightly for you to see, pointing at it, and so on
- *Vocalizations*: attempting to use his voice, cooing[21]

Eye gaze    *Gestures*    *Vocalizations*

At this stage, children's communicative attempts can be placed into three categories:

1. *Behavior regulation*: attempts to satisfy basic needs and wants. For example, a preverbal child "asks" for food or a toy by reaching for it and looking at his caregiver. Or he

indicates that he wants to be held by his mother by reaching out to her or by crying if someone else picks him up.
2. *Social interaction*: attempts to gain an adult's attention. For example, while sitting in his highchair, a baby may take a bite of food, touch his mouth, look at his father, and grin. He uses gestures and eye contact to try to get his father's attention.
3. *Joint attention*: attempts to show an adult objects or events and to persuade the person to comment on them. For example, while a child's mother reads to him from a picture book, he might point to something on the page, look at her, and say, "Uh-uh!" He wants her to name the item.[22]

Within these three broad categories, children use various communicative acts for different purposes. Examples of behavior regulation include requesting or protesting food or objects. A child knows that if he looks at you and throws his bowl of cereal, you probably won't serve him another bowl. Examples of social interaction include greetings, showing off, "calling" for someone, or babbling about favorite items. Examples of joint attention include directing someone's attention to objects, to pictures in a book, to interesting things noticed in the room, or to the need for help in situations that can't be handled alone.

For years researchers have been studying the ways in which parents interact linguistically with their children, and studies show that a facilitative style benefits language development more than a directive style. Parents who use a facilitative style follow their children's lead and give them many chances to try to communicate. Parents who use a directive style choose the objects of play and the subjects to talk about, and they overanticipate their children's needs.[23]

To initiate a communicative act, join your child on the floor as he plays with his toys. Choose a musical wind-up toy or some other toy that requires your help to function and that runs down on its own. Wind it up and let it play. When it stops, wait for a moment and see what happens. If the toy interests your child, he may make eye contact with you, he may gesture toward the toy as if to say, "Again," or he may coo. If he does one of these acts, great! Reward him by winding up the toy. Make sure to say the words he'll eventually use, like "More?" or "Again?" If he can combine two of the three communicative acts, that's even better. For example, if he can point to the toy and coo at it, directing the act to you, he's communicating nonverbally.[24]

Keep an eye out for other opportunities for similar communicative acts. As your baby develops, he can communicate increasingly complex messages. For example, he might request a rattle at age 9 or 10 months, but can't comment on a toy or event until age 13 months.[25] Play time is the best time to encourage communication, because you're both having fun and looking at the same objects. In addition to musical wind-up toys, try squeak toys, bubbles, or any toy or book that requires your help to make it perform. When your child gets a little older and can bring you his empty cup for refills, for example, wait for him to make a communicative act before responding. Always use the words to describe what he wants, but keep it simple: "Oh! More juice?" These early interactions reinforce the social part of communication.

As your child grows, you can modify this strategy to help him say the words you know he understands. For example, if you've heard him use *mo* for *more*, wait for him to say it before filling his cup with milk. When he says *mo*, make sure to model the appropriate expansion. "More milk?" Praise him for using words, and reward him by filling his cup. As your child acquires more words, you can also use this strategy to lengthen his utterances. A frequent request around my house is "I wan' more." "More what?" I ask. "More juice." My son smiles when he says this, proud that he can say the words.

Here's the bottom line: Start encouraging communication before your child can say his first words. Create situations in which he can communicate with you using eye gaze, gestures, and vocalizations, and model the words he'll eventually use on his own. Research shows that the rate at which babies communicate intentionally, or how often and how effectively they use communicative acts, predicts how they'll use expressive and receptive language skills one year later.[26] Preverbal communication skills seem to be a precursor to preschool

General Ways to Enhance Language Development

language skills, which seem to be a precursor to later reading skills. It appears likely preverbal communication skills are the earliest indicator of reading achievement, and new research is working hard to prove this theory.[27]

Learning to Recognize Your Baby's Gestures

In the early stages of development, most children can use gestures like reaching, showing, and giving before they can use words. Other gestures (pointing, conventional, and symbolic) come later, about the same time as your child's first words. Your baby probably can't fully understand the gestures he makes at first. Over time, he not only understands the gestures, but also learns to use them intentionally.

There are two types of gestures: deictic gestures (pronounced DIKE-tic) and representational gestures. A baby uses deictic gestures to show someone the focus of his attention. There are four types of deictic gestures:

1. *Showing*: holding up an object for someone else to see
2. *Reaching*: extending an arm toward a desired object, while sometimes opening and closing fingers
3. *Giving*: transferring an object to another person
4. *Pointing*: extending an index finger toward an object of interest[28]

Showing   *Reaching*   *Giving*   *Pointing*

Babies use showing, reaching, and giving gestures the earliest, around age 8 to 14 months. Babies generally point around age 12 to 14 months.[29] When your baby first starts using gestures, he might simply fuss and reach for a desired object. As he figures out how to involve you in the process, he refines his use of gestures, often coupling them with vocalizations and eye gaze. Instead of crying when something is hard to reach, he eventually uses a gesture to show you he's interested in an object.[30] My son, for example, used to cry when he couldn't fit the plastic shapes into the matching holes of his toy. Eventually he learned to look at me and vocalize a frustrated, "Doe, doe." I responded with an empathetic look and said, "It's hard to make it go down, isn't it? Can I help you?"

Representational gestures usually emerge around the same time as the first words (age 12 to 14 months). In addition to drawing another person's attention toward an object, person, or event, representational gestures convey some additional meaning about the item. Babies imitate representational gestures at first, but eventually use them intentionally to communicate. There are two types of representational gestures:

1. *Conventional*: used as social greetings or markers. Examples include waving hello or good-bye, blowing kisses, nodding your head yes or shaking it no, and so on.

    Conventional

2. *Symbolic*: used to convey some meaning, usually by representing a characteristic of the object or event. For example, a baby may move his hand in a flying motion to signify a bee.[31] Sign language is an extension of symbolic gestures that parents teach their babies during the preverbal stage. (See Chapter 7.)

    Symbolic

Babies become more adept at using gestures just a few months after beginning to use them. They usually progress from using a gesture in only one situation to using it in various situations to convey different meanings. For example, your baby might initially imitate a buzzing bee only when being read to about bees. Later he might use the gesture to tell you there's a bee outside or to ask you if there's a bee in the house when he hears Grandpa's snoring. This progression occurs as your baby learns that symbols represent objects—an important precursor to the first-word stage.[32] It's important that parents and caregivers recognize and respond to gestures, and realize gestures convey meaning preverbally the same way words do verbally.

Using Natural Situations to Help Your Baby Communicate

Each day you and your child enjoy routines while eating, bathing, playing, going to bed, and so on. These routines help your child know what to expect, and they reinforce skills recently learned. Once your child learns a particular routine, he concentrates less on the action and devotes greater attention to what you're saying during the event.[33] An unexpected interruption in a routine can capture your child's attention and become an excellent opportunity to encourage communication.

My younger son, for example, loved to be wrapped up in his "train" towel after bath time. We established a routine of wrapping him up, holding him in front of the mirror, and singing a Thomas the Tank Engine song together. If the train towel was in the laundry or if I forgot to sing the song, he'd do something to let me know things weren't right. When he was two, he'd look at me and say, "Mommy seen?" When he was three, he'd say, "I wanna sing Thomas."

This kind of responsive environment helps the timing and frequency of a child's early communicative acts, which predict later language development.[34] Other predictors include how effectively babies communicate their needs (especially with gestures and sounds), how babies play with objects, and how well they seem to understand words and facial expressions.[35]

A typically developing child naturally finds ways to communicate preverbally. A child who doesn't try to communicate preverbally, however, especially benefits from numerous social routines and an environment in which he's encouraged to ask for what he wants. This type of child also benefits when an adult follows the child's lead during play. Research shows that when an adult names objects and actions an infant is focused on, the child learns words rapidly.[36] When a child begins to use a communicative act as frequently as once per minute, he's close to saying his first words.

Ways to Stimulate Your Baby's Early Communicative Attempts

Gather some of the following items and keep them near your baby's toys. Avoid testing your child with the items. Instead, use them as props to encourage preverbal communication.[37]

- Play a musical toy that stops or winds down automatically. When it stops, wait for your child to "ask" you to turn it on again.
- Blow a kazoo or whistle, then set it down and wait for your child's response.
- If your child has a favorite social game (like Ride-a-Horse), go through the routine a couple of times, then stop and wait for your child's response.
- Play a jack-in-the-box a few times, then put it down and wait for your child's response.
- Play with a wind-up bath toy a few times while your child is in the bathtub, then let it float until your child "asks" you to wind it up again.
- If your child enjoys a routine of putting toys in the bathtub before getting in himself, put the toys somewhere out of reach so he'll be encouraged to "ask" for them.
- If your child enjoys bubbles in the bathtub, don't automatically put them in. Wait for him to show you he wants them.
- Use a toy containing several pieces, like a puzzle, stacking rings, nesting blocks, and so on. Hand three or four pieces to your child one by one, then give him an object that doesn't go with the toy. See how he reacts.
- When your child gets out of the bathtub, give him a choice between two towels. Let him indicate which one he wants.
- Have your child look at himself in a child-safe mirror. Then say, "Where's Baby? There he is!" Look in the mirror yourself and say, "Where's Mommy? There she is!" Go back and forth a few times, then place the mirror in your lap and wait for your child's response.

You'll discover hundreds of other opportunities to encourage your child to communicate. Remember, you don't have to hear a word to experience communication. If your child points to what he wants and looks at you expectantly, he's communicating! Make sure to respond to his request so he learns that communication gets results.

General Ways to Enhance Language Development

Ways to Stimulate Your Child's Later Communicative Attempts

As children develop their motor skills, they begin to fulfill their own needs, which may reduce their need to communicate. At age 18 months, both of my sons could open the refrigerator door and pull out the Hershey's Syrup and other favorites from the bottom shelves. At that point, I needed to encourage communication more creatively. Here are some ideas:

- When the batteries run out in your child's favorite toy, don't replace them until your child "asks" you to fix the toy.
- Put nonperishable snacks in a basket on a shelf where your child can see them but can't get at them without your help. Put your child's favorite books and toys out of reach for the same reason.
- Put your child's art supplies in a transparent container only you can open.
- Place colorful magnets up high on the refrigerator so your child must "ask" for help to reach them.
- Put on a funny hat or sunglasses. Your child will probably want to try them on. Wait until he "asks."
- Give your child two choices of music to play, like train songs or bear songs. Let him decide.

Withholding objects and giving choices in playful situations like these eventually leads your child to make regular, independent requests for objects and actions. You'll generally have more success withholding toys playfully. Withholding food, drinks, or other necessities could backfire. (Recall the example on page 7 in which the boy threw a tantrum when his mother withheld a drink of milk until he said the word *milk*.) If your child displays any frustration while you're withholding an item, model the desired request and give him the item.

Also avoid holding out for requests your child isn't developmentally ready to provide. If your child uses primarily gestures and vocalizations, and if you withhold a toy, be sure he understands the word that represents that toy. (If you've asked him to bring you the toy before, and he's picked it out of a pile of toys, he probably understands the word.) As your child begins to replace vocalizations with words, you can expect from him a request that's more verbal before you fulfill it.

Eventually your child must learn that there are times when he should fulfill his own requests. When he gets to this stage, don't expect him to ask you for objects he can obtain himself.[38] Doing so would seem unnatural, and language is best learned in natural situations. Of course, just because your 18-month-old can open the refrigerator door doesn't mean you want him refilling everybody's apple juice during dinner! You always need to balance promoting language development with promoting independence and other appropriate behavior.

Techniques to Help Your Baby Want to Communicate

I encourage parents and caregivers to think prevention when it comes to their children's speech and language development. Language delays may occur no matter what parents do, but it's important to encourage language development to prevent unnecessary, avoidable delays. Parents should also avoid being overzealous or demanding, expecting more than a child can produce, and not seeking professional help when needed. Know what skills a child typically should master at certain ages. (See Chapter 4.) Here are some more techniques to encourage your child to communicate:

- **Intersection of gaze** involves establishing eye contact with your baby. Get your child's attention by moving your head into your child's line of vision and waiting until you establish eye contact. You can phase out this technique as your child begins to regularly initiate and maintain eye contact (around age 12 to 14 months).
- **Modeling** reinforces and enhances your baby's communicative attempts with vocalizations or gestures.[39] You can use your voice to repeat sounds your baby uses (like *ba*). If your child is beginning to say words, it's important to model the correct speech sounds. (See page 11.) Verbal modeling naturally encourages your child to talk. You can

also use gestures to encourage your child's preverbal communication skills. For example, if a frog hops into the sandbox as you play with your child, you might model the pointing gesture by pointing to the frog. Or you might model the American Sign Language gesture *frog*.

- **Prompting** should be used only when your baby is highly motivated to communicate. Some signs that your baby wants to communicate include alertness, smiling, maintaining eye contact, and showing interest in playing with toys. For some babies these signs might appear right after the first morning feeding. Other babies may be more interested in communicating after a bath or an afternoon nap. If you're face to face with your baby and he seems eager to interact with you, then prompting can be helpful. There are two types of prompts:[40]

    - *Time-delay prompts* are nonverbal actions used to interrupt a routine. For example, if a parent and child are taking turns blowing bubbles, the parent might interrupt the routine by holding the bubble wand and looking expectantly at the child until he initiates a request to continue.

    - *Verbal prompts* are questions or requests used to elicit general or specific responses. For example, an open-ended question such as, "What are you doing?" is designed to elicit a general response. "Please look at me" is designed to elicit a specific response.

Always reinforce your child's attempts to communicate intentionally. For example, if your child points to the jar of bubble bath while vocalizing, you could smile and say, "You pointed at the bubbles!" or, "Would you like some bubbles in your bath?" As with all behaviors, positive reinforcement of communication encourages further attempts.

Another way to reinforce your child's communicative attempts is saying what your child is trying to say. This technique is called linguistic mapping. For example, if your child holds up a stuffed animal and vocalizes, you might say, "It's a bear!" Linguistic mapping can contribute significantly to vocabulary development.

As your child begins to consistently communicate with eye gaze, gestures, and vocalizations (usually around age 12 months), you should begin to phase out your preverbal techniques, like intersection of gaze, and start using techniques appropriate for the next level of language. (For example, you might stop repeating your child's vocalizations and start using single words.) Also, once your child learns to use gestures, you won't need to model them anymore. In addition to linguistic mapping, continue using other techniques—like providing an environment that encourages communication, following your child's lead, and establishing more social routines—as your child grows.[41]

Scaffolding describes the ways in which parents support their children's development by guiding them, assisting them, and preventing them from becoming frustrated. A parent scaffolds for a child by drawing him into a particular task and showing him what parts of it are manageable. The parent helps the child recognize the goal of the task, provides enough help so the child doesn't become frustrated, and signals when the goal is achieved.[42] For example, a father may show his two-year-old son how to hit a baseball off a tee. He shows the boy how to put the ball on the tee, how to hold the bat, and how to swing the bat to hit the ball. If the boy becomes frustrated because he doesn't have the motor skills to put the ball back on the tee, the father scaffolds the task by placing the ball on the tee so the boy can concentrate on what he does best—swinging the bat.

When referring to speech and language development, scaffolding involves supporting the child's language level and helping him strive for the next level. For a child who isn't yet using words, scaffolding involves using facial expressions, intonation, and gestures; imitating his behavior; interpreting his emotions or intention; modeling a more sophisticated behavior; expanding on his behavior; giving simple verbal directions; and asking a question or offering help.[43]

For a verbal child, scaffolding a task allows for the highest level of response without frustrating him. Caregivers can tailor their support strategies to meet their children's needs at a particular age. For example, when sharing a favorite book with your 12-month-old son, you read slowly and point to the pictures on the page. When your son is age 18 months, you read the sentences slowly and insert a pause before the last word of the sentence, allowing him to complete the sentence if he can and is interested. If he doesn't respond, you provide the word. For many parents, scaffolding comes naturally, and most typically developing children learn language with ease.

Good Verbal Techniques to Help Your Child's Language Development

Researchers developed the following verbal techniques to help children who have trouble learning language. Although typically developing children don't need these techniques to learn language, they nonetheless facilitate language development and may prevent problems. Remember: if you want to encourage your child to communicate more, you should follow his lead, respond accordingly, and provide a predictable environment.[44] Also remember to pause, look expectantly at him, and recognize his communicative intent.[45]

Researchers disagree on which of the following techniques is most effective, and they don't know whether one technique or a combination of them works best to enhance language development. You don't have to use all the techniques with your child. Even small changes, like increasing the amount of time you spend talking to your child, can affect your child's language skills dramatically.[46]

- **Self-talk** occurs when you describe to your child what you see, hear, do, think, or feel.[47] For example, as you are making lunch, you might say, "I'm making my lunch. I'm opening the can of soup, pouring it in the pan, and stirring it up. There—now we wait until it gets warm." You can also use self-talk when your child seems to be focusing on what you're doing. This type of modeling is great for the preverbal period.

- **Parallel talk** occurs when you describe what your child is doing.[48] For example, you might say, "Tommy is playing with his truck," or, "You're petting the cat." Parallel talk models the language that describes the child's immediate focus of attention without requesting a response from him. This is another good technique for the preverbal period.

- **Expansion** involves taking a child's incomplete utterance and developing it into a complete sentence.[49] Expansion should preserve the order of the child's words and the child's intended meaning. For example, if your child says, "Daddy eat," you might expand it by saying, "Daddy is eating his supper." Expansion adds meaning and depth to your child's utterance and helps him pay attention to a topic he has initiated. It's a great way to help your child learn grammatical forms like plurals, possessives, and verb tenses. Once you begin to use expansions, they'll become a natural way of communicating with your child.

- **Recasting** is similar to expansion in that it preserves the perceived meaning of the child's utterance while adding new information about sentence formation.[50] Unlike expansion, recasting changes the original order of the words. You might change a declarative sentence into a question, a question into an exclamation, and so on. For example, your child might say, "I wan' milk," and you might respond, "Do you want some milk?" Recasting also models a correct grammatical form after your child has said an incorrect one.

For example, imagine that your three-year-old asks you for more milk for his bowl of Cheerios. While you're pouring the milk, a couple of drops spill on the place mat. Your tidy child notices right away. "Mom, you spill the milk." You reply, "You're right. I spilled the milk." In this case, you've modeled the correct verb tense without drawing attention to the fact your child used an incorrect one, a common error in three-year-olds. Avoid giving your child the impression you're correcting his language. If a child feels his language is being corrected, especially in a way that seems intimidating, he'll be less likely to comment.

Research shows that recasting can help children focus on grammatical skills, but recasting is not absolutely necessary.[51] It simply helps a child focus on a new grammatical structure using the same words.[52] It's a nonintrusive, conversational technique you can use during daily activities like playing, reading, diaper changing, and so on.

- **Extension** maintains a topic of conversation without necessarily expanding the child's utterance into a complete sentence. Instead, extension adds information to develop a topic.[53] For example, if your child says, "Bird," you might extend that observation by saying, "A pretty red robin." Extensions are fun to use when you want to develop a topic your child has initiated. They also provide an excellent opportunity to increase your child's vocabulary.

- **Open-ended questions** are designed to elicit multiword responses. For example, while reading a book to your child, you might say, "Why is the boy petting the dog?" instead of "What is the boy petting?" Be careful not to give your child the impression you're quizzing him. Outgoing children usually enjoy the chance to pipe up with responses. Introverted children, on the other hand, could view this type of question as intimidating. If your child is easily intimidated, avoid open-ended questions or ones you already know the answer to. Studies show that "real" questions (those you *don't* know the answer to) elicit more frequent responses from children, suggesting children pay closer attention to these types of questions.[54]

One of the main reasons why these techniques work is that they develop the *child's* topic of interest, not the parent's. Another reason is that they don't require your child to produce corrected forms of language.[55] For these reasons, parents should use these techniques both to stimulate language in a child who's delayed and to augment development in a child who's acquiring language typically.[56]

When Are Speech Sounds Learned?

Many parents have questions about their children's inability to say certain sounds correctly. The following chart shows what researchers have learned about the typical pattern for acquiring speech sounds. This chart provides a *general* guide to when children acquire speech sounds, so use the information with caution. The age ranges are statistical averages based on an evaluation of many children. Each bar begins at

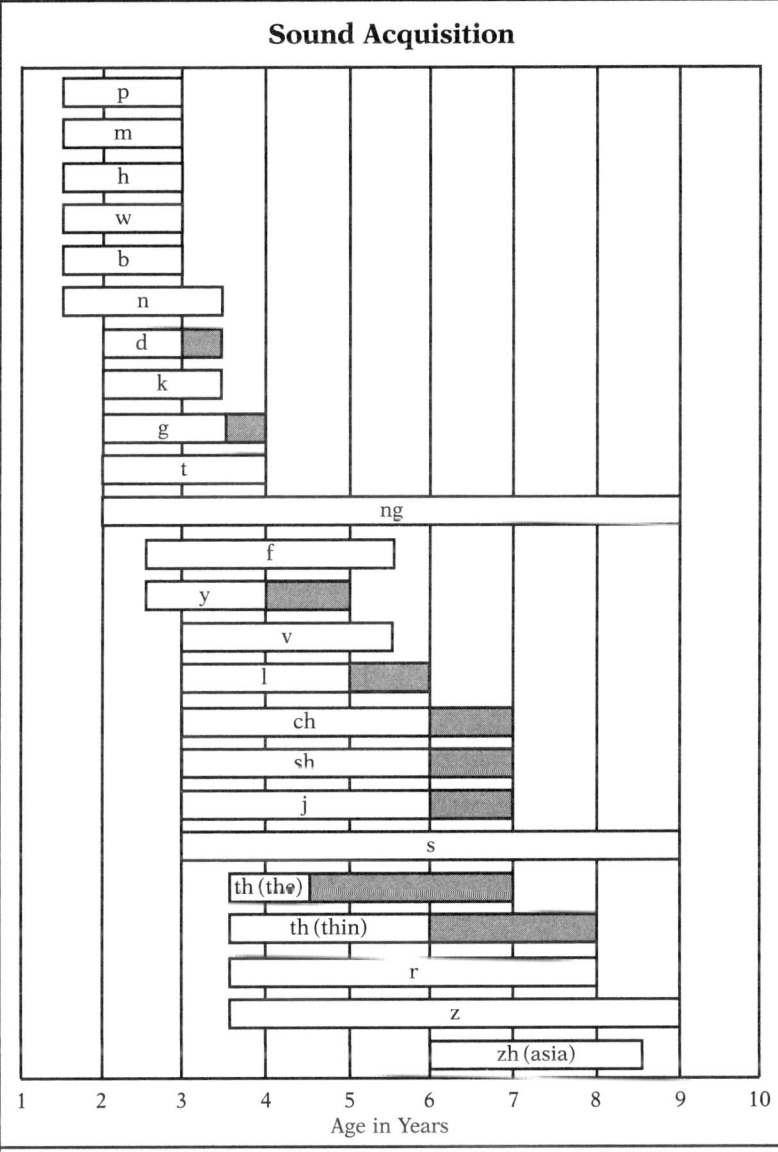

Sound Acquisition

Sound	Age Range
p	
m	
h	
w	
b	
n	
d	
k	
g	
t	
ng	
f	
y	
v	
l	
ch	
sh	
j	
s	
th (the)	
th (thin)	
r	
z	
zh (asia)	

Age in Years: 1–10

From A. Smit and others, "The Iowa Articulation Norms Project and Its Nebraska Replication," *Journal of Speech and Hearing Disorders* 55 (1990): 779–98. Used with permission. Data for children under age three and for the *zh* sound was supplemented by E. K. Sander, "When Are Speech Sounds Learned?" *Journal of Speech and Hearing Disorders* 37 (1972): 55–63. Used with permission.

Shaded areas indicate the time some boys needed to acquire certain sounds.

General Ways to Enhance Language Development

the age at which 50 percent of the children uttered the sound correctly, and ends at the age at which 90 percent of the children uttered the sound correctly. The bars don't necessarily reflect the performance of an individual child. Some children have very good pronunciation at age two, while others continue to struggle at age five. In either case, the children may still be within the range of normal.

Studies that look specifically at the production of speech sounds don't necessarily say anything about children who have phonological processing problems. Some children have trouble producing only a few isolated sounds, while others have a larger number of speech errors that show themselves in patterns. For example, a child might omit the beginning consonant of many of his words. In these cases, speech-language pathologists try to treat the pattern of the speech problem rather than the production of the individual sounds. (Phonological processes have their own age ranges for what's considered normal and are discussed further in Chapter 3.) Decisions about whether a child shows developmental problems are based on his entire sound production, not just on isolated sounds. Additional factors come into play as well, like his frustration level, environment, overall intelligibility, and emotional issues.

Consonant Clusters

Consonant clusters are made up of two or three consonant sounds that appear together in a word. Generally, consonant clusters are among the last sounds children acquire. There's a typical sequence of development (see the following chart), but individual development varies from child to child and is often marked by reversals and revisions until consonant clusters are acquired.[57] Your child may be able to pronounce a particular consonant cluster for a while, but may regress and make substitution errors until he can master the sound. Some research has suggested children develop consonant clusters at the ends of words earlier than at the beginnings.[58] Recent studies, however, show that two-year-olds can produce some consonant clusters at the beginnings of words.[59]

Consonant Cluster Acquisition

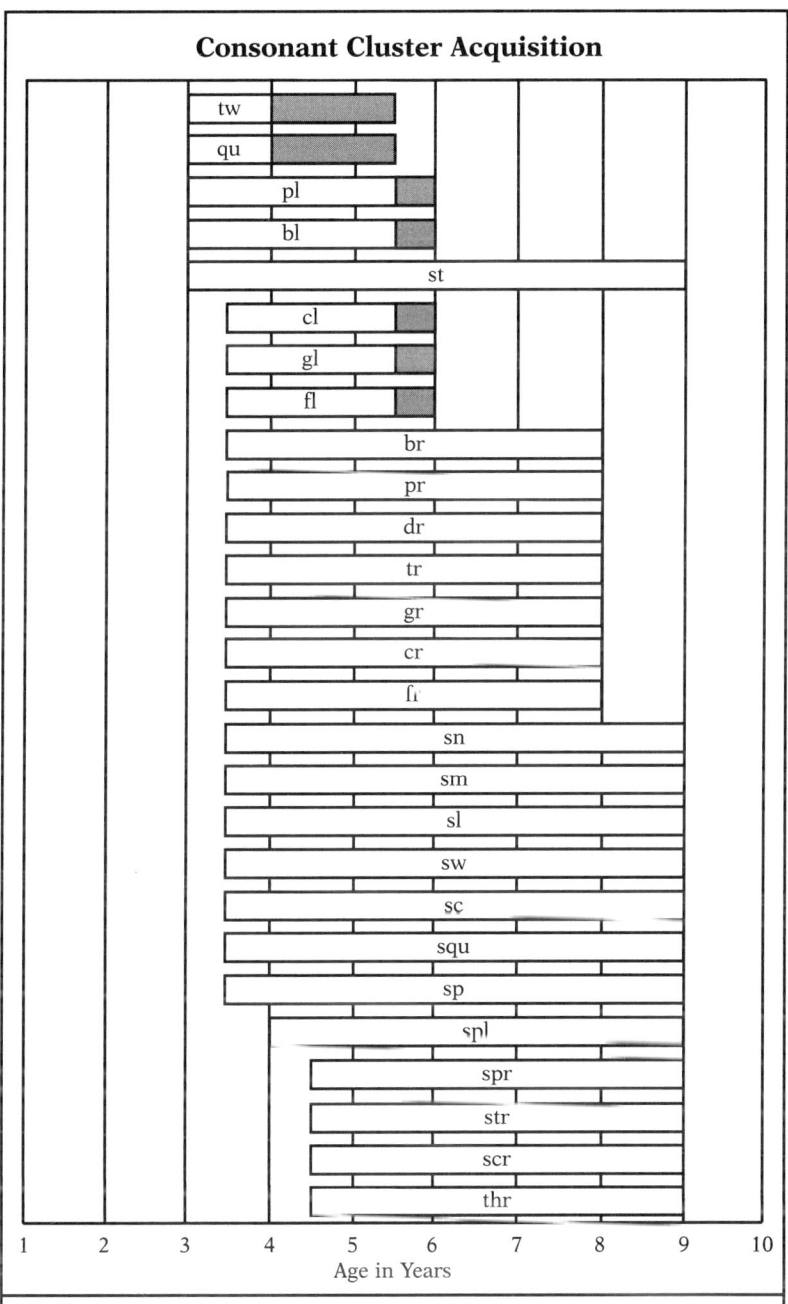

tw	
qu	
pl	
bl	
st	
cl	
gl	
fl	
br	
pr	
dr	
tr	
gr	
cr	
fr	
sn	
sm	
sl	
sw	
sc	
squ	
sp	
spl	
spr	
str	
scr	
thr	

Age in Years: 1–10

From A. Smit and others, "The Iowa Articulation Norms Project and Its Nebraska Replication," *Journal of Speech and Hearing Disorders* 55 (1990): 779–798. Used with permission.

Shaded areas indicate the time some boys needed to acquire certain consonant clusters.

General Ways to Enhance Language Development

Some two-year-olds produce clusters that match adult forms. Others produce clusters that don't exist in the language.[60] For example, some two-year-olds can produce the cluster *fw* at the beginnings of words, but there aren't any words in the English language that begin with *fw*. Other examples include *pw* and *bw* at the beginnings of words. Use these charts with caution and know that as children acquire speech sounds, they often go through stages during which they plateau and regress.[61]

Chapter 2

Significant Influences on Language Development

Gender

Research suggests that boys and girls acquire language differently. Most studies show that girls are slightly more advanced than boys in the early stages of speech and language development. Girls tend to articulate more clearly than boys, and they tend to use more nouns, naming games, role-playing, and abstract speech. Girls lead boys in every major language category—number of words produced, number of words understood, number of words used in combination, sentence complexity, and maximum sentence length—but they tend to develop only one to two months ahead of boys.[1] This small difference between genders, however, doesn't mean late language development in boys is never a cause for concern.[2] If you're worried your son may have a problem, talk to your doctor about screening tests.

I remember taking my two-year-old son to a hands-on museum with a friend and her daughter, who was about six weeks older than my son. When we passed the dinosaur collection, I was amazed that the girl could repeat *stegosaurus* perfectly after hearing her mother say it only once. Although my son's speech was understandable, he hadn't yet mastered consonant clusters. I had to remind myself that this girl's ability didn't mean my little boy wouldn't be articulate. Boys tend to place more emphasis on action words early on, and they catch up on other parts of speech later. Many have wonderful talents for making sound effects.

As boys and girls mature, the differences in *how* they use language become more apparent. Girls tend to enjoy talking to dolls and role-playing with them. Boys tend to enjoy activity-oriented games that have winners, losers, and elaborate rules. Boys sometimes use speech to tell stories and jokes and to interrupt and challenge each other. Girls, on the other hand, tend to engage in activities that don't have winners and losers. They tend to emphasize taking turns and sharing their thoughts and feelings.[3]

Research suggests that the ways parents interact with their children affect language development. Studies show that mothers tend to use longer and more complex sentences with their daughters than with their sons. Mothers also tend to talk to girls about abstract concepts like feelings and emotions.[4] (These tendencies don't appear in every family.) Parents should try to expose their children—both boys and girls—to various language situations and styles to make development well rounded.

Birth Order

Research suggests a minor but significant relationship between birth order and language skills. One large study found that language skills weakened a little as the number of a child's birth order increased.[5] In other words, a second-born child seems to have slightly weaker language skills than her first-born sibling had at the same age. This difference may be due to the changing amount of verbal interaction between parents and children as a family grows. Having more children vying for attention makes it difficult for parents to provide the same amount of verbal interaction that they gave their first-borns to their subsequent children. Nonetheless, parents should try to give each child verbal stimulation that's appropriate to the child's developmental level.

Younger siblings aren't always at a disadvantage when it comes to language acquisition. They tend to pick up pronoun usage more readily than first-borns.[6] They also have more language models to choose from (their older siblings, for example), and they can acquire a lot of language just by listening. Studies show that two-year-olds can learn nouns simply by overhearing them, and two-and-a-half-year-olds can learn verbs by overhearing them.[7]

I'll never forget the time I overheard my toddler sons telling each other knock-knock jokes. My 18-month-old said, "Naa, naa," and my three-and-a-half-year-old replied, "Who's there?" My younger son said, "Di do," and my older son said, "Di do who?" Then they both erupted into giggles. Sibling interactions like this not only make wonderful memories, but they also help younger children learn the rules of conversation, even before their pronunciation is fully developed. Generally speaking, the older the sibling, the better the model. If your children are close in age, make sure each—especially your youngest—gets plenty of modeling from you to consistently reinforce correct forms of speech and language.

Children only two years apart can be worlds apart when it comes to language comprehension. If you enjoy reading books with your children together, your younger one(s) may not have the attention span or language competence to understand the words. If a younger child seems distracted, try to share an age-appropriate story with her after the family story is finished.

Multiple Births

Twins and higher-order multiples often are born prematurely and have low birth weights and health problems. Researchers suggest that these children face various communication challenges. Specifically, these children tend to exhibit typical phonological processes longer than normal. (See pages 61–64.) For example, typically developing singletons leave off the last consonant of words (saying *bu* instead of *bus*) until they're age 39 months. Multiples might continue to leave off the last consonant until they're age four or older.

Multiples may also show unusual phonological processes not seen in typical development, like deleting many initial consonants, distorting vowels, and adding unnecessary consonants to a word (for example, saying "a-shway" for "away"). These unusual processes can make their speech seem unintelligible at times.[8] Twins are more likely to understand each other's mispronunciations than those of nonsiblings the same age.[9] Researchers once described this phenomenon as "twin

Significant Influences on Language Development

language," but they now think these unusual processes are immature or deviant language forms.[10] Instead of using special "words" only they can understand, multiples probably show extended or unusual phonological processes.

Exhibiting immature or deviant language forms doesn't mean multiples will have speech and language delays. To help these children, parents must enhance their children's language development and provide good modeling. (Depending on their age and language development, older siblings may be helpful models, too.) Most interactions between parents and multiples involve at least three people—parents interact with the group, not with the children individually. For this reason, parents should find ways to spend time with each multiple alone to help the children's individual development.

Lastly, research also shows that parents of multiples tend to use a more directive style of speech, not a facilitative style, when interacting with their children. Remember that a facilitative style helps language development much more than a directive style. (See page 14.)

Parents

During the first 8 months, babies begin to learn that their behavior affects their world. When parents respond to them, babies form an attachment because they know that their needs will be met. When babies feel secure, they tend to explore more, which may enhance language development.[11] Exploration naturally leads to preverbal communication as babies show their parents the objects they've found.

When your baby begins exploring, she has a very short attention span. She learns more from your comments about something she finds than about something you introduce to her. It's easier for your child to analyze and understand what you're saying about an object that both of you are focused on.[12] It doesn't matter *what* you're saying; instead, it's important that you're talking about what *your child* is focused on. You're helping her develop joint attention skills. (See page 14.)

Studies show that talking about a child's interests helps language development.[13] Focusing on the child's topic of interest is especially important around age 12 to 36 months, when a child typically acquires lots of new words. Research shows that redirecting a child's attention away from her topic of interest doesn't help improve her vocabulary.[14]

After your baby attempts to communicate with you, it's natural for you to respond. Modeling the words that convey the meaning of your baby's communicative act is called linguistic mapping.[15] Once your child talks more frequently (around age 16 to 22 months), you can expand her chosen topic by recasting her sentences or expanding them. (See pages 25–26.) When parents talk to their children, they expose them to lots of different words and expressions associated with many objects in their environment. The more a child hears different words in different situations, the more expansive her vocabulary will become, establishing a foundation for complex concepts and relationships she'll need to know and express later.[16]

After your child acquires enough words to say short sentences, it may seem as though she talks all day long. Try to respond whenever you can, giving her good eye contact to reinforce her attempts. Often it'll be tough to understand what she's saying. Look at her body language, facial expressions, and gestures for clues. If you still can't understand what she's saying, take her by the hand and ask her to show you what she means. If you can understand a word or two, repeat them to her so she knows some information is getting through to you.

Be honest with your child when you don't understand what she's saying. Don't say, "Uh-huh," "That's nice," or "Okay" when you don't know what she means. Pretending to understand your child won't fool her, and it sends her the message that you're not interested in what she's saying. Such a message could lead your child to make fewer communicative attempts. Let her know the words you do understand. Also, sign language can help both you and your child tremendously. (See Chapter 7.) The more you can reinforce your child's communicative attempts with appropriate responses, the more her language develops.

Parents may harm their children's language development by trying to speed it up. Overtly correcting or trying to modify a child's normally developing speech could backfire. Some researchers speculate such pressure can be especially harmful for children who tend to worry about making mistakes.[17] Parents can better serve their children by understanding and taking advantage of communicative opportunities. If there is a problem with language development, parents, caregivers, and health care providers must recognize when the normal progression of babbling, gestures, and eye contact is *not* taking place. The sooner a professional can diagnose a child with a communication problem, the more effective intervention will be.[18]

Childcare

Childcare environments can encourage or hinder a child's language and cognitive development. The quality of interaction between caregivers and children may be the most important factor to consider when deciding on childcare. For example, if your child interacts primarily with her peers without receiving modeling from a caregiver, her speech and language development may not be properly nurtured. Children can acquire good receptive skills by overhearing conversation between adults or by watching TV, but these types of stimulation aren't always appropriate or adequate in childcare settings. Parents should strive to find a childcare environment that's warm, loving, and that satisfies a child's physical, social-emotional, cognitive, and linguistic needs.[19]

Childcare Centers

Several decades of research shows that high-quality early-childhood programs help children's cognitive and social skills.[20] Children participating in high-quality childcare bettered their expressive and receptive language skills.[21] Long-term benefits include improved math skills, more focused attention, and fewer problem behaviors.[22] Children also gain pre-literacy skills (see Chapter 6), self-control, and a higher motivation for learning. High-quality childcare during the infant and toddler years is generally connected to higher overall cognitive skills. Economically disadvantaged children or those at risk for developmental problems are especially likely to benefit from the complex play and language models provided in childcare centers.[23]

The National Association for the Education of Young Children (NAEYC) has established an accreditation program that's raised the quality of early-childhood education in the United States. The NAEYC grants accreditation to childcare centers and other early-childhood programs that meet certain standards and demonstrate a commitment to ongoing evaluation and improvement. If your local childcare center meets all the criteria of accreditation, it's well on its way to helping your child's language development.

One of the NAEYC requirements is that lead teachers have a degree in early childhood education. To ensure that caregivers are well trained in child development and are aware of young children's needs, the NAEYC requires teachers and childcare providers to attend continuing education workshops to remain current in their field. Caregivers must be aware of each child's developmental level and adjust their speech models to accommodate each child's needs. They must also work closely with families to ensure the well-being of each child.

A well-trained caregiver can't meet every child's needs unless the ratio of children to caregivers is reasonable. If the ratio is too large, the quality of care may be compromised. The smaller the ratio, the more stimulation a child receives, which leads to better overall language development.

Recommended Staff-Child Ratios

AGE	MAXIMUM GROUP SIZE	RATIOS
Infants (0–12 months)	8	1:4
Toddlers (12–24 months)	12 10	1:4 1:5
Toddlers (24–30 months)	12	1:6
Toddlers (30–36 months)	14	1:7
Three-year olds	20	1:10
Four-year-olds	20	1:10
Five-year-olds	20	1:10
Kindergartners	24	1:12
Six- to eight-year-olds	30	1:15
Nine- to twelve-year-olds	30	1:15

Adapted from the *Accreditation Criteria & Procedures of the National Association for the Education of Young Children*, http://www.naevc.org/accreditation/naeyc_accred/info_general-components.asp#F (accessed November 7, 2003).

After confirming a childcare center is accredited, set up an informational interview with the director and talk to some of the teachers. Ask about the center's philosophy and how it's applied in the classroom. Find out what a typical day is like and how much attention is given to each child. Ask what the teachers do when they aren't involved in structured activities. Do they go around from station to station and talk to the children individually? Do they sit and play at eye level with the children? When touring the center, make sure to visit the other rooms in addition to the one your child would be in most of the day. To confirm the center's information, meet with parents who have children enrolled at the center.

Play should be at the heart of a childcare center's curriculum. Play gives children the opportunity to manipulate objects, learn about the world, interact socially, express and control their emotions, and develop symbolic capabilities (see page 17).[24] Teachers promote learning by creating a playful environment that's conducive to discovery and exploration.[25]

Make sure potential childcare centers provide opportunities for your child to play alone, quietly, and actively. It's important for children to play alone occasionally and learn how to entertain themselves. Playing alone allows children to set the pace, solve problems, make choices, and deal with the consequences of their decisions. Children also need quiet time to play with their fingers and toes, discover books, experiment with music, and explore language. And they need active play to develop large motor skills and get the wiggles out!

When children play together, work on projects in small groups, and talk with other children and adults, their development and learning is enhanced.[26] Penny Warner, child development expert and author of *Baby Play and Learn*, suggests that playing with others is important because it enables children to observe new ways to explore toys and interact socially.[27] Childcare centers should have areas set up to give children a chance to learn different skills in small groups. Examples include a storytelling area complete with puppets, felt boards, and characters; a reading/library area stocked with age-appropriate books; an arts-and-crafts area; a building area containing blocks and other building materials; a practical-life area containing housekeeping materials; and so on. Storytelling and pretend play allow children to play different roles and to think about future roles as well as present ones.[28] For older toddlers especially, pretend play can teach important lessons about interacting in everyday situations.

Because children need high-quality adult language interaction to expand and extend their utterances, interaction between caregivers and children in small groups is especially important. Small groups encourage children to initiate conversations, change topics, and respond to open-ended questions.[29] Small groups allow caregivers more opportunities to engage in conversations with children one on one. These early relationships children have with their caregivers best predict children's social skills.[30]

Besides structured, child-centered play, childcare centers should provide social events and times when groups come together to sing songs, dance, listen to music, and read books. Because pre-literacy is so important, written or printed language should appear in many activities. Children should be encouraged but not required to participate in stories that are read. They should be given opportunities to ask questions and make predictions about the story whenever it's appropriate for their age group. Whenever possible, conversations should be two-way instead of listening-only.[31] Some childcare programs send home fun art projects and other crafts that are great conversation starters for parents.[32]

Home-Based Childcare

Many parents choose home-based childcare instead of childcare centers. Not all states require licensing for home-based providers, but many that do provide ratings that parents can use to evaluate the providers according to the state's standards. The National Association for Family Child Care (NAFCC) regulates accreditation programs for home-based daycares by assessing six areas in its evaluations: relationships, environment, activities, developmental learning goals, safety and health, and professional and business practices. Don't be afraid to ask potential providers about licensing, accreditation, and education.

Home-based daycares typically involve smaller ratios of providers to children, which means more opportunities for

Significant Influences on Language Development

one-on-one interaction between children and adults. Children also benefit from a warm, natural setting that's similar to their home environment. Parents may also consider hiring a nanny, sitter, or au pair to provide in-home daycare. Advantages of this option are that the child remains in her own home, receives lots of one-on-one attention, and avoids exposure to other children's germs. Some parents go one step further and hire bilingual nannies to give their children the opportunity to acquire a second language.

How Does Childcare Affect a Child's Speech and Language Development?

Some parents worry that a daycare environment may harm their children's speech development, especially when other daycare children have speech problems like lisps or stuttering. Children constantly change their speech patterns to match patterns they hear.[33] Remember, though, that *you* are your child's first and most important model for speech and language. As long as your child steadily hears the correct forms from you, the influence of incorrect forms should be temporary. When given a choice between correct and incorrect speech models, a child is more likely to follow the correct model because that's the one she hears most often.[34]

Parents may also wonder how different dialects affect their child's speech development. Other people's speech patterns tend to influence our speech from time to time. For example, having grown up in the South, I found myself shortening my vowels during my first visit to New York City. When I didn't, I got lots of amused looks. Our feelings and perceptions about the listener affect, often unconsciously, our rate of speech, articulation, intonation, and so on. You might notice subtle differences in the way your child speaks after spending time with other children at daycare. These dialectal changes are usually temporary and may occur only when your child is around the daycare children.

If you have a language-delayed child who's home with you most of the time, your pediatrician may encourage you to place your child in a daycare program that allows her to interact with other children and adults, and communicate her needs to them. This interaction usually facilitates language development as long as the daycare provider doesn't overanticipate your child's needs. If your child has special language needs, convey these to your daycare provider. Your child may be able to receive speech services at daycare, if necessary. If your normal-hearing child is signing with you, your provider should learn the signs you're using and use them with your child to further reinforce her communicative attempts.

TV

The American Academy of Pediatrics (AAP) recommends that children two years and older watch less than two hours of TV per day, and children younger than two years shouldn't watch TV at all. Furthermore, the AAP recommends that parents remove TV sets from children's bedrooms and engage their children in more interactive activities, like talking, playing, singing, and reading.[35] Despite these recommendations, studies show that a large number of children start watching TV at an earlier age and they watch it more often. These early viewing patterns continue into childhood.

One study reported that children who watched more than two hours of TV per day at age two were more likely to watch more than two hours per day at age six.[36] According to 2001 Nielsen Media Research data, the average preschooler watches nearly three and a half hours of TV per day. School-age children watch an average of three hours per day.[37] These figures don't include time spent watching movies or playing video games. A 1999 study found that the average American child spent an average of six and a half hours per day watching various media.[38] This figure is almost a half a child's waking hours!

Active learning is better than passive learning. Children under age six learn best by discovery and hands-on experiences, not by watching TV. To increase a child's vocabulary and knowledge of sentence structure, having her listen to stories that are read by an adult or older child is better than having her watch TV. Talking with parents and other adults is one of the most effective ways a child can enhance her vocabulary and help her overall language development.[39]

A main problem with TV programs is that very few talk directly to children. Some educational programs use Child-Directed Speech (CDS) to stimulate language development, including *Mister Rogers' Neighborhood* and *Sesame Street*.[40] But the programs don't comment on the *child's* topic of interest.[41] For example, if your child is watching a show and sees a character crossing a river, she might not focus on this action even though the character is talking about what he's doing. Instead, your child might focus on why the bridge is broken, what another character is doing, or something else going on in the background.

When young children watch shows that don't use CDS, they simply observe others' conversation. They don't listen as intently to the subject matter because it's always explained by the actions on the screen. If they miss a sentence because of noise in the room, they can easily get back into the program by using its visual cues. They learn to rely more on these visual cues than on the key linguistic information.[42]

Studies have examined the relationship between TV viewing and the development of grammar skills. The results are mixed. Some studies found that the more TV a child watched, the lower her language score was. Other studies found that when a child watched *educational* TV programs, her use of sentences and exclamations in spontaneous speech was slightly improved. Overall, there seems to be little evidence children are learning better grammar skills by watching TV.[43]

Other studies have focused on the effect TV viewing has on vocabulary growth. One study found that children who watched *Barney & Friends* acquired more vocabulary, especially nouns, than nonwatchers.[44] Other studies' findings suggest that children can learn words and their meanings from TV programs, especially if there's a lot of discussion following the program. This suggestion may be important at two levels of development: (1) when children are learning lots of words for the first time (around age 12 to 36 months), and (2) when children are learning to extend, enhance, or restrict the meanings of words they've already heard (around age three to five years).[45]

Many young children actively participate as they watch TV. This participation usually occurs when an adult watches TV with them. When children have a viewing partner, they may occasionally call attention to objects on the screen. Some children ask questions or repeat what they've heard. Some preschoolers frequently laugh at appropriate moments during a show and repeat parts of the dialogue.[46] This kind of active TV viewing with an adult can help learning because it simulates the conditions of joint attention (see page 14).

Be wary of allowing your young child to watch movies and programs that feature baby talk. On one hand, letting your child watch a movie that features a little baby talk can be harmless, because she gets considerable modeling from you. On the other hand, with all the wonderful movies and programs available, why choose one that contains a poor language model? While baby talk may be necessary to reflect a character's personality, a toddler isn't old enough to understand such humor. Children around age five can better understand why a particular character talks like a baby. Similarly, movies and programs that humorously model stuttering or other speech problems may be misconstrued by an impressionable preschooler, who may not understand such speech is incorrect until she's older.

Children pay attention to whatever parents put in their environment. To be a good language model, be aware of what you point out and discuss as you watch TV with your child. If, for example, you encourage your child to pay attention to a character who displays good manners but who also refers to himself in the third person, your child may ignore the manners and instead start to refer to herself in the third person. Pronouns often confuse children, and exposure to incorrect pronoun usage could make it harder for your child to learn correct usage. The fact that a child normally chooses correct language forms (because she hears them most often) reminds parents of the importance of correct modeling.[47]

Young children don't always understand what they see on TV, which may make them fear the situations depicted.[48] As children get older, fears arising from fictional shows decrease while fears arising from nightly news programs increase.[49] Studies show that parents underestimate their children's exposure to "scary" media; children are often frightened by programs their parents wouldn't describe as scary.[50] Be aware of what and how much TV your child watches and know its possible effects on her. Talk to your child about what she sees on the screen and try to reassure her when she seems troubled by what she's viewed.

As a parent, I know limiting TV viewing can be hard, especially when you or your child is sick or when weather prohibits outdoor activity. But the more we allow our children to remain glued to the set, the more they'll become attached to it and dependent on us to find them another activity after they're done watching TV.[51] After many years of pleasant TV experiences, children might think of TV as an easy, attractive source of entertainment that's more satisfying than books.[52]

I believe parents should follow the AAP's advice and limit their children's TV viewing to occasional family programs watched together with an adult. Educational shows that use CDS are good choices because they promote vocabulary development and pre-literacy skills. Some TV programs can introduce your young child to characters like Winnie-the-Pooh and Big Bird, which gives her new make-believe friends to engage in conversation and imaginary play without needing the TV.

Even though TV might help your child with some parts of language development, there's *nothing* to suggest it could ever be as helpful as adult interaction and reading. One mother reported that only one month after turning off the TV, her child went from saying two-word utterances to singing full songs. After three months, the child was retelling stories, using nine words in a sentence, and engaging in lots of imaginary play.[53] Here's one way to sum up the relationship between TV and language development: "If you think of the environmental influences on language development as a four-course dinner, TV should appear as one of the options on the dessert cart."[54]

Computers

If you own a computer, your child is bound to be attracted to the screen and will want to play with the keyboard. According to the U.S. Department of Commerce, 90 percent of school-age kids can log on to computers at school or at home.[55]

Companies have even started marketing computer products for younger children, including children's keyboards that fit over regular keyboards so children can have their own buttons to push.

What's the right age to introduce your child to the computer? Although software developers recommend introducing babies and toddlers to computers, child development experts encourage parents to wait until children are age three, because computers don't match the learning styles of the very young.[56] Before age three, children don't have the sophisticated eye-hand coordination required to operate the mouse and keyboard with confidence and ease. They also lack the cognitive skills necessary to operate a program independently. For babies and toddlers, using a computer is mostly a passive experience because most of the thought and effort is supplied by someone else.[57]

One experience toddlers might enjoy with adult supervision is watching computer-animated storybooks. Studies have found that CD-ROM storybooks can help improve some parts of literacy, including verbal ability, comprehension, and motivation to read.[58] Such technology shouldn't replace traditional storybook reading, but you can use it to supplement the literary experience.[59] The same precautions that apply to TV also apply to computer-animated stories. Children may tend to rely more on the visual information than the language. The time you spend discussing the computer characters and the action will enhance language development.

Many preschools have computers to introduce young children to the technology. Developmentally appropriate computer programs can be a fun way to reinforce concepts like letter recognition, shape recognition, number recognition, basic math skills, new vocabulary, color concepts, and pre-literacy skills. School age children who use computers have shown improved motor skills, enhanced mathematical thinking, increased creativity, higher scores on tests of critical thinking and problem solving, and higher scores on standardized language assessments.[60]

Although some parents worry that computer use may hinder social skills, a rich social context can be built around the computer. Encourage your child to play on the computer with a sibling or friend without using headphones.[61] Children can also work together to comment on stories and figure out how to solve problems. Educational, age-appropriate software that allows children to create stories or outcomes can stimulate discussion and improve social skills.[62] In fact, studies show that children are nine times more likely to socialize at the computer than when working with puzzles together.[63]

As with other types of media, computer use can be abused. American children typically spend between one to three hours at a time on a computer. Children who spend more than three hours at a time in front of a monitor may suffer early vision problems caused by eyestrain; however, children who use computers for less than three hours at a time appear to suffer no related vision problems.[64] Parents should turn off the computer after forty minutes to an hour of use. Even though the patterns on the screen or the sounds from the speakers may attract babies and toddlers, remember that children need to explore a wide variety of items and activities.[65] They learn more by using all their senses in exploration than by using just a few while sitting in front of a colorful screen.

The National Association for the Education of Young Children (NAEYC) agrees that when used appropriately, technology can enhance children's cognitive and social abilities. But computers should be used to supplement, not replace, highly valued early-childhood activities and materials like arts and crafts, blocks, sand, water, books, writing materials, and dramatic play.[66]

Chapter 3

Common Concerns about Language Development

This chapter tackles the most common issues raised by parents about the development of their children's speech, language, and oral motor skills. The two most common concerns are ear infections and hearing loss. Other concerns include auditory processing problems, pacifier use, use of sippy cups, tongue-tie, and common speech problems like lisps and stuttering. I also discuss possible reasons for a language delay and ways that you can find professional help.

Ear Infections

About 80 percent of children age four and younger experience fluid in their ears.[1] When there's no infection, this condition is called otitis media with effusion (OME), and it can affect one or both ears. In 60 to 70 percent of cases, this condition clears up within thirty days of diagnosis, with or without antibiotics treatment.[2]

One reason why OME is one of the most common childhood illnesses is because of the shape and size of the Eustachian tube, the small canal that equalizes pressure between the middle and outer ear. In adults, the tube is longer, narrower, and more vertical than in children, and it's kept closed by the spring action of cartilage.[3] In young children, the tube is shorter, wider, and more horizontal, which makes it easier for fluid to build up. Congestion or swelling can easily block the end of the tube, which tends to remain open in infants. Children who develop fluid in the ear may show symptoms like irritability, pulling on the ear, or crying. Some children show no symptoms at all.

OME may not cause problems if it occurs for a short time and clears up on its own. If the fluid becomes infected by a bacteria or virus, an ear infection can develop. This condition, called acute otitis media, can be painful and may cause symptoms like fever (100°F to 104°F), yellow or white discharge from the ear, loss of balance, and hearing problems. If you suspect your child has an ear infection, visit your doctor, who may prescribe antibiotics if the infection is bacterial. An untreated ear infection can sometimes cause serious problems, especially in children age two and younger. Your doctor will monitor the fluid to make sure the infection is clearing up. Once the infection clears up, some fluid may remain in the middle ear for about three months. This condition is usually painless and disappears on its own.

Sometimes a child with fluid in his ears experiences a mild, temporary hearing loss, which may make him miss language or confuse the language he hears.[4] He may be less responsive when spoken to and may speak up less often. A parent, in turn, may not catch the cues necessary to establish the facilitative style that's best for language learning.[5] If your child experiences many ear infections with residual fluid during the first two years, watch for signs of hearing loss. Recurrent ear infections don't necessarily mean your child will have a language delay,[6] but be aware of the risk and talk to your doctor about options for dealing with the illness. Have your child's hearing tested if you have *any* doubt about his hearing ability. Your doctor may also order a test called tympanometry, which tests the condition and movement of the ear drum and helps detect middle ear disorders.

If ear infections and fluid buildup persist, your doctor may refer you to a specialist, who may recommend putting tubes in your child's ears. Pressure equalizing (PE) tubes are surgically inserted through one or both of a child's eardrums. The tubes remain in place for anywhere from a few months to over a year, and most eventually work themselves out.

Research shows that the recurrence of otitis media in children age two and younger is much higher for those who attend group daycare.[7] Parents with children in group daycare must watch for symptoms of otitis media and hearing loss. There's no way to completely eliminate your child's risk of ear infections, but here are some ways to help reduce it:

- Don't smoke while you're pregnant, and keep your child away from secondhand smoke. The toxic chemicals in the smoke can irritate the lining of the Eustachian tube, creating mucus that may collect behind the eardrum and become infected.[8]

- Consider breastfeeding your newborn as long as possible to protect against otitis media. In one study, infants who were never breastfed had about twice as many episodes of otitis media as infants who were exclusively breastfed for four or more months.[9] In addition to preventing ear infections, breastfeeding prevents many other health problems and is excellent for parent-child attachment, oral motor development, and cognitive development. If you're planning to bottle-feed, make sure you hold your baby's head so his ears are above mouth level. This position ensures that liquid won't go through the Eustachian tube and into the middle ear. Don't place a bottle in bed with him.

- Try not to expose your child to other sick children, if possible. Reducing exposure helps prevent bacterial and respiratory infections.

- Beginning at age 6 months, restrict your baby's pacifier use to just before bedtime. Discontinue use altogether by age 10 months. Children who use pacifiers less frequently have 33 percent fewer ear infections (see pages 54–55).[10]

- Help your child develop good hand-washing habits.

- If your child has allergies, do your best to keep allergens (pet dander, dust, and so on) to a minimum in your home. Preventing allergic reactions helps prevent tissue swelling that could lead to ear infections.

- Talk to your doctor about the pneumococcal conjugate vaccine (PCV), which has been added to the recommended childhood immunization schedule. One PCV, Prevnar, helps prevent serious bacterial infections like meningitis and pneumonia, and it also reduces the number of common ear infections, the number of recurrent ear infections, and the need for PE tubes.[11]

Hearing Impairment

Hearing impairment affects children in varying degrees, from minimal reduction in one ear to no hearing in either ear. The effects of hearing impairment on your child depend on two important factors: the severity of the loss and the age at which it occurs.

Hearing impairment can occur for different reasons at different ages. In the United States, an average of thirty-three babies each day (or twelve thousand each year) are born with significant hearing impairment, making it the most frequent birth defect.[12] Sometimes a child loses his hearing through an illness or accident. If a child loses his hearing after developing speech, the hearing loss is less likely to affect his speech and language skills than if he were born with hearing impairment. The earlier the hearing impairment is detected, the earlier intervention can occur.

Parents must watch for signs of hearing impairment in their infants. Only half of children with hearing impairment have a known family history of hearing problems. Several federal agencies—including the National Institutes of Health (NIH), the National Institute on Deafness and Other Communication Disorders (NIDCD), the Centers for Disease Control and Prevention (CDC), and the Health Resources and Services Administration (HRSA)—strongly recommend universal hearing screening. The American Speech-Language-Hearing Association (ASHA) and the American Academy of Pediatrics (AAP) also recommend that your newborn receive a hearing screening before leaving the hospital. Two tests may be used to screen a newborn's hearing:

- Auditory brainstem response (ABR): This test measures how the brain responds to sounds. Clicks or tones are played through earphones into the baby's ears. Three electrodes placed on the baby's head measure the brain's response.
- Otoacoustic emissions (OAE): This test measures sound waves produced in the inner ear. A tiny probe is placed inside the ear canal to measure the response (echo) when clicks or tones are played into the baby's ears.[13]

Both procedures are quick (about 5 to 10 minutes), painless, noninvasive, and may be done while your baby is sleeping or lying still. If you don't receive the results before leaving the hospital, call your doctor's office to confirm them. If you can't have your newborn's hearing screened at the hospital, you can have it done anytime thereafter.

If your baby fails one or both tests shortly after birth, he doesn't necessarily have a hearing impairment. Further testing is done to confirm a problem, including a more thorough hearing and medical evaluation. Follow-up tests should be done as soon as possible, preferably before your baby is age 3 months. If babies diagnosed with a hearing impairment receive services before they're age 6 months, they have a better chance of developing language (spoken or signed) at the same rate as their hearing peers. If your child shows any of the following warning signs, talk to your doctor about scheduling a screening. Early detection is the key to preventing or minimizing language delays.[14]

Signs of Hearing Impairment

Birth to Age 3 Months

- Awakens to your touch but not to your voice
- Doesn't smile when spoken to
- Doesn't startle at loud noises
- Doesn't seem to recognize your voice and quiet down when crying

Age 4 to 6 Months

- Doesn't try to turn toward a sound made at eye level
- Responds to comforting only when held
- Doesn't pay attention to music
- Shows little interest in babbling or imitating sounds
- Doesn't respond to speech sounds, footsteps, or noise-producing toys by stopping his activities to listen

---

Common Concerns about Language Development   51

> **Signs of Hearing Impairment** *(cont.)*
>
> Age 7 to 12 Months
>
> - Doesn't turn and look in the direction of sounds
> - Doesn't respond when spoken to
> - Ignores a ringing telephone or doorbell
> - Seems startled to see a person nearby
>
> Age 12 to 24 Months
>
> - Doesn't imitate speech, or speech is very unclear
> - Doesn't follow simple directions
> - May respond to very loud noises, but doesn't respond to speech
> - Uses gestures rather than speech to express needs
>
> Adapted from *Ear Infections and Language Development* (American Speech-Language-Hearing Association, 2000).

Auditory Processing Problems

Hearing problems include a group of disorders that involve the outer, middle, and inner ear and the neural pathway to the brain. When a child has difficulty understanding the signals that his ears send to his brain, this difficulty is called an auditory processing disorder. This disorder is sometimes misdiagnosed as attention deficit hyperactivity disorder (**ADHD**). Although these disorders share the symptom of a short attention span, auditory processing disorders don't respond to the medications that often help a child with **ADHD**. Children suffering from auditory processing disorders are frequently described as "not listening," "unable to follow directions," or "unable to learn from information they hear."[15] Symptoms include the following:*

- Frequently asks a speaker to repeat what's been said
- Has trouble understanding requests, especially if there's background noise
- Has difficulty with longer directions involving several steps

- May understand the words he's heard, but mixes up the order and gets the information confused
- Seems to have selective hearing, or listens only to topics that interest him
- Seems to understand the last part of a verbal message, but doesn't remember the first part
- Frequently fails to respond to someone's comments, or provides a peculiar response
- Has difficulty repeating words or numbers in a sequence
- Frequently repeats what he's been told, but doesn't seem to comprehend the message
- Has problems with sound awareness and reading[16]

If your child shows one or more of these symptoms, talk to your doctor about scheduling a screening to rule out a hearing problem. If hearing isn't the problem, get a referral to a speech-language pathologist to determine if your child has an auditory processing problem (as opposed to a different type of learning disorder). An auditory processing problem can be serious. It may require a team of professionals to make an accurate assessment and determine an appropriate treatment. In the meantime, here are a few things you can do to ease your child's frustration and help improve communication:

- Get your child's full attention before speaking to him.
- Limit background noise when talking to your child.
- Talk to your child only when he's in the same room.
- Make eye contact when talking to your child.
- Talk slowly and keep your sentences short.
- Ask your child to repeat your instructions to make sure he's understood them.
- Encourage your child to ask for clarification if he's confused about something you've said.
- Praise your child for being a good listener.[17]

Pacifiers

Pacifiers can serve a purpose in the first few months of life. They may help soothe an infant and satisfy his sucking reflex when he isn't hungry. Pacifiers also help infants who have difficulty establishing good sucking patterns. There comes a time, however, when pacifier use may lead to oral motor and speech development problems. I encourage parents to discontinue pacifier use after their children are age 10 months, and preferably before the children have several teeth.

Contrary to popular belief, giving a child a pacifier won't prevent him from sucking his thumb. It's natural for a baby to suck his thumb for the first few months; this behavior usually disappears on its own as the child matures. If you let your child get used to always having something in his mouth, he may start sucking his thumb when you take the pacifier away.[18]

How do you get rid of the beloved binkie? I know some mothers who collected all the pacifiers in their homes and told their children that they'd be giving the pacifiers to the new baby down the street, then tossed them in the trash. Some parents punch pinholes in pacifiers to make them less enjoyable to suck. Others simply throw them all away so they won't feel tempted to give in during those difficult first days of withdrawal.

Some pediatric dentists advise parents to limit or eliminate their children's pacifier use after age 6 months. Other professionals suggest that parents use a pacifier only to calm a fussy baby and then remove it when the baby is calm or asleep. Parents may need to replace the pacifier with a favorite blanket or a beloved toy that their children can hold for comfort. If your child is attached to his pacifier, try limiting its use to bedtime until you can wean him from it completely.

Studies show that children who used pacifiers less often had 33 percent fewer ear infections.[19] The reasons are two-fold: First, pacifiers are difficult to keep clean, especially when they're used all day long. In addition to ear infections, bacteria found on pacifiers could make a baby more susceptible to diarrhea. (Honey can also be contaminated with certain bacteria and shouldn't be used on a pacifier.) Second, pacifiers increase saliva production, which favors the presence of fungi and alters the types of bacteria present in the mouth. When your child sucks constantly, there's a higher risk the germs will be transmitted into the middle ear.

New studies are beginning to suggest that pacifiers may also increase the risk of deformities in your child's mouth. Some children may develop a cross bite or other alignment problem that requires orthodontics to correct.[20] Pacifiers may also harm the development of the muscles of the mouth. Pacifiers generally make a baby use his tongue in a front-to-back motion. As a child grows older, his tongue needs to move in all directions. If your child can't move his tongue from side to side proficiently, he could have difficulty eating solid foods. If he has trouble moving his tongue up, down, or back, he could be at increased risk of developing speech problems.[21]

Not all children who use pacifiers will develop these problems. But it makes sense to lower the risk by reducing your child's pacifier use after age 6 months, then eliminating it within a few months thereafter. Keep in mind that without a pacifier in his mouth, your child will be more likely to babble and attempt first words.

Sippy Cups

The American Academy of Pediatric Dentistry has said that children should use sippy cups sparingly and only as a transition from bottles to regular cups. While sippy cups are great for keeping your home clean and your car dry, there are some drawbacks in allowing your child to drink from them exclusively.

Drinking from sippy cups immerses your child's front teeth in liquid. Even if you don't give him sweetened drinks, remember that many unsweetened drinks, like milk and natural fruit juices, still contain sugar. Children who carry around sippy cups and drink sugary beverages from them throughout the day may have a higher risk of developing tooth decay. This risk increases if children are allowed to fall asleep with a sippy cup. At bedtime, a child produces less saliva and doesn't swallow as often, which allows the sugar in the liquid to collect on the child's teeth. It's best to limit your child's drinks (other than water) to snack time and mealtime. It's also a good idea to help your child learn to use a straw, especially for sugary beverages. Perhaps most importantly, parents should teach their children good tooth-brushing habits, especially at bedtime.

Another problem with sippy cups is that certain cup styles may not promote the oral motor strength that's needed for speech development. Hard-spouted cups encourage a child to move his tongue forward and backward. But children must also develop adequate side-to-side and up-and-down tongue movement to help them eat solid foods and improve speech and swallowing.

Some clinicians who've worked with children with oral motor problems have found soft-spouted cups work better to encourage active lip movements while drinking. The best cups for promoting appropriate oral motor function have a slit or small holes (not a spout) in a recessed lid that snaps into the top of the cup. With this type of cup, the child uses jaw, lip, and tongue movements as if drinking from a regular cup.[22] This type of cup, however, is not as popular as the sippy cup and may be hard to find.

Cups with built-in straws are also a good idea. Sucking through a short straw promotes better oral motor strength and a stronger swallowing reflex. The straw should be cut so only a half-inch fits into the child's mouth. This straw length allows the child to use his lips to suck the liquid. He then uses tongue movements to swallow, as with a regular cup. If he uses the straw improperly (places it too far back and onto his tongue), the sucking can encourage immature front-to-back swallowing.

Oral Motor Development

From infancy through early childhood, babies' oral motor skills develop rapidly. The muscles of the jaw, lips, tongue, and cheeks learn to work together to bite, chew, swallow, and produce speech sounds. The oral muscles also learn to work with muscles from other parts of the body to coordinate various functions. For example, the production of speech requires muscles in the larynx. Muscles in the diaphragm, chest, abdomen, and back support respiration, creating a smooth air flow for speech.

It's important that babies have lots of oral motor stimulation. One of the main ways babies learn about objects in their environment is by putting them in their mouths. Giving your infant safe toys that come in lots of different shapes, sizes, and textures is a great way to help his oral muscles become more coordinated. Be aware that if your baby has never put his hands, feet, or toys into his mouth by age 4 to 5 months, he may have skipped an important stage of development,[23] and your doctor should examine your baby's oral motor development.

Typically developing infants have a bite reflex that helps them develop jaw movements for chewing. You can observe this reflex, which tends to disappear between ages 9 and 12 months, by sticking your finger in an infant's mouth and feeling the surface of his gums. His jaw will close and open rhythmically as he munches on your finger. Munching, the first step toward chewing, involves moving the jaw up and down, and the typically developing child between ages 5 and 7 months can munch on toys.[24] Chewing on toys helps your baby make the connection to chewing food.[25]

Chewing helps develop jaw muscles for eating, drinking, and speaking. The ability to move the tongue and lips at the same time usually emerges around age 6 to 7 months and is well established by age three.[26] Gradually, the child's tongue begins to move from side to side in an increasingly controlled way. Rotary chewing, the last stage of chewing development, involves coordination of vertical, horizontal, diagonal, and circular movements of the jaw, which typically develops by age 15 months.

A child's active lip use is typically well developed by age 10 months.[27] To help promote your child's lip use, spoon-feed your infant by placing the spoon in his mouth levelly. When you remove the spoon, avoid tipping it upward. Instead, let your infant use his lips to clean it.

Babies are ready for finger feeding as soon as they can coordinate hand and mouth movements to explore food (usually around age 8 to 12 months).[28] After an infant gets his front teeth (typically between ages 6 and 10 months), he's ready to take a bite of food. Your baby should be able to take a bite of a soft cookie by age 9 months and a hard cookie by age 18 months.[29]

Sometimes a delay or disorder causes a weakness or a lack of coordination of oral muscle groups. Inappropriate patterns may develop and cause difficulties in feeding, swallowing, and/or speaking. Here are some warning signs:

- Lack of muscle tone (or very tense tone) in the cheeks, jaw, tongue, or lips
- Frequent choking on food or liquids
- Difficulty keeping lips closed
- Weak chewing and swallowing
- Oral/facial hypersensitivity (for example, extreme dislike of having his face or nose wiped)
- Hypersensitivity to changes in the textures, tastes, smells, or temperatures of foods you offer
- Difficulty imitating mouth movements
- Drooling profusely at any age or drooling even minimally past age two
- Not developing speech on schedule[30]

If you think your child is having trouble with his oral motor skills, seek help from a speech-language pathologist, who can assess his oral motor function and work closely with you to provide the best treatment.

Tongue-Tie

Tongue-tie, also known as ankyloglossia, is a congenital condition that's characterized by an unusually thickened, tightened, or shortened frenum (the flap of tissue that runs from the floor of the mouth to the underside of the tongue). This condition limits tongue movement during feeding and may harm both speech and dental health.[31] A child with tongue-tie usually has a V-shaped notch or heart shape at the tip of the tongue when he sticks it out or cries. (When crying, a child lifts his tongue enough inside his mouth to reveal the notch or heart shape). Tongue-tie occurs in less than 5 percent of the population, with a male to female ratio of 2.6:1.[32]

    Some children seem genetically predisposed to tongue-tie.[33] Research has noted that the condition is less common in adults than children, which has led some to hypothesize that certain cases of ankyloglossia might improve with age.[34] As a child grows, the tongue grows longer and thins out at the tip. Research hasn't documented, however, that the frenum stretches or breaks so the tongue can move easily.[35]

Infants born with severe ankyloglossia may have trouble latching on to the breast because they can't stick out their tongues far enough to assume the correct position. In one study, 25 percent of infants with mild or moderate tongue-tie had trouble getting latched on or staying on the breast. For this reason, surgery should be considered as an option for those babies who have continued difficulty with breastfeeding.[36] If an infant doesn't have trouble feeding, many doctors wait and see if the tongue compensates for the condition on its own. In the past, surgery was done more often than required. Current medical opinions about surgery range from caution to enthusiastic support.[37]

Carmen Fernando, a researcher specializing in tongue-tie, has found that speech symptoms associated with tongue-tie vary widely in children. Her studies have shown tongue-tie may affect clarity of pronunciation, fluency in speech production, and quality of speech sounds. She's noted that tongue-tie distorts other sounds in addition to tongue-tip sounds because it alters airflow out of the sides of the mouth.[38]

Fernando developed an assessment that doctors can use to determine whether a patient needs surgery. This assessment includes gathering a case history and examining factors like cosmetic appearance, oral hygiene, dental health, feeding skills, tongue movement, oral sensation/awareness, speech, and emotional status.[39] In certain cases of ankyloglossia, tooth decay results from being unable to clean the teeth and sides of the mouth with the tip of the tongue.[40] Some dentists feel if ankyloglossia is causing problems in permanent teeth, it's best to schedule surgery as soon as possible.[41]

Usually within a week of an infant undergoing tongue-tie surgery to solve breastfeeding problems, mothers notice weight gain in their infants as well as a reduction of breast pain while feeding them.[42] For children over age three, speech therapy is often needed following surgery, since by that time tongue-tie has caused problems that don't correct themselves without supervised oral motor exercises. Delaying surgery may commit some children to longer periods of speech therapy to solve the speech problems caused by limited tongue mobility.[43] In most cases with older children, a combination of surgery and speech therapy is effective.[44] If you suspect your child has tongue-tie, a physician and a specialist familiar with the assessment of the condition should evaluate your child.

Common Speech Problems

Children experience various speech problems as they grow. You should be familiar with a few important terms so you can accurately describe what your child is doing to your child's doctor or speech therapist. Speech errors are generally classified into four types:[45]

1. *Substitutions* occur when a child substitutes one sound for another. For example, he may say "doe" for "go," or "wun" for "run." Substitutions are the most common errors in children's speech.
2. *Distortions* occur when a child attempts to say a sound but can't pronounce it accurately. For example, he may try to say "dinosaur," but the *s* might sound more like *sh* or *z*.
3. *Omissions* occur when a child deletes a speech sound from a word. For example, he may say "ca" instead of "cat," or "fooball" instead of "football."
4. *Additions* occur when a child inserts an extra speech sound into a word. For example, he may say "cerzeal" instead of "cereal," or "Sarzah" instead of "Sarah." Additions are the least common errors in children's speech.

These errors can occur in different positions in words: the initial position (first sound), the medial position (middle sound), or the final position (last sound). In a word like *rabbit*, *r* is the initial consonant sound, *b* is the medial consonant sound, and *t* is the final consonant sound.

Lisps

Lisps are one of the most common speech errors and can be categorized into two basic types.[46] A central lisp (interdental) occurs when a child's tongue protrudes between the front teeth and the airflow is directed forward and down toward the middle of the tongue.[47] When a child tries to say *s* or *z* sounds, they get converted into a *th* sound (for example, he pronounces "sun" as "thun"). Many children have a central lisp until they're about age four and a half, and many outgrow it on their own.

A lateral lisp occurs when air comes out around the sides of the tongue instead of the middle. The result sounds like a slushy *s* or *sh* sound (for example, *sun* sounds like *shun*).[48] This type of lisp isn't part of the normal developmental progression and doesn't tend to disappear on its own.[49] A speech-language pathologist is trained to provide therapy to help the child fix this problem. Discriminating between correct and incorrect pronunciations is one of the first steps. See page 221 for "The Spider Shines Her Shoes," a song that contains some of the commonly lisped sounds. Singing this song can be a fun way to listen to the differences among sounds.

Phonological Processes

Children simplify complex speech sounds when learning language. The fancy term for these simplifications is *phonological processes*. Children don't simplify language haphazardly; they do so methodically. At times, children apply as many as two or three processes to one word, so analyzing them all when attempting to diagnose or rule out a speech problem can get pretty complicated.

Following is a list of the basic processes children use when developing speech. These processes aren't errors in your child's speech patterns; they're stages he goes through on his way toward developing adult speech.[50] As your child matures and acquires more sophisticated language skills, he'll suppress these processes. Developing correct pronunciation is a long task, and you may notice your child backtracking occasionally.[51] It's important that you understand the normal processes and know the ages at which they usually disappear so you can spot an emerging problem.

Sometimes children produce unusual phonological processes that aren't consistent with typically developing speech. For example, it's common for some children to delete the *h* sound at the beginning of words for a short time. Some children with disordered phonology, however, delete many or all consonants at the beginning of words for longer periods of time.[52] In such cases, speech-language pathologists examine numerous samples of a child's phonological processes to determine if he's using typical or atypical patterns.

Reduplication
A child pronounces a word by repeating the same syllable twice. This process should disappear by age two and a half.

"dog" → "dah-dah"
"water" → "wa-wa"

Context-Sensitive Voicing
A child replaces a voiceless sound with a voiced sound. (Voicing refers to the rapid vibration of the vocal cords, which occurs in some sounds but not in others. For example, *t* and *d* are pronounced almost exactly the same way, with the tip of the tongue touching the alveolar ridge behind the upper teeth. The only difference is that *d* is voiced and *t* isn't.) This process should disappear by age three.

"toe" → "doe"
"pat" → "bat"
"cat" → "gat"
"fun" → "vun"

Word Final De-voicing
A child replaces a voiced sound with a voiceless sound in the final position of a word. Again, all aspects of the sound production are correct except for voicing. This process should disappear by age three.

"dog" → "dok"
"sad" → "sat"

Final Consonant Deletion
A child leaves the last consonant off a word. This process should disappear by age three years, three months.

"bus" → "buh"
"bed" → "beh"

Fronting
A child replaces sounds made in the back of the mouth (*k*, *g*, and *ng*) with sounds made in the front of the mouth (*t*, *d*, and *n*). Sometimes a child replaces sounds made in the middle of the mouth, like replacing *sh* and *zh* with *s* and *z*. This process should disappear by age three and a half.

"key" → "tea"
"go" → "doe"
"sheep" → "seep"

Consonant Harmony
A child changes one consonant in a word to make it similar to another consonant in the word. Sometimes a child changes the consonant to match another consonant exactly, and sometimes he changes it to match a sound made in the same part of the mouth. In the second example below, the *j* is changed to a *g*, which is made in the same part of the mouth as *k*. This process should disappear by age three years, nine months.

"cat" → "tat"
"joke" → "goke"

Weak Syllable Deletion
In a word with two or more syllables, a child leaves out the syllable with the least stress. This process should disappear by age four.

"elephant" → "ephant"
"spaghetti" → "ghetti"

Stopping
A child replaces certain sounds (*f, v, s, z, sh, zh, th, h, j, ch*) that are hard to pronounce with sounds called "stops." "Stop" sounds are made by temporarily stopping the airflow from the mouth. Examples include *p, b, t, d, k,* and *g*. This process should begin to disappear for some sounds by age three, but other sounds may continue to be simplified until age five.

"this" → "dis"
"sun" → "tun"
"chip" → "tip"

Gliding

A child replaces the *r* and *l* sounds with *w* or *y* sounds. This process might disappear by age five. Some children, however, may continue to have difficulty until age seven.

"ride" → "wide"
"light" → "white"
"little" → "yittuw"

Cluster Reduction/Simplification

A consonant cluster is two or more consonants appearing together, like *br* or *str*. A child might delete all the consonants in a cluster, delete only one, or substitute one for another that's easier to say. Some children suppress this process by age four. Research suggests, however, that children master very few clusters by age four. They master the majority of clusters by age six or seven, and they may not master some clusters until age eight or nine. Children master consonant clusters containing three consonants (*scr*, *str*) at a later age than clusters containing only two consonants.[53] Consonant cluster reduction/simplification is one of the most common and longest lasting processes that occur in language development.

"bread" → "ed" (cluster reduction)
"bread" → "bed" (cluster reduction)
"bread" → "bwead" (cluster simplification)

Vocal Abuse

When children are young, they enjoy exploring their voices. Boys especially love to mimic animal sounds and sounds from their environment—trucks, cars, sirens, screams, squeals, and so on. Let your child have his fun, but the sooner you have him use an "inside" voice rather than an "outside" voice, the better. If your child strains his voice all day, he could develop chronic hoarseness. Some children who yell excessively both inside and outside their homes have chronic hoarseness. Many frequently imitate animal and machine noises, and are habitually loud talkers. Others sing frequently and talk incessantly.

If your child seems to be hoarse regularly (apart from those times when he has a respiratory infection), it could be a symptom of vocal abuse, or it could be a symptom of allergies.

Talk to your doctor about this problem, as vocal abuse could lead to permanent damage. Avoid encouraging your child to use his voice to show off or to be funny. Try to plan more quiet time for a particularly noisy child, and encourage him to curb the habits that may strain his voice. I realize this is no small task. Many children don't understand the difference between "inside" and "outside" voices until after age three. To help your child understand, illustrate the difference by contrasting loud animals (lions and bears) with quiet ones (mice and rabbits). To help your child quiet down, you might say, "Let's use our mouse voice in the car today." Or you could play a game by putting your finger to your lips and making the *sh* sound.

Stuttering

Stuttering is a condition in which the flow of speech is broken by abnormal stops (no sound), repetitions ("st-st-story"), or prolongations ("sssstory"). It may also involve unusual facial and body movements associated with the effort to speak.[54] A person who stutters understands perfectly well what he wants to say, but involuntary behaviors disrupt the flow of speech. Stuttering is sometimes called disfluent speech (as opposed to fluent speech, in which words are produced smoothly and effortlessly). Some children go through a stage of disfluency in early speech development. Even adults occasionally repeat words, phrases, and sounds, but these disfluencies aren't usually identified as abnormal and aren't a cause for concern.

Researchers still don't understand exactly what causes stuttering.[55] It may result from different causes in different people, or it may occur only when certain factors combine. The initial cause of stuttering may differ from what perpetuates or aggravates it.[56] Possible causes of stuttering include stress, major life changes, uncoordinated speech muscles, slow or fast language development, poor modeling by parents and others, and some parents' demanding expectations for a child's quick response when spoken to.[57] Genetic predisposition plays a role in stuttering,[58] but your child won't necessarily develop the problem if it runs in your family. Research has discovered that physical and intellectual behavior don't cause stuttering in children.[59]

In some children, disfluency occurs around the time they're figuring out how to put a sentence together (around age three). If proper word order and sentence structures are new to a child, he may pause or repeat words as he thinks about what he wants to say. For example, he might say, "My, my bear fell behind the bed." Or he might insert pauses by saying *um*: "My, um, bear, um, fell behind the bed." Try not to worry about this behavior, and avoid calling attention to it. The more you comment on disfluent speech, the more self-conscious your child may become and the more pressure he may feel to speak fluently. It's best simply to model fluent speech and to praise your child when he speaks fluently.

If your child struggles to complete a sentence without stuttering, be a great listener. Maintain eye contact and try to listen patiently to *what* your child is saying without focusing on *how* he says it. Resist finishing your child's sentences for him. Try not to interrupt him, and don't tell him to slow down, stop, or try to relax. Waiting calmly can be difficult, but your patience will lower his stress level. Encourage others to be patient with him, too, and avoid firing questions at him without giving him enough time to answer. It's also important that you and others slow your rate of speech and not be in a hurry to communicate.

Avoid inadvertently modeling disfluent speech during attempts to help your child speak clearly. For example, if your disfluent child is saying *bamato* instead of *tomato*, avoid correcting him by saying, "t-t-t-tomato." Instead, say something such as, "Yes, that's a pretty tomato. Hey, that starts with the *t* sound. Tomato."

Most children outgrow stuttering. Studies show that 65 to 75 percent of children recover without treatment within two years of the onset of stuttering. As many as 85 percent of children eventually recover on their own.[60] In many cases, however, it's not clear whether a child will recover without treatment. It may be possible to prevent stuttering from developing into a problem if it's treated early.[61] Research shows that a child's chances of outgrowing a stuttering problem decrease depending on the child's age, the severity of the problem, and the length of the disfluent period.[62]

Watch for warning signs of severe disfluent speech, like repetitions of parts of a word ("b-b-b-b-b-b-bat"), especially if the number of repetitions is five or more. Listen for the vowel sound *uh* in your child's repetitions ("buh-buh-buh-buh-bat"), and watch for prolongations of sounds ("shhhhhhhhhhare"). If your child shows these signs for more than three months, schedule a consultation with a speech-language pathologist. Also look for signs that your child is tense, embarrassed, or self-conscious about his speech. Sometimes children move their eyes to the side or blink during a stuttering episode.[63] They may also nod their heads or stomp their feet. If your child shows signs of frustration or irritation while speaking, a formal speech evaluation may be necessary.

Warning signs don't necessarily mean a child has a stuttering problem. But the signs mean that he may develop a problem unless some intervention takes place.[64] A speech-language pathologist can determine how often a child is stuttering, how long the stuttering occurs, and whether the disfluency puts him at risk for a continued problem. Sometimes a therapist may suggest waiting for six months, then reevaluating a child's situation. The decision to begin treatment is based on each child's behavior. If a child has been stuttering for eighteen months or longer and shows some of the other warning signs, too, a speech-language pathologist may recommend treatment.[65]

Why Children Experience Language Delays

From walking to talking, some children reach milestones later than others. In all areas of development, there are ranges of what's considered normal. Most children fall within typical boundaries, but a surprising 30 percent of children fall within "outer" boundaries, and 10 percent are "abnormally" late in reaching at least one significant milestone (even though there may be no diagnosis given).

About 10 to 15 percent of children are late bloomers in speech and language development.[66] Some researchers define a late talker as a child who hasn't reached a fifty-word vocabulary and isn't using two words together by age two.[67] Although some late bloomers catch up on their own, at least half experience persisting language delays.[68] Researchers continue to search for predictors that may help distinguish, at an earlier age, children who will outgrow a delay from children who will require intervention.

Here's a review of the five major areas of child development:

1. Large motor skills: the ability to control and coordinate large muscle groups (trunk, shoulders, hips, neck, arms, and legs) that enable actions like sitting, crawling, and walking
2. Small motor skills: the ability to control and coordinate small muscle groups (mouth, eyes, hands, fingers, feet, and toes) that control actions like speaking and seeing as well as holding and manipulating objects
3. Speech-language skills: the ability to understand and use language to communicate and to fulfill basic needs
4. Perceptual-cognitive skills: the ability to think and process information obtained through the senses
5. Social-emotional skills: the ability to relate to people and to one's surroundings[69]

Language and perceptual-cognitive development are closely related during the early learning period. Throughout early childhood, a child processes new experiences and continually reshapes, expands, and reorganizes his mental makeup.[70] He learns basic cognitive skills like imitation, cause and effect (understanding that certain behaviors have predictable outcomes), means to an end (understanding what needs to be done to accomplish a task, and knowing the most effective means of doing so), object permanence (understanding that an object still exists when it's out of sight), and symbolic play (pretending that one object stands for another).[71]

Cognitive abilities and comprehension skills are related in early language development.[72] For example, after your baby masters object permanence and means to an end, he can distinguish himself from objects and people. He understands the relationship between objects and people who are present and those who aren't. He learns how to involve adults in his quest for what he wants and needs, often by using gestures to communicate. If he's sitting by himself, he understands that he can play only with the objects he can reach. If a parent is in the room, however, he understands that he has access to objects he can't reach *if* he communicates his desire for them to the parent. As a child's cognitive abilities increase, they affect later language skills like vocabulary and sentence structure.[73]

Though cognition and language are related, there are cases that illustrate that they develop as two completely separate processes. Some children with average to above average intelligence and otherwise typical development may have an extraordinarily difficult time learning to talk. These children are said to have Specific Language Impairment (SLI), in which language disorders are the primary disability and no other diagnosis or reason can be found. Most children with SLI don't have a speech disorder. Their difficulties are more language based, and they require intervention to solve problems understanding and using words in sentences. It's possible that children with SLI also have unintelligible speech because of difficulty learning correct sounds. Children with SLI are different from those who suffer from secondary language disorders caused by another condition (for example, mental retardation, autism, hearing impairment, cerebral palsy, or brain injury). About 5 to 7 percent of five-year-olds have SLI, and it affects more boys than girls. There's also growing evidence that genetics contribute to the occurrence of the disorder.[74]

A complete medical history is vital when determining the cause of a language delay in a late bloomer, because various factors can prevent a child from reaching milestones on schedule. If a child is born prematurely, he may not meet the milestones that his chronological age suggests. In fact, it's normal for premature babies to need as much as a year or two to catch up to their peers. Speech-language pathologists will often evaluate the premature child based on his adjusted age (counting from his due date) rather than his actual age (counting from his birth date) until age two.

Language delays are sometimes seen in children who have illnesses that require long-term hospitalizations. These children frequently have neither the energy nor the opportunity to interact sufficiently with others. In some cases, they may have also undergone procedures that have limited their speech and/or language development, like a tracheostomy. Temperament, personality, and individual learning styles may also account for late-blooming language. Research also suggests that there may be a genetic reason for language delays.[75]

If your child's speech is delayed, look for specific warning signs: Does he make eye contact, smile, play with toys, and interact with others? Does he understand what's being said to him? Does he regularly use gestures or noises to make his needs and feelings known? Research on late talkers indicates that those who understand words and use eye gaze, gestures, and sounds are likely to catch up without intervention.[76]

It's common to wait until a child is age 18 to 24 months before beginning a formal evaluation of his speech and language skills. New research indicates, however, that speech-language pathologists may be able to identify at-risk children earlier based on their preverbal behavior. If your child seems to have trouble using eye gaze and gestures to get what he wants, if he doesn't babble or use other sounds, he may be at risk for a language delay. Other red flags include your child's incomprehension of what you say or his inability to use objects. Even if your child does well with these tasks but still has trouble with sounds and words, he may need help.

Early intervention is important because a child's capacity for learning certain parts of language, which are regulated by brain maturation, is fixed by age three. The first three years are a peak period of development during which the child's brain has twice as many synapses (nerve connections) as an adult's. As a child's brain is stimulated, the synapses are strengthened; if a synapse is used repeatedly in the early years, it becomes permanent. If it's used rarely or not at all, it's unlikely to survive. These reasons are why children need consistent emotional, physical, cognitive, and language stimulation, starting from birth.

Unfortunately, many children who need early intervention may be falling through the cracks.[77] Having language-delayed children begin educational programs at age three or four to boost school readiness may not be enough.[78] You may be surprised to learn that one in three children in the United States enters kindergarten unprepared to learn. Most of these children lack the vocabulary and sentence structure skills that would allow them to participate fully in the classroom.[79]

For this reason, language delays should be addressed early. If a child is diagnosed with a problem and given help when he's young, a better prognosis can be expected. It's always a good idea to bring any concerns to your doctor's attention and have your child evaluated. Although there might not be a diagnosable reason for a delay, your child may need help from a speech-language pathologist. For further information on services in your area, contact your state's early intervention program.

Developmental Delays

Developmental delay is a broad term that's used to describe a lag in physical, cognitive, behavioral, emotional, or social development. Often a child with a mild delay will catch up on his own without intervention. A language delay, however, is sometimes the first sign of a more serious disorder. Disorders are severe delays that require intervention and don't usually resolve themselves. Early signs of a language delay may suggest that a child is at risk for certain learning disorders, behavior disorders, mental retardation, or social-emotional impairments (like autism, schizophrenia, or Asperger's syndrome).

Developmental delays show themselves in different patterns. Sometimes children will progress in the same sequence as typical children, but reach milestones later than expected. Often a specific diagnosis or explanation can't be found for the delay. Another pattern is a child who's specifically delayed in one or more areas, like reaching both speech and physical milestones late. Still other children may follow a hit-and-miss (rather than successive) pattern, reaching certain milestones but being unable to do other tasks typical of that level.[80] For example, a child may have good large motor skills but can't hold a crayon without breaking it because his small motor skills aren't developed.

Children with developmental disorders may have trouble integrating information. They may use all their cognitive skills to monitor and understand conversations, leaving little energy for learning new language skills.[81] Some of the known reasons for developmental disorders involve problems with the brain and nervous system. Sometimes brain cells don't develop properly, make insufficient connections, or are damaged before birth or at birth. Another possible cause of developmental disorders is a learning disability. This disability is seen in children who have problems with the way their brains absorb, process, and respond to information. Other causes of disorders include early trauma or abuse, physical problems, sensory loss, genetic disorders, multiple handicaps, and mental retardation.[82]

When you first realize that your child might have a developmental disorder, it can be distressing. Try to create a stimulating environment for your child and encourage him to participate in community activities at whatever level is appropriate from him. Children with developmental disorders need more opportunities to interact and communicate with others, even though providing such opportunities can be challenging. Seek out support groups so you can contact other families facing the same challenges. Remember: you'll help your child immensely by seeking professional help as early as possible.

Seeking Professional Help

This book isn't meant to take the place of professional evaluation and services. If your child shows some of the warning signs mentioned, don't hesitate to seek professional help. Depending on where you go to receive services, there could be waiting lists, and time is precious. In addition to conducting a formal hearing test and developmental assessment, your doctor may refer your child to a speech-language pathologist for a formal speech and language evaluation.

Some children who start out with a limited problem continue to experience language problems later. Children with early language delays are often at higher risk for developing reading problems.[83] For this reason, many preschool caregivers screen children for early language delays, because language and literacy go hand in hand. Remember that the earlier a child is diagnosed with a problem and intervention takes place, the better the prognosis.[84]

The government has passed the Individuals with Disabilities Education Act (IDEA) to ensure that early intervention services are available to any child suspected of having significant physical, speech-language, perceptual-cognitive, or social-emotional developmental problems, starting at birth. Each state has early childhood intervention programs available through either its health or education department. The programs are free in some states, and other states require payment on a sliding scale. You should find listings for programs in your county in the government pages of your phone book. If you have trouble finding resources in your area, consult the National Information Center for Children and Youth with Disabilities (NICHCY). (See Appendix B.) If your child is age two or younger, you'll be given information from the early intervention services office. Children age three to five are usually referred to a speech-language pathologist from the local public school system for assessment.

Children with significant delays may qualify for government programs. If your child doesn't qualify because he has only a moderate delay, there are other places you can take him for services. Ask your doctor for the name of a respected therapist or clinic in your area. If you have trouble finding a speech-language pathologist, contact the American Speech-Language-Hearing Association. (See Appendix B.) It's also a good idea to call your insurance company and find out exactly what services and expenses it covers. Many insurance companies now cover speech and language evaluations and treatments. Depending on the state where you live, some clinics require that you have a physician's referral.

A college or university offering speech-language pathology and audiology programs usually has a speech, language, and hearing clinic on or near campus. Evaluations and treatments are often conducted by students who are supervised by certified professionals. Many of these programs offer sliding scale benefits for services rendered. Occasionally universities conduct speech and language studies in which they ask children to participate at no cost. You might ask if any studies are currently going on. Some organizations like Easter Seals provide subsidized treatment programs. Early intervention is the key to solving speech and language delays and to helping children learn to their greatest potential, so seek professional help as soon as you suspect a delay in your child's language development.

Chapter 4

Language Development Facts and Warning Signs

This chapter explains the sound production, vocabulary, and overall language ability of typically developing children at certain ages. It also discusses what these children can comprehend at each stage. In addition, each section contains a list of possible warning signs of a delay that parents should keep in mind.

Children develop language in fairly predictable patterns, and most children reach important milestones at about the same age.[1] Milestones are based on statistical averages, and there's a wide range of normal when it comes to a particular skill. When reading about your child's current age group, make sure to read about the age groups before and after it, too. You'll notice that starting at age 8 months, the average number of words understood and produced at each age varies considerably.[2]

Don't expect your child to reach each set of milestones completely or on time. Each child has an individual learning style that's heavily influenced by her environment and biological makeup. Consider the information for each stage as a *guide* to development, not a set of rigorous standards children must meet at specific ages. Children commonly have spurts of development: Their development explodes, plateaus, and regresses before they master certain skills.[3]

The information for each stage will give you an idea of what to expect with your child's language development and can help you identify possible signs of a delay. Remember that certain skills may lag behind as others emerge. Just because your child exhibits one or more warning signs doesn't necessarily mean she has a problem. If you think your child shows serious signs of a delay, talk to your doctor about a referral to a speech-language pathologist.

Birth to Age 2 Months

Expression

Newborns make many reflexive vocalizations like coughing, sneezing, grunting, groaning, and burping.[4] They also make pleasure sounds during feeding that involve soft phonation of the vocal folds but no real vowel or consonant sounds. Around age 6 weeks, infants begin to smile in response to external stimuli. At age 2 months, they begin cooing with consonant-like and vowel-like sounds as they learn how to route airflow through their noses.

As every parent knows, infants also cry and fuss to show displeasure. At this age, crying indicates a general pain, discomfort, or need, but it doesn't *intentionally* communicate the specific cause of a problem. Crying alerts parents to investigate the problem; in turn, the parents' response can help the infant learn that her actions affect her world. Responding promptly to your baby's cries creates a safe, predictable world for her. Your baby continues to cry to express her needs because she knows it gets results, a fact that encourages further language development as she grows.

Crying also helps an infant become accustomed to the airflow across her vocal folds and to the changes in her breathing patterns. Since speech sounds originate at the level of the larynx, this early stimulation is important.[5] Infant cries vary in pitch (high and low) and intensity (loud and soft), and they relate the level of distress and the urgency of the need. Interpreting an infant's cries involves listening to the pitch, intensity, duration, and pauses between the sounds. It's also helpful to look at an infant's facial expressions and the movement of her arms and legs.[6]

It becomes much easier to interpret a baby's cries at age 5 or 6 months. Observation, patience, and experience help you learn what your baby is saying with her cries. Although a baby expresses different cries during the first 8 months, she won't realize that different cries can yield certain results—and won't intentionally produce them to get these results—until she's 9 months old.

Comprehension

Newborns respond to human voices. A parent's voice usually calms a newborn because it's familiar to her. Newborns are already beginning to distinguish different speech sounds, and new sounds capture their attention. Because babies so easily adapt to noises by tuning them out, your baby may react to a new sound only once or twice. To respond to sounds, infants may pause while sucking (or fussing) and widen their eyes.[7] By age 2 months, your baby can turn her head and look in the direction of your voice. Here's a tip to help placate a baby on a particularly fussy evening: Take her on a walk outside. The new, interesting sounds may distract her enough to calm her.

Warning Signs

- Doesn't coo by making vowel-like sounds
- Doesn't startle in response to a loud sound
- Doesn't try to look at you when you talk to her

Age 3 to 4 Months

Expression

An infant cries when she needs something. Adults can distinguish the level of distress in an infant's cry, although it's difficult to tell what the different cries might mean at this stage.[8] An infant also increases the amount of cooing she does during the day. You might hear her coo with a long vowel-like sound. She starts to make some of these sounds when you interact with her. You may hear an occasional consonant-like sound—possibly a front-lip sound like *p*, *m*, or *b*.[9] She may vary her pitch occasionally and may even try to imitate your tone. She smiles when she sees you, and you may even hear squeals, raspberries, trills, and chuckles. The more you talk to her, the more she vocalizes back to you. Pause occasionally to let her interject coos and other sounds. You're participating in your first proto-conversations. These first instances of turn taking are so exciting!

Comprehension

At this age, your baby shows more and more signs of comprehension. She moves her head and/or eyes when she hears a voice, and smiles at the person speaking to her. She can differentiate between a friendly and an angry voice.[10] As she becomes aware of the different ways she can use her tongue and lips, it may sometimes seem as if she's listening to her own voice.

Warning Signs
- Doesn't make cooing noises with vowel-like or consonant-like sounds
- Doesn't respond to your soothing voice or turn her eyes or head toward a sound source
- Doesn't smile

Age 5 to 6 Months

Expression

Your baby's cooing begins to change at this stage. She might experiment with different combinations of consonant-like and vowel-like sounds. This experimentation is an important part of language development. Research shows that babies who produce more babbled utterances with various consonants and vowels build a better foundation for later word production.[11] Essentially, babbling is practice for speech. The more often a baby shapes her mouth to produce particular sounds, the more automatic these movements become, and the easier it is to make them later when she tries to produce words.[12]

At this age, your baby may combine vowel-like sounds with consonant-like sounds made in the back of the throat (similar to *k* and *g*).[13] She may begin to vocalize while playing with toys, and may experiment with other sounds during play. She may buzz her lips to make a "raspberry" sound, and she squeals when she's happy. She may experiment with contrasting sounds (loud and soft, fast and slow, high and low, and so on). She may even begin to imitate some of your sounds.

Comprehension

At this age, your baby seems frightened by an angry voice and responds with happy squeals to a friendly voice. She can laugh at funny faces and toys. She can smile, respond to her name, and vocalize to an image in the mirror. She moves her eyes and turns her head to find voices in the room, and she starts to recognize familiar household sounds, like a pet dog's panting or someone opening a door.[14]

Warning Signs

- Doesn't babble with both consonants and vowels
- Doesn't respond by vocalizing a sound when you talk to her
- Doesn't follow moving objects or look for the source of a sound
- Doesn't stop her activities to listen to speech sounds, footsteps, or noise-producing toys

Age 7 to 8 Months

Expression

At this age, babbling becomes more variable. As your baby learns to better control the airflow through her vocal tract (throat, mouth, and nose), vowels and consonants begin to sound more recognizable. Your baby mainly experiments with strings of repeated consonant sounds ("da-da-da-da"), although you might hear some variable strings, too.[15] Sound play increases, and your baby may be able to imitate gestures and the tone of adult speech.[16] Sometimes parents interpret *da-da* or *ma-ma* as their babies' first word. Actually, it's a little early to call it a word. A baby babbles continuously at this age, but she can't yet communicate intentionally. At the beginning of this stage, your baby may produce sounds made in the front of the mouth (*p*, *b*, *m*, and *w*), since they're easiest to pronounce. You may also hear *k* and *g* sounds.

Comprehension

At this stage, your baby's comprehension improves all the time. She listens to speech and begins to recognize some

Language Development Facts and Warning Signs

words. You can tell she understands by the way she looks for objects and people who are named. She also listens more closely to her own speech and begins to make it match the patterns she hears. Words begin to have some meaning for your child at around age 6 to 10 months, but she still relies primarily on nonverbal contextual cues (a gesture or the direction of an adult's gaze) to get the meaning of a word.[17] Individual patterns of development are already evident at this age. The largest vocabulary study to date found that babies' understanding at age 8 months ranges from just a few words to as many as seventy-five, with the average being around twenty.[18]

Warning Signs
- Doesn't string together sounds when babbling
- Doesn't look at people who are talking to her
- Doesn't seem to recognize her name
- Doesn't enjoy interactive games like Pat-a-Cake

Age 9 to 10 Months

Expression

At this age, a baby begins to imitate adult speech. She uses vocalizations and gestures in different combinations. She vocalizes distinctly for particular requests, even if she isn't using words yet. She can finally communicate intentionally—albeit preverbally.[19] She uses eye gaze, gestures, and vocalizations to make comments, request items, signal for help, or seek attention.[20] She expresses pleasure by smiling and laughing while looking at adults.

Her use of gestures may include giving you objects to see, reaching toward you, and showing you objects she's interested in. She may hold out her hand to "ask" for food and vocalize at the same time. She makes all sorts of fun sounds including coughs, hisses, tongue clicks, and raspberries. She begins to use an early nonsense language (called jargon) and strings of various consonants like *pee-pie*, *ma-ba*, *wa-da-ga*, and *wa-wy*. She experiments with pitch and loudness, imitates siblings, vocalizes back to you, enjoys social games like Peek-a-Boo, and loves to laugh at funny sights!

Comprehension

At this age, your child's comprehension allows her to follow simple instructions like "Wave bye-bye." She shows you she comprehends more fully by responding more specifically to your speech. For example, when it's time to take a bath and you say, "Let's take off your shirt," she may respond by raising her arms. Or she may crawl toward you when you ask her to come. She's extremely interested in toys that make noises, and she listens attentively to them. When she's engrossed in play, she may not hear what you're saying. She can concentrate on only one task at a time, so it's best to wait until you have her attention before attempting to communicate. At this age, your child pays closer attention to the sounds of the language she hears most often (her native or birth language) and pays less attention to other languages.

Warning Signs

- Doesn't babble frequently and imitate some of your sounds
- Doesn't use gestures and sounds to get help or attention
- Doesn't turn toward you when you call her name
- Doesn't understand words used frequently, like *bye-bye*, *Mommy*, or *Daddy*
- Doesn't smile or enjoy social games like Peek-a-Boo

Age 11 to 12 Months

Expression

At this age, your baby can imitate inflections, rhythms, and facial expressions. She uses more gestures with increasing sophistication. She continues to use eye contact along with gestures and vocalizations to produce different combinations of communicative acts. Her rate of communicative acts is also increasing. One sign that she's close to saying words is her use of communicative acts as frequently as once per minute.[21] She continues to babble frequently throughout the day and she shows signs of understanding the rules of conversation. She may stop babbling when you talk to her, and then start again when you're finished. She may seek your attention by calling to you, and may answer when you call her.

This is an exciting stage because many babies speak their first words now. Don't worry if you don't hear those first words right away; the normal range for first words is age 9 to 18 months. Infants at this age typically use proto-words, "pretend" words used consistently to represent objects. Babies use proto-words when they first realize there's a relationship between a word and an object.[22] For example, a child may call the family cat "mau." Once a child starts to use proto-words, a growing number of real words starts to appear in her vocabulary. For a while, your child uses proto-words and real words together.[23]

Many parents wonder how they'll know when their babies have uttered a first word. Researchers agree that the first word should (1) have a clear vowel sound similar or identical to the one used in the actual word, (2) be a single production followed by a period of silence so it can't be confused with babbling, (3) be used consistently to refer to a person, thing, or situation, and (4) be used in a conversation with someone.[24]

Comprehension

Comprehension at this age includes a child's quicker recognition of her name and the ability to follow simple verbal directions accompanied by gestures. For example, you might say, "Pick up the bear," as you point to a teddy bear. Your child also reacts to your saying "no." She begins to identify some of her body parts, if you provide the appropriate gestures. She can also scan her environment to look for the sources of sounds. Children at this age are also interested in manipulating objects (for example, trying to drink from a cup, eat with a spoon, brush with a hairbrush, and so on).[25] The gap between comprehension and expression continues to grow. On average, an 11-month-old's understanding exceeds fifty words, but she can produce only up to three words.[26]

Warning Signs

- Doesn't gesture or make sounds to get what she wants
- Doesn't babble frequently
- Doesn't look at people who are talking to her
- Doesn't turn her face to look at something you're pointing at or talking about
- Doesn't understand simple words used frequently

Age 13 to 14 Months

Expression

At this age, your toddler practices words she knows and mixes them with jargon. She generally has at least three simplified words in her vocabulary. You may notice her using the same word for different objects or people. For example, she may use *ba* to refer to *ball*, *bath*, and *baby*. Don't think that she can't differentiate among them; she knows what object she's referring to with each *ba*. You can likely distinguish your baby's words by noticing her gestures in context. She may use additional gestures like pointing, waving, blowing kisses, and hugging. Reinforce each communicative act by responding to her *intended* message. Also, whenever you understand what she's trying to say, model the word so she'll learn how to pronounce it.

Your child may expand her babbling to sounds made in other areas of the mouth besides the lips. She may add *n*, *t*, *d*, and *h* sounds. She also begins inserting words into long strings of babbling. She picks up on sounds made by other children and tries to imitate them. She also imitates more and more words and sounds in her environment, including adult words and non-speech sounds.

Comprehension

Even though your child may use only three or four words at this age, she may understand sixty words or more. She still needs to hear words several times so she can learn how to produce them. She can point to clothes, people, toys, and animals you name. But she still needs your help (with gestures) to comprehend what you're referring to. One important skill your baby has learned by this age is sensory integration, the ability to concentrate on words and sounds in the foreground and tune out background noises.[27] If your child can't focus on a particular sound, she may become overstimulated by all that she hears.

Warning Signs
- Doesn't babble in strings
- Doesn't point to and name favorite toys (using simplified words)
- Doesn't initiate social games like Peek-a-Boo
- Doesn't look at objects or people you're talking about
- Doesn't use gestures to ask for help or attention
- Becomes easily frustrated if her communicative attempts aren't understood

Age 15 to 18 Months

Expression

Your child continues to practice words she knows and mixes them with jargon. She typically has at least a four-word vocabulary at 15 months, and her vocabulary gradually develops, averaging roughly ten new words a month for several months. She has at least a twenty-word vocabulary by 18 months. Some children can say fifty or more words at this time. As children approach the fifty-word level, some experience a sudden vocabulary growth spurt. Others experience this spurt between fifty and a hundred words. Some children may not experience a spurt at all; rather, they gradually and steadily acquire many new words.[28] All three patterns of development are typical.

Your child still uses lots of sounds, gestures, and proto-words. She can identify some of her body parts and refer to them by name. Her words sound a little clearer, but she probably still leaves the ends off. She may hum and sing spontaneously. She may play simple question-and-answer games like asking about the names of unfamiliar objects. Late in this stage and into the next (at 18 to 24 months), your child may still use a particular word to refer to several things. She may still overextend the meaning of *ball*, for example, to refer to marbles, eggs, apples, and so on.[29]

Comprehension

Your child comprehends more and more words each day. At 16 months, a child's comprehension ranges widely, from 92 to 321 words, with the average being 169.[30] Your child can identify most of her body parts. She can finally recognize familiar objects by name, even when these objects are out of sight. Before, she could understand words only with the help of gestures and context.

Your child also starts to categorize words at this age. The most common categories include people (parents, siblings, grandparents, self), games (Peek-a-Boo, Pat-a-Cake, Ride-a-Horse), routines (bath time, mealtime, bedtime), familiar objects (household items, toys), clothing, animals, body parts, and action words.[31] She also starts to pay attention to your conversations for longer periods of time and interact with you for a couple of turns.

Warning Signs

- Doesn't use single words
- Doesn't initiate looking at a book
- Doesn't enjoy games or social routines
- Doesn't imitate animal sounds or other non-speech sounds
- Doesn't look at you or make gestures or sounds to show you what she wants
- Shows increased frustration at not being understood, sometimes by throwing a tantrum
- Makes fewer attempts to show you what she wants

Age 19 to 24 Months

Expression

At this age, a child's vocabulary blossoms. Your child most likely experiences a burst of vocabulary growth shortly before or during this stage, and by 24 months she typically has a 200- to 300-word vocabulary.[32] Your child learns five to ten new words a day and can name common objects. By age two, about half of what she says should be understandable to a stranger.[33]

Researchers have identified two distinct styles for learning language: referential and expressive. Some children lean strongly in one direction or the other, but most exhibit features of both. These styles, which are most pronounced at around age 20 months, are seen in the types of words children prefer early on.[34]

Some children notice nouns and acquire first words more readily. These children prefer to label people and objects in their environment. When combining words, these children tend to use real words (and less jargon) in short sentences. Such children have a referential style and are sometimes called "noun lovers."[35] Other children prefer personal-social words and phrases used in routines, such as "I want it," "One more time," and "Where did it go?" They also tend to use more jargon. These children have an expressive style and are sometimes called "noun leavers."[36]

Both styles are equally effective for learning language. Children who prefer a referential style tend to use more clearly articulated single words in the earliest stages of development. Those who prefer an expressive style attempt to produce whole sentences, regardless of whether they can say the words clearly. These differences between styles tend to equalize over time, and children acquire large vocabularies regardless of what style they use initially.[37]

Parents who are aware of their children's learning styles may be better able to adjust their own styles to match their children's. If you're not sure what style your child prefers, don't worry. Her language development won't suffer. If, however, you have a referential child who loves to learn the names of objects and people, you can make it easier for her to acquire vocabulary by labeling things, repeating your child's labels, and describing your environment. You may also use fewer conversational fillers (like *um, so,* and *you know*) and use fewer references to objects that aren't present (using these references better supports an expressive style[38]).

If your child enjoys the phrases associated with social routines and play, you might increase your expressive modeling by using phrases such as "Hi," "Bye," "Please," "Let's go," "My turn," "See you later," and "Thank you." A child with an expressive learning style may also pay more attention to your intonation and may vary her intonation more to express her words.[39]

Whatever style your child prefers, she most likely begins to put two words together between 18 and 24 months (for example, "Go night-night," "More juice," and so on). A two-year-old can produce various consonant sounds and syllable shapes (different combinations of vowels and consonants). For example, a cv (consonant vowel) syllable would be the word *no*, and a cvcv (consonant vowel consonant vowel) syllable would be the word *mama*. On average, a child this age uses nine to ten different consonants sounds in the initial position of words (like *b, t, d, k, g, m, n, h, w, f,* and *s*) and five to six different consonant sounds in the final position of words (like *p, t, k, n, s,* and *r*).[40]

Comprehension

At this age, your child better understands long sentences. She might surprise you by responding to your statements with appropriate actions. When it's time to eat, she may run to her highchair. She even starts to comprehend sentences in different situations, generalizing her understanding. She continues to comprehend many more words than she can express. She can answer simple questions such as, "Where's your cup?" If, however, you ask her a question involving a more abstract concept (like "when," "how," or "why"), she may answer as if you'd asked her a "what" question. For example, if you ask her, "When did John eat?" she may say, "A cracker." When your child is this age, there's no use asking her why she did something. She just won't understand. She can, however, understand things like possession, simple amounts (one or many), directions (up and down), some colors, and two-step commands. She can comprehend shapes and match familiar objects, and she responds rhythmically to music with her whole body.

Warning Signs
- Has never produced a two-word phrase
- Doesn't frequently imitate new words or phrases she hears
- Doesn't follow simple directions such as "Come to Mommy"
- Shows considerable frustration in expressing her needs
- Doesn't effectively use gestures to communicate
- Doesn't engage in imaginary play (feeding a teddy bear, putting her doll to bed, and so on)

Age Two to Three Years

Expression

During these important years, both expression and comprehension continue to blossom. Once your child has acquired a few hundred words, your words alone begin to cue her to produce more words.[41] She doesn't need as many gestures to carry on a conversation. By age three, she has a 900- to 1,000-word vocabulary and can produce three- to four-word sentences.[42] Her vocabulary has increased tenfold over a 15-month period.[43]

At this age, your child's vocabulary grows at an astonishing rate. Some studies indicate that children learn five new words per day from age 18 months to six years, and then increase to twenty new words per day after that.[44] Other studies suggest that children learn ten new words per day until age six, and continue to learn many new words daily until age seventeen.[45] One researcher estimates that children learn one word every two waking hours from age 18 months to adolescence.[46] Despite the different growth patterns they suggest, these studies all point to the importance of modeling lots of new words for your child's ever-growing vocabulary.

At this age, your child uses simple sentences, each containing a subject and verb. She plays with words and sounds, and talks about the present. Her words are clearer than the proto-words she used early on. By age three, 75 percent of what she says should be understandable to a stranger.[47] She may put the ends on some of her words, which makes her speech much more understandable. For example, *kno* may change to *knock*. She begins to suppress some of her phonological processes. The tendency to label items with a double sound (water → *wa-wa* or dog → *dah-dah*) typically disappears by age two and a half. Voicing and de-voicing processes (*toe* → *doe* or *dog* → *dok*) also disappear.

It's normal for children this age to continue simplifying difficult sounds. For example, children may not pronounce the *r* sound correctly until age seven; most change the *r* to a *w* (*rabbit* → *wabbit*). Other difficult sounds that children may simplify include *t, y, th, l, v, ch, sh, j, ng, s,* and *z*. Children also simplify several consonant clusters at this age. Some two-year-olds produce certain consonant clusters correctly, while some eight- to nine-year-olds struggle to master them.[48] (See pages 28–30.) Expect your child to reduce or simplify many consonant clusters. At this age, my son Brent simplified his name to "dent" because he couldn't pronounce the *br* cluster.

Starting at around age two, your child uses negative forms (*no*), simple questions ("What's this?" or "Where go?"), personal pronouns (*I* and *mine*), and prepositions (*in* and *on*). She may not, however, use these forms correctly each time. Your child may also begin to use regular endings on words, like *-ed*, *-ing*, and the plural *-s*.[49] She starts to distinguish between the names of animals and the sounds they make. As she approaches age three, she chatters away in three- to four-word sentences, and her word order shapes up. Some of her utterances are hilarious! Try to write them down so you can enjoy them later.

Comprehension

Your child typically can follow two-step commands, match primary colors, and understand the concept of two. She understands the meaning of prepositions like *in, on,* and *under*. She also can understand other concepts like simple opposites (big and little). She starts to comprehend strings of words without needing extra cues from her environment.

Your child's symbolic play (pretending that one object is another) shows new levels of sophistication as she combines several actions using the same toy. She can comprehend several actions in a row, so describe a series of actions for her to try. She might enjoy stirring and scooping pretend food with a utensil and using it to "feed" a teddy bear. Or she might "drive" a toy train up a mountain, through a farmyard to greet the animals, and into the engine shed to put it to sleep.

Warning Signs

- Doesn't have a vocabulary of fifty words
- Doesn't produce two-word phrases frequently
- Doesn't ask questions
- Has a difficult time being understood by strangers
- Doesn't respond to simple yes-or-no questions
- Doesn't like to play pretend games
- Doesn't combine several actions during play

Age Three to Four Years

Expression

At age four, a child typically has a vocabulary of 1,500 to 1,600 words. She asks various types of questions, uses increasingly complex sentence forms, and can recount stories and events from the recent past. She can also count to five and understand the concept of three. A child this age knows the primary colors and can identify some coins.[50] Some of the more difficult speech sounds start to emerge, like *t*, *y*, and voiced *th* (as in *the*). It's common for boys to have trouble with these sounds and not acquire them until age five to seven. By age four, some girls may be able to pronounce some of the easier consonant clusters like *tw* and *qu*.

By age three years three months, your child no longer deletes the final consonant of words. The fronting phonological process (substituting a front sound like *t* or *d* for a back sound like *k* or *g*) starts to disappear around three years six months. By age three years nine months, the consonant harmony process (changing one consonant in a word to another consonant that's similar to one already appearing in the word, like *forgot* → *gogot*) also starts disappearing.

Many three-year-olds have trouble selecting the proper negative form for a particular context. For example, they use *no, not, can't, don't,* and *won't* interchangeably. This error is normal. Another common error is overextending the grammatical rules for regular forms.[51] For example, children learn the rule for forming the past tense of regular verbs without having it explained to them. They may occasionally apply the rule, however, to irregular verbs (for example, saying *eated* instead of *ate*). They also learn the rule for forming the plural of regular nouns, but they may occasionally apply it to irregular nouns (saying *gooses* instead of *geese*). Model irregular forms as much as possible so your child can learn them.

Your child combines simple phrases to make longer sentences. She's also learning conversational tools that allow her to answer questions on a particular topic.

Comprehension

The number of words your child understands at this age is amazing. She not only recognizes common nouns and verbs, but also many adjectives, especially contrasting ones like *heavy* and *light*. Your child understands many shapes and sizes and can answer questions about her immediate environment. She understands where things are in relation to other objects. For example, she might say, "The ball is under Daddy's chair." She may still have difficulty understanding "how" and "why" questions, although she understands the other "wh" questions (who, what, where, and when). At times, her comprehension is very literal. For example, she may think Sunday is the only day the sun comes out.

Warning Signs

- Doesn't use three- to four-word phrases and sentences

- Doesn't use grammatical suffixes to form common plural forms (*-s*, *-es*), past tense forms (*-ed*), and present progressive forms (*-ing*)
- Frequently acts as if she doesn't understand what you've said
- Repeats or echoes everything she hears, but with little or no comprehension
- Doesn't engage in pretend play
- Doesn't enjoy sharing books
- Has an extremely short attention span, even for brief activities

Age Four to Five Years

Expression

By age five, your child's vocabulary typically exceeds 2,100 words. She can tell long stories and discuss her feelings. Her sentences are grammatically correct 90 percent of the time. She embeds short phrases into other phrases and uses at least four words in an average sentence. She can define objects by their use, express basic information about where she lives, count to thirteen, and pronounce most sounds.[52] For girls this age, more consonant clusters emerge, including *pl*, *bl*, *cl*, *gl*, and *fl*. Boys, however, may need another year for these clusters to appear.

By age four, your child pronounces whole words consistently, instead of leaving out the weak or unstressed syllables. The stopping phonological process (replacing difficult sounds with "stop" sounds, like *this* → *dis*) also disappears by the end of this stage. At this age, if your child is mispronouncing a sound that occurs in her name, consider consulting a speech-language pathologist, since this mispronunciation may embarrass her when she starts school. You can understand everything she says at this age, although she occasionally may confuse her word order and she still may overgeneralize grammatical rules. Her conversational skills still have several constraints at this age. For example, she can answer a question and focus on a topic of interest, but she can't really carry on a sustained dialogue.

Comprehension

By this age, a child typically doesn't have problems focusing on a speaker even with background noise going on. She can comprehend three-step commands, concepts like *before* and *after*, and numbers greater than three. By age five, she knows her own right from left, but can't necessarily distinguish them in others. She develops an understanding of temporal concepts like *today*, *tomorrow*, *yesterday*, *morning*, *afternoon*, *noon*, *night*, and *day*. She begins to understand the relationship between part and whole. She's still learning about relative size concepts like *big*, *bigger*, and *biggest*.

She still interprets sentences that don't have standard word order (subject-verb-object) as if they did. For example, she interprets the sentence "The squirrel was chased by the cat" as "The squirrel chased the cat." At this age, she's mastered most early language concepts like colors, shapes, simple opposites, prepositions, and simpler forms of speech, but her skills will continue to grow throughout childhood and adolescence.

Warning Signs

- Doesn't ask several questions a day
- Has difficulty formulating sentences, as shown by word omissions, confused word order, or deleted word-endings
- Can't retell a simple story that links several thoughts together in an orderly sequence
- Can't talk about the past and future
- Can't follow instructions involving three or more steps

Age Five to Six Years

Expression

By age six, your child typically has a vocabulary of 2,600 words. Many of the remaining sounds emerge, especially for girls, including *ch*, *sh*, *j*, de-voiced *th* (as in *thin*), *r*, *ng*, *s*, and *z*. Some children may still have trouble with consonant clusters, particularly *s* clusters (*sp*, *st*, *sc*, *sm*, *sn*, *sw*, *sl*, *squ*, *spl*, *spr*, *str*, and *scr*) and *r* clusters (*pr*, *br*, *tr*, *dr*, *cr*, *gr*, and *fr*). Many children pronounce these clusters correctly at this age, but a few won't accurately pronounce them until age eight or nine. Some children continue to glide *r* and *l* sounds until age seven (see page 64).

Your child can form many complex sentences. Her conjoined sentences consist of two or more clauses joined by *and* or *but*. Some sentence structures are still difficult for her, especially those containing embedded phrases that begin with *if* and *so*. Also, some words ending in *-ing* are difficult for her to form. She can use all of the grammatical parts of speech to some degree. She can name the days of the week in order and count to thirty. She can verbalize her ideas and the problems she faces without frustration. She can tell a story containing several parts in the right sequence. She loves jokes and simple plays on words.

Her conversational skills can take several turns at this age. She can initiate and maintain a conversation; however, if something she's said needs clarification, she may not be able to provide it. At this age, she tends to repeat her sentence when it isn't understood. She may not be able to elaborate or provide additional information unless it's specifically requested. She's also learning to communicate in the classroom, which involves a different set of skills (answering questions, staying on a topic that the teacher has initiated, not interrupting, and so on) than those needed for regular conversation.

Comprehension

At this age, your child probably understands between 20,000 and 24,000 words.[53] Her auditory and visual attention spans have improved tremendously, and she can filter out unnecessary information and concentrate on the task at hand. She can better comprehend the parts of a sentence and understand them as a whole, rather than relying on word order for comprehension. For example, she doesn't misinterpret the sentence "We can play in the pool after we change clothes" as "We can play in the pool, and after we can change clothes."

Warning Signs

- Can't verbalize her name and basic information about where she lives
- Doesn't attend to a task for more than a few minutes
- Becomes frustrated during shared reading time
- Struggles with pre-literacy skills like rhyming and sound recognition

Age Six to Seven Years

Expression

When your child reaches this age, the concepts underlying *how* she uses speech (semantics and pragmatics) become more evident. Semantics refers to the types of words she chooses and the meanings and uses of these words. Pragmatics refers to how your child uses words to meet her needs and participate in conversation. Babies use pragmatics at a basic level to learn that they can influence someone's behavior to get what they want or need. A child's social use of language grows more refined over time. At age six or seven, she typically not only initiates and maintains a conversation, but also repairs it by adding new information when a breakdown occurs.

When your child is age seven, you start to notice subtle changes in how she participates in conversation and uses language to her benefit. For example, she's less direct in her requests at times, preferring polite hints such as, "These cookies look really yummy." Improved conversational skills help her learn to introduce, maintain, and change the topic of conversation with various listeners.[54]

As your child's cognitive abilities grow, she learns to appreciate the perspectives of others. More difficult language concepts emerge, like the use of irregular verbs, multiple meanings for words, and idioms (for example, "Cut it out"). Don't worry if she occasionally uses an incorrect verb form or plural form. These are the rules of language children violate most often and will eventually learn to follow.

At this age, your child begins using indirect requests instead of blunt commands. For example, if she's gathering books at the library while you're talking to someone, she might say, "I could use some help here," instead of, "Carry these." As she progresses through school, she may pick up slang from her peers and use it in her speech.

Your child can predict the sequences of events for stories and tell a four- to five-part story. Some words that might cause sentence structure problems include *tell*, *ask*, and *promise*. These words tend to interfere with the normal rules about where to place subjects, verbs, and direct objects in a sentence. For example, in the sentence, "Tina promised to bake Jennifer a birthday cake," the baker is different than in, "Tina asked Jennifer to bake a birthday cake." These subtle contrasts take a few years for the school-age child to comprehend. Your child continues to work on the passive sentence form, and probably won't master it until she's about age ten.

Comprehension

By this time, your child's basic comprehension of everyday conversation typically is in place. Activities like reading and writing further stimulate her comprehension of abstract concepts. She begins to be aware of figurative language including similes, metaphors, idioms, and proverbs (although proverbs usually aren't well understood until adolescence[55]). She also understands humor better, and her sense of humor will eventually become more and more abstract. Her use of abstract language grows more refined throughout adolescence.

Your child comprehends increasingly longer sentences that contain embedded phrases. She now understands concepts like *because* and many of the more difficult suffixes, like *-ist*, *-er*, and *-man*. She understands the adverb ending *-ly*. By age seven, your child also understands more difficult grammatical forms like irregular noun-verb agreement (for example, "The deer are running"). One of the goals of first grade is helping children learn to listen to and comprehend a story well enough to retell the plot and describe the main characters.

Warning Signs

- Can't express herself in conversation with friends and peers
- Has difficulty forming sentences
- Can't focus on a task for at least ten minutes
- Has difficulty learning to read

One Last Thought on Normal Language Development

Understanding normal language development helps parents and professionals identify children who might be late bloomers and those who might face more serious language challenges. It's important to remember that just because your child exhibits one or more warning signs, it doesn't mean she has a developmental problem. Don't substitute the advice in this chapter for a professional evaluation. If you have any concerns about your child's language development, talk to your doctor and seek advice from a speech-language pathologist.

Chapter 5

Enhancing Your Child's Language Skills at Each Stage

This chapter discusses specific ways you can create a rich language environment that helps your child's language skills develop naturally to their greatest potential at each stage. You'll learn about the best games to play, the best books to read, and the best verbal strategies for stimulating your child's skills.

When you interact with your child, remember to focus on *his* object of interest. Children (especially younger children) get more information from comments about objects that are right in front of them. If you show your child a flashcard of a ball while he plays with cars and trucks, you ask him to think abstractly about the ball, which won't mean as much to him at that moment as playing with the cars and trucks.

Children learn best from play, from everyday experiences at home, and from simple outings in their communities. Keep in mind, though, that children don't learn language the same way they learn numbers, colors, and letters. They *acquire* language naturally through interactions and modeling. When you engage in activities like singing, rhyming, and finger plays with your child, you use language in ways that make it fun and easy for him to acquire it naturally.

Birth to Age 2 Months

Newborns often leave their parents feeling exhausted. Constant feedings and diaper changes, combined with sleepless nights, can turn lives upside down. Providing verbal stimulation may be the last thing on tired parents' minds, but it's crucial for a child's development, especially during the first few years.

Scientists have recently shown that the brain grows dramatically in the early years, producing billions of neurons and other brain cells, and hundreds of trillions of synapses (connections between these cells).[1] Interactions stimulate and reinforce the synapses between neurons. If stimulation continues, neurons fully connect with other neurons. If there's no stimulation, neurons and synapses wither and die.[2] (Some elimination of unused neural circuits, however, is necessary to streamline children's neural processing and make the remaining circuits operate more quickly and efficiently.) Talking and playing often with your baby encourages healthy brain development and helps develop his language skills.

Carrying on a one-sided conversation with your newborn might seem silly, but he does listen to what you say and the way you say it—and he learns a lot from it! Infants are intensely curious about their world, and everything their parents do and say expands their knowledge and experience.[3] Think of language stimulation as something that occurs naturally all day everyday.

What can you talk about to your newborn? Talk about where he lives, who his relatives are, what you're doing, and so on. Talk while you're feeding him, changing his diaper, dressing him, doing laundry, grocery shopping, making supper, and so on. Pretend he understands everything you say, and use Child-Directed Speech (CDS). (See page 10.) Babies listen to CDS for longer periods of time than they listen to regular speech.

At this age, your baby can make pleasure sounds, coo, respond to human voices, and distinguish different speech sounds. Try to respond to your baby's hiccups, burps, grunts, and groans. Even though he can't yet communicate intentionally, responding to his noises shows him that different sounds receive different responses.

Hold your baby often, talk to him, and watch him search for your voice. Indicate your surprise when he discovers your mouth is the source of the sound. Sing to your baby while rocking him to sleep. Most lullabies have the same rhythm as a relaxed heartbeat, which may be why they're so calming. Encourage older siblings to participate in the bedtime routine by singing lullabies or reading stories to your baby.

Infants like to look at interesting objects with bold, contrasting colors (especially red, black, and white), and objects with different angles and curves attract their interest.[4] Babies seem to especially prefer studying human faces. Allow your baby to study your features. He may concentrate on your hairline, if there's a sharp contrast of color between your hair and skin. Or he may zone in on the angle of your nose. Keep about eight inches from his face so he can see you clearly. Infants also like to imitate facial movements. Model simple movements like opening your mouth or sticking out your tongue. Slowly repeat each movement a few times, and see if your baby tries to mimic the gesture. Near the end of the second month, hold an object about eight inches from your baby's face. Move it slowly up and down and side to side to encourage him to follow it with his eyes.

Your baby lets you know how much stimulation is enough. If stimulation is adequate, he's active and alert. If he's understimulated, he may fall asleep or cry for attention. If he's overstimulated, he may close his eyes, turn away, become irritable, tense up, or arch his back.[5] By watching for these cues, you can provide the right amount of stimulation.

Age 3 to 4 Months

At this age, your baby reacts to face-to-face interactions, so exaggerate your facial expressions while talking to him. Pause occasionally to give him an opportunity to respond. (These interactions with pauses are called proto-conversations and are the earliest forms of turn taking.) Accept any vocalization (including cries, coughs, sneezes, and burps) as your baby's contribution to the conversation. He may also make higher and more variable-pitched coos. Use the same pitch to imitate the sounds he makes, and follow his reactions. See if he spontaneously imitates your sounds.

Babies find comfort in daily rituals (feeding, dressing, bathing) and social routines (rhymes, games, songs). When coupled with proto-conversations, these routines encourage social development and turn taking—important prerequisites to language development. Perform daily tasks in the same way so your baby can learn what to expect. For example, when you bathe your baby, name a few of his body parts in the same order each time: "Here are your eyes, ears, nose…and toes!"

Then tickle his toes and laugh. When he's used to the pattern, an interruption may make him react. Pause after washing his nose and look at him expectantly. See if he gives you a sign that he knows you've stopped talking or he knows the tickles and laughs are coming. Then provide the tickles and laughs as usual. At this age, your infant pays attention for longer periods of time, but be wary of providing too much stimulation.

During infancy fluid can build up in your child's ears, so it's a good idea to monitor his hearing. Does he startle at loud noises? Does he respond to your voice? You might squeak a toy or ring a bell at his side and see if he turns to look at it. Encourage your baby to use his sight and hearing to track an object by rolling a colorful, noisy ball or other object in front of him. If you suspect a problem with your child's hearing, consult your pediatrician. Your pediatrician also should continue to informally screen your baby's hearing at routine checkups.

Some researchers recommend crossover activities at this age. Crossover (or cross-lateral) activities involve crossing your baby's arms or legs over to touch his opposite arms or legs.[6] Because each side of the brain controls the opposite side of the body, crossover activities encourage the two sides of the brain to communicate with each other.[7] Cross your baby's hand to touch his opposite knee or foot, then switch. Do these actions to the beat of a rhyme or song. (See page 203 for more crossover activities.) Some researchers doubt the benefits of crossover activities, but children seem to enjoy them, especially when coupled with rhymes.

I believe it's never too early to do musical activities with babies. Helping a child learn to keep a steady beat provides a solid foundation for later musical experiences, and studies show that emphasizing rhythms and beats fosters a child's reading skills.[8] Help your baby learn the rhythm of a rhyme by clapping his hands or feet together on the beat. He can also learn to recognize the steady beat of music by listening to rhythmic speech and nursery rhymes. There's a wonderful video series called Babies Make Music, which contains rhymes put to simple rhythms that are great to recite when you're massaging or talking to your baby.[9] (See Appendix C for more information.)

It's *never* too early to begin reading to your baby. Books provide new objects for babies to touch, new topics to explore, and stimulating illustrations to study. Small vinyl books or board books are great. Many have mirrored pages. Babies love to focus on new faces and enjoy seeing their own expressions in a mirror. Also look for textured books that enhance learning by allowing your baby to feel a different texture on each page. Some picture books contain only colorful images designed to capture your baby's attention. You fill in the words!

Reading Suggestions

- Choose colorful books with interesting illustrations.
- Read phrases with an animated, singsong voice.
- Pay special attention to objects that interest your baby.
- Put the book down when your baby loses interest.

Age 5 to 6 Months

When your baby is this age, continue to talk to him often during daily routines. Speak slowly and keep your sentences very short. Continue to engage in proto-conversations with him by pausing, looking expectantly, and waiting for him to respond with a coo or facial expression. This stage is a good time to introduce a few signs if you plan to use gestural communication. (See Chapter 7.) When modeling signs to your baby, make sure to say the words that signify the objects or actions represented.

Your baby can make a wide range of sounds, including raspberries, squeals, and sounds that contrast in pitch (high/low), intensity (loud/soft) and duration (long/short). He also expresses new emotions like surprise, excitement, and frustration. He's very interested in objects in his environment, and in making sounds toward those objects. Get down to his level and play with the objects he's interested in. Expose him to a variety of sounds, and help him try to locate the sources. Imitate the sounds he makes, and see if he repeats them.

Sing lots of songs to your baby and let him look in a child-safe mirror to see his expressions. Children this age can begin to enjoy finger plays like Whoops Johnny, Open-Them-Shut-Them, Pat-a-Cake, Itsy-Bitsy-Spider, and Five-Little-Monkeys. There are hundreds of finger plays and rhymes. (Visit your local library for resources.) Finger plays enhance your child's self-expression.[10] In addition, they:

- Encourage your baby's verbal participation
- Help him learn to follow directions
- Increase his manual dexterity and small motor control
- Develop his listening skills
- Enrich his vocabulary
- Increase his attention span
- Teach concepts like order, sequence, and numbers
- Provide relaxation

You'll probably need to move your baby's fingers for him during the finger play, but he'll enjoy the rhythm of the rhyme or song and the interaction with you. Eventually he'll learn to make the movements himself (around age two to three).

Select plenty of picture books from your local library or bookstore, or make your own with pictures cut from magazines and glued onto sheets of paper. Point to objects and name them as your baby looks at them. His interest may not last more than a few minutes at a time, but let him look at picture books every day. When my first son was 6 months old, I made a miniature scrapbook featuring photos of him, Mommy, Daddy, our pets, our house, and our relatives. I gradually added laminated pictures of storybook characters that interested him. I also attached items of different colors, textures, and shapes to the scrapbook with Velcro. He loved to hear the sound as he ripped off each item, then feel its texture before putting it back in place. As he grew older, we added new pictures so he could continue enjoying his scrapbook.

Reading Suggestions
- Choose short, simple picture books and board books.
- Read short phrases aloud slowly.
- Point to people and objects, and name them.
- Make a special time every day to share a book.
- Keep reading time brief.
- Quit when your child's attention begins to wane.

Age 7 to 8 Months

When a child is this age, his babbling become more variable and proto-conversations begin to sound more like adult conversations. Parents naturally become more selective in their responses, giving more attention to speech-like babbling and less attention to reflexive sounds (cries, coughs, sneezes, and burps).[11]

Your child may begin crawling to explore his environment. Get comfortable on the floor with him, and label everything you see. Talk about colors, shapes, textures, body parts, sounds, weight, function, and concepts like opposites and directions. Continue to use finger plays and other social games, and add new ones, like hiding objects under blankets and letting your child look for them. At this age, a baby begins to understand that a whole object exists even though he can see only part of it (a precursor to object permanence—see page 68). He'll try to find an object by looking under something that partially conceals it.[12]

Interruptions in social routines create situations that allow your baby to make a communicative act (mostly gestures at this age). For example, if you've established a routine of playing Ride-a-Horse, play the game a couple of times, then pause and look expectantly at your baby. See if he gives you any sign (gesture, eye gaze, or vocalization) that he knows you're about to bounce him up and down again. Wait for him to perform one or more of these actions, then reward him by playing the game again.

Continue repeating the sounds your baby makes. At this age, he listens closely to your utterances and compares yours to his. Show interest in other sounds, like a ringing doorbell or a barking dog, so your baby may show an interest in them, too.

Your baby still has a relatively short attention span, but it's important to read to him several times a day. He can now hold books and turn the pages. Point to objects on the page as you read their names. Take time to show your baby family photos in albums and scrapbooks. When talking to your baby, keep your sentences short, say them slowly, and use them in context.

Continue singing to your baby and add new songs, like "Old MacDonald Had a Farm" and "The Wheels on the Bus," to your repertoire. Even though some words might be beyond your baby's understanding, he'll focus on the gestures and sounds you make. You also teach him to look at you while you sing.

Reading Suggestions

- Choose short, simple picture books.
- Read short phrases aloud slowly.
- Point to and name the people and objects in a book.
- Choose books that have different textures for your baby to feel.
- Choose lift-the-flap books.
- Try to read to your baby several times a day.
- Quit when your baby shows signs of overstimulation.

Age 9 to 10 Months

At this age, your baby starts communicating his thoughts and requests *intentionally*, and he begins the transition toward saying his first words. Talk to him as much as possible, and respond to the sounds he makes. Continue to sing songs and read nursery rhymes to him. You may grow bored with reading the same rhyme over and over, but the repetition helps your child learn. Continue playing the social games you've been enjoying. Because your baby understands object permanence now, have him look for objects that are completely hidden by other objects.[13]

By now, your baby is accustomed to the way you play a certain game. When you interrupt the game by pausing, your baby not only notices the disruption but also "asks" you to continue by using eye contact, gestures, and vocalizations. If your baby isn't making eye contact regularly, move your face into his line of vision. Don't say anything; just smile. If he doesn't maintain eye contact, prompt him verbally by saying, "Look at me" in a friendly tone.

Continue reading picture books and naming the pictures you see. Show your baby how to point at objects by modeling this gesture. He probably won't start pointing until he's older than 12 months, but seeing you do it will help him learn the gesture. He can use other gestures, like showing you objects he's holding because he wants you to see them or comment on them. Use this opportunity to model the names of the objects. For example, if your baby holds up a plush animal, you might say, "Look! A puppy!" The more he hears you name an object, the more likely he is to say that name in the near future. Occasionally, see if your baby can look at objects you name when he's not holding them.

Continue modeling contrasting concepts. At this age, many children can pull themselves up to standing, so you should have ample opportunities to label *up* and *down* many times a day. Continue enhancing your baby's comprehension skills by pointing to and naming family members, pets, body parts, and so on.

Begin to use puppets with your baby. Buy them or make them by drawing faces with markers on old socks, mittens, or small paper lunch bags. Pretend the puppet is talking to your baby, and encourage him to "talk" back to the puppet. If your baby doesn't vocalize often, try some of the activities below to help him discover his voice.

Activities to Help Your Baby Discover His Voice

- Help your baby discover his tongue and lips by letting him lick jam, ice cream, or yogurt off his lips. Or let him suck on a Popsicle.

- Use a child-safe mirror to show your baby how to wiggle his tongue.
- Make silly faces and noises together. Smack your lips, inflate your cheeks, or blow raspberries. Lead the way and then let your baby take a turn. Be sure to imitate any sounds he makes.
- Use toys that surprise, like a jack-in-the-box, because they're more likely to make your baby vocalize. Other toys that make noises or pop up might encourage your baby to vocalize a sound. Whenever he vocalizes (and any vocal sound counts!), reward him with hugs and praise.
- Take out a toy that has moving parts or that makes a sound. Play with it a few times, then stop and look at your baby expectantly. Wait until he vocalizes a request to continue. When he does, reward him with hugs and kisses, and play with the toy again.
- Vocalize a lot when playing with plush animals, vehicles, bells, airplanes, and other toys that lend themselves to noisemaking. Encourage your baby to imitate you.
- Play with a toy phone by making ringing sounds and talking into it.
- Model the sounds associated with certain feelings and situations. For example, say, "Ah!" when fireworks explode; "Pop!" when bubbles hit the ground; "Ow!" when you hurt yourself; "Oh!" when you're surprised; "Roar!" when you look at a picture of a lion; and so on. Use facial expressions, gestures, and exaggerated pitch changes to match.
- Sing to your baby using babbling sounds *(la-la-la)*. Encourage him to join in.
- While your baby plays with musical instruments or pots and pans, vocalize the sounds the instruments make. For example, a triangle goes *ting-a-ling-a-ling,* a drum goes *boom-boom,* cymbals *crash,* and so on. Insert these sounds into a story or song you create. This activity also introduces your baby to the names of the instruments.
- Once your baby begins using sounds to communicate his needs or signify objects, start associating these sounds

with actual words. For example, if your baby says *mmm,* associate it with *Mom* by modeling the word and using a gesture like pointing to Mom. If he says *ku,* associate it with *car* or whatever you think he's describing by showing him the object and modeling the word. These actions reinforce the idea that language has meaning.

- Instead of asking your baby a yes-or-no question, give him a choice, which shows him you expect him to respond to your question. For example, say, "Would you like milk or juice?" Even though he can't repeat the word, he might show his preference with a gesture, eye contact, or a vocalization.
- Use puppets, which are great for teaching role-playing, turn taking, and first words.[14]

Using these activities to encourage vocalizations helps your child get used to making meaningful sounds, which in turn will help him say words. Typically developing children between ages 9 and 15 months begin to comprehend simple books based on the pictures that accompany the text. At these ages, children don't directly associate printed words with the story being presented in a book, and they may only marginally pay attention to key words within the story being read.[15] For this reason, use picture books that contain only one word on each page. Once you know your child comprehends the word, expand it into a simple phrase. For example, instead of saying "Ball," you might say "Little ball" or "Blue ball." Resist the urge to read more complex books to your child at this time.

Reading Suggestions

- Choose short, simple picture books.
- Read short phrases aloud slowly.
- Point to and name the people and objects in the book.
- Stop and wait to see if your baby will "comment" on something in the book.
- Choose books that have textures for your baby to feel.
- Choose lift-the-flap books, and play Peek-a-Boo with them.
- Choose books that contain fun sounds.

Age 11 to 12 Months

At this age, your child begins to use his first recognizable words meaningfully and consistently. Researchers believe that children initially learn words based upon context and association. For example, when your child participates in a game like Pat-a-Cake with you, he may hear and remember the word *pat* as a part of the game. The next time you play, he may say the word because he links it to the game. Eventually, he learns to use the word in different contexts because he *hears it used* in different contexts. This progression occurs for most words at this early stage; however, some children can use certain words in different situations as soon as they learn them.[16] The ability to expand a word's usage beyond its original context improves as your child better understands various situations, language concepts, and words modeled in various contexts.[17]

Your child is also learning how to use words to draw attention to, comment on, and request objects. Encourage him to point to something and say its name. Don't, however, ask him to repeat a word. Indirect methods of eliciting responses are much more effective. For example, if your child shows by his gestures and vocalization that he wants something (like a toy), show him the toy, model the word, and wait a few seconds to give him time to vocalize before you give it to him. Be careful not to frustrate him by waiting too long.

Continue to label everything you see using one-word models. Labeling is important because your child needs to comprehend an object's name before he can use the word meaningfully. Eventually your child will follow simple commands and retrieve requested objects because he can comprehend the words.

Gestures also can help your child comprehend what you say. I used to play a bathtub game with my son to help him comprehend the names of objects. I'd name the objects as he played with them in the tub. When it was time to get out, I'd ask him to help me put away the toys. I'd ask him to show me or give me an object, and I'd point in its direction. He didn't always respond correctly, but the game was fun to play because it helped him learn to listen. We started with two objects and added more until he could identify about twenty-five. Once I was sure he comprehended an object's name, I began to model it in different contexts. He started saying the word in no time. When engaging in these types of activities, be playful. Don't use the activities to test your child's comprehension.

When your child begins to use words, help him learn nouns by naming the objects he focuses on.[18] Don't restrict your activity to labeling nouns; encourage other types of words as well, like adjectives, adverbs, verbs, and greetings. Try to model common, useful words like *big, little, more, again, gone, bye-bye, go, here, up, down, on,* and *off.*

Children tend to understand verbs earlier than they can express them. This tendency may result from parents who encourage the understanding—but not the expression—of verbs. Parents often ask children to eat, drink, come, go, climb, look, do, or catch, but they don't often give kids the opportunity to say these words. Young children might not be able to focus on the verb while performing the task.[19] A child can learn verbs when a parent mentions the action right before the child performs it.[20] For example, a parent might say, "Look, here's the cookie dough. *Stir* it. Can you *stir* it?" This prompting encourages the child to say, "I stir it" or something similar. The parent can then respond, "That's right, you can *stir* it," and reinforce the verb after the child has performed the action.

Sometimes children learn vocabulary by simply overhearing words. In many cultures, children learn most of their words in this way. Don't underestimate a child's ability to learn language by listening to real-life social situations.[21] For example, you may be surprised at the number of words your child picks up as he listens to your interaction with a salesclerk or your conversation with a friend in the park.

A child often uses his first words to refer to many (sometimes inappropriate) things. For example, your child might use *light* to refer to a light and to tell you to turn it on. He might use *TV* to refer both to the TV and to the remote. He might use *night-night* to refer to darkness and to the time to go to sleep. In addition to overgeneralizing the meanings of words, children sometimes undergeneralize the meanings. For example, a child might use *cookie* to refer only to his favorite sugar cookies and not to the chocolate chip cookies sitting on the table. Children use most first words for fairly specific purposes: to request something, to name objects or people, to control the behavior of someone else, or to express emotion. Your child will spend the next eight to nine months sorting his first words into their appropriate grammatical categories.

Continue engaging in social games, outings, songs, nursery rhymes, and reading with your child. Use the strategies in Chapter 1 to help your child say the words he knows.

At this age, your child tries to greet people socially, perhaps using a nonverbal "hi" (eye contact, vocalization, smile) or trying to wave good-bye. Don't be disappointed if these attempts occur too late for the other person to appreciate them (after the person has walked away, for example).

A good way to help your child learn the concept of "gone" or "bye-bye" is to make a picture book of your child's favorite characters, animals, and people. Leave each left-hand page blank. As you turn to a blank page, say, "Gone" or "Bye-bye" to the previous picture. You can also use the picture book for naming. When your child has learned how to name an object, have him name it, turn the page, and say "gone." He'll eventually expand his expression to two-word phrases such as "Ball gone."[22]

Reading Suggestions

- Pick short, simple books with two- to three-word sentences.
- Make your own picture books of your child's favorite things.
- Don't worry about finishing every book you begin.
- Follow your child's lead.
- Talk about the pictures that interest your child.

Age 13 to 14 Months

Your child touches everything now and explores new sights, sounds, and textures. Take him outside and let him discover nature. Talk about the rough texture of the bark and the beautiful colors of the leaves. Listen for leaves crackling beneath your feet, birds singing, and crickets chirping. Provide lots of labels so he can learn the names of natural things.

During mealtimes, talk about the different foods, and draw his attention to each food as you name it. Offer him a choice of foods to eat by holding up two items and naming them. Label different types of clothing as you dress and undress him, and name your own clothing: "Look; I'm putting on my socks." Remember to label items in different settings to show your child that word meanings extend to other situations (for example, say at his grandparents' house, "Papa is taking off his socks").

Continue playing the social games you've been playing (nursery rhymes, songs, outings, and so on). These routines make a child's world predictable and safe, and you can use them to encourage your child to make communicative attempts. (Remember to avoid overanticipating his needs!) Children learn by repetition, and your child may now start to supply the last word of a line of a rhyme. At this age, children love rhymes and songs about their body parts, including "Head, Shoulders, Knees and Toes" and "Teddy Bear, Teddy Bear, Turn Around." Sing these songs slowly and give your child time to point to each body part. Children this age also love to scribble (a precursor to understanding the meaning of print). Give your child crayons and paper, and talk to him about what he's coloring.

Many babies this age take their first steps, and some can walk quite well. It's harder to find quiet time for reading once your child starts walking, but try to read together several times a day. Surround your child with books. I have a basket of books my sons can look at whenever they want. I also have special books with delicate dust jackets they like to carefully remove, and ones I've saved from childhood. It's always a treat for them to choose one of the special books, which are usually reserved for bedtime. Library books are a big hit, especially ones they've picked out themselves, and they enjoy new books much more than candy or toys.

By now, your child's attention span is long enough to allow him to sit through a short book. You may feel grateful that you can finally read through an entire book! Keep in mind your *child's* needs, however. The time spent rushing through a book just to finish it may be wasted for him if it's read too fast. Let him point to objects as you name them, if that's what he wants to do.

Look for books that have one or two words on each page or that contain activities to do, like lift-the-flap books. If there's a special picture on every page, encourage your child to find it. You want him to enjoy reading time, so choose books he can understand, and don't make him remain sitting in your lap when he's obviously had his fill of reading time.

Reading Suggestions

- Lengthen your child's attention span by letting him have a snack during the story.
- Give your child something to hold that relates to the story (a puppet, a plush animal, and so on).
- Let your child turn the pages and touch the pictures.
- Pause while reading to let your child examine every picture he finds interesting.
- Use an animated voice while reading, and make all the sounds that bring the story to life.

Age 15 to 18 Months

Libraries can be great places for children this age. Many libraries have programs that encourage children to sit in their parents' laps and listen to stories. Some programs play songs between stories and provide other activities to maintain children's interest. Library outings also provide opportunities for parents and children to socialize, explore new topics, and learn new songs. Continue singing with your child at home. At this age, children really enjoy making big gestures associated with songs.

Play time provides an excellent opportunity to model words. When you play with your child in the bathtub or sandbox, name all the toys, and model some verbs, too. Try to provide several different toys from the same category, like three different trucks, so your child learns that *truck* refers to more than just his favorite one.[23]

Continue to use short sentences to describe what you see and do. At age 18 months, your child can put two words together, so model two-word phrases for him. When he asks for something using only one word, use one of the strategies discussed in Chapter 1 to help him expand his utterance. (See page 25.) If he says only "milk" to ask for milk, model phrases such as, "More milk." Praise your child for putting words together.

Pretend play emerges at this age. Show your child how to use objects imaginatively. For example, show him how to pretend to feed his plush animal, give it a drink, change its diaper, and put it to bed. This pretend play helps him learn symbolic play (using certain objects to represent other objects). Show him how to pretend that a box is a car that's going down a road made of blocks. Give him a toy phone and have him pretend to call Grandma. Model some of the words he might use on the phone, like *hello, good-bye, fine,* and so on.

Introduce new social games that model new words, like knock-knock jokes and Hide-and-Seek. Introduce water play. Fill a large bowl or tub with water and gather child-safe items from your kitchen (like plastic containers, a funnel, and measuring cups and spoons) or plastic toys. Let your child play with the items in the water. Show him how to pour the water into different containers. Label concepts like *wet, dry, full,* and *empty.* Pretend to make a rain shower and talk about what animals and people do when it rains. (Watch your child carefully around water, of course.)

Take advantage of everyday outings to expand your child's vocabulary. When you grocery shop, name the foods as you select them. See if your child can name them as you point to them. Plan frequent outings to the playground, zoo, circus, fair, library, mall, marina, aquarium, farm, museum, and so on.

At the end of the day, ask your child if he remembers what he saw or did. If he doesn't express a word or two about what happened, give him a short summary of his activities. This reminder helps him develop his short-term memory skills. At evening reading time, choose a book that talks about something your child did during the day. By this age, your child can follow directions to help you pick up toys and books.

Reading Suggestions

- Read rhymes and stories containing real and nonsense words.
- If you know your child is familiar with a story, omit the last word of a line and see if he can supply the word or a vocalization.
- If your child doesn't want to listen to the words being read, just comment on the pictures together.
- Let your child initiate comments about pictures he sees in the book.
- If your child has a favorite book, read it to him whenever he wants.

Age 19 to 24 Months

Encourage your child to tell you about the things he sees and does. He now can follow more complex directions, such as, "Bring me the big ball, please," or, "Put your crayon on the table." Make a simple game out of following directions, like playing Simon Says. This stage is a good time to begin modeling the words that describe how various objects function. For example, show your child a broom and say, "We use a broom to sweep the floor."

You don't need expensive toys to stimulate your child's development. All you need are interesting activities that capture his attention. Children learn when they bang on pots and pans, when they drop objects from highchairs, when they smell interesting aromas, and so on. They engage all their senses to learn about their environment.

Use play dough to show your child how to form different shapes. Make your own play dough by mixing one tablespoon of vegetable oil with a cup of water. Stir in two cups of flour and a half-cup of salt. Knead the mixture until it forms a dough. Add a little more flour if the dough is too sticky, or a little more water if it's too dry. Show your child how to make different animal shapes with the dough. Encourage him to make creatures, and have the creatures "talk" to each other. Start modeling counting and the concept of the number two. Show your child how to count objects made from play dough.

Let your child paint with washable water-based paints, and talk about the colors. Show your child how to dip the brush in the water and then in the paint, and then how to paint with it on the paper. Talk about cause and effect: "When we put the brush in the water, it gets wet." Talk often about opposites like big and little, wet and dry, up and down, in and out, empty and full, light and dark, and so on. Demonstrate these concepts in real situations rather than discussing them when they come up in a book. Remember, children learn best by *doing!*

Show your child how to sing, clap, and keep the beat as you enjoy music together. Continue to sing songs and recite nursery rhymes, especially ones that reinforce concepts your child is learning. Buy some toy musical instruments or make your own. (See page 204.) Let your child play with maracas, finger cymbals, castanets, tambourines, jingle bells, whistles, harmonicas, and drums. Talk about the different sounds they make. Musical instruments are great for modeling concepts like loud and soft, high and low, and fast and slow. Get your child interested by saying, "Let's bang the drums," or, "Let's blow the whistle." You can play a modified version of Simon Says by taking turns telling each other what instrument to play.

At this age, your child begins to understand the power of language. He may try to influence your actions throughout the day. For example, he may stand at the refrigerator and say, "Want milk." When you reach for it, he may say, "Want juice," and grin. He also begins to have more influence on how you share stories. When you look at books and magazines together, he may want to flip back and forth between two pages and name his two favorite animals. Humor him, of course, and expand his utterances by describing what the animals are doing in the pictures. This type of interaction allows you to focus on your child's topic of interest.

Try to notice what style your child uses to learn words. (See page 86.) If he uses a referential style, help him by labeling

Enhancing Your Child's Language Skills at Each Stage

things, repeating his labels, and describing his environment. If he uses an expressive style, help him by using short phrases and lots of intonation. For example, say, "Up you go" when putting him in his highchair. If you don't know which style he uses, continue to model language naturally as you play with him.

Avoid asking your child to say certain words or phrases to show off for family or friends. Even outgoing children often remain silent and make faces when asked to perform in front of others or on the phone. Resist the urge to prod your child to talk. Soon enough he'll carry on conversations without your help.

Reading Suggestions

- Make the story as exciting as possible while your child is paying attention.
- Make a puppet or some other item to go along with the story. Let your child hold the item while you read. If he wants, let your child act out the story with the item.
- If your child wants to flip back and forth between two pages in a book, let him do it as long as he's interested.
- Don't worry if you don't finish a book.

Age Two to Three Years

By this age, your toddler becomes increasingly independent. His short-term memory skills have increased, so he attempts to say longer sentences. Try to stay one step ahead of him by modeling four- or five-word sentences and occasionally challenging his comprehension with more complex sentences. For example, instead of saying, "I saw a dog," say, "I saw a big white dog. He was chasing a small brown dog around a tree!" Talk about how objects and people are similar and different. Try to expand the topic of conversation while fulfilling your child's request. For example, if your child says, "I want cracker," say, "I want a cracker, too. Would you like a round one or a square one?" You reinforce your child's language skills when you acknowledge his reason for communicating.[24]

Children this age enjoy puzzles. At first, try the ones with knobs on the pieces. Use language during the activity whenever possible. Talk about the colors, shapes, and objects on the pieces. Count the pieces as your child puts them in their correct places. To help your child learn prepositions, get a cardboard box and some of your child's toys. Place the toys in different locations around the box (above, below, beside, over, under, inside, on, and so on), and talk about where they are.

If your child has trouble pronouncing a particular sound, don't correct him explicitly. Just model the correct sound as you expand or extend his utterance. Another way to model a sound is to read a book that repeats the sound often. For example, if your child can't produce the *h* sound correctly, you might read *Horton Hears a Who!* by Dr. Seuss. Therapists use this technique to help children hear the differences among sounds. One of the first steps to learning a new sound is distinguishing it from other sounds.

Create your own language games that help your child learn to pronounce sounds. Make a "surprise box" containing toys whose names all begin with a certain sound. Have him reach into the box and try to guess the toy without pulling it out. Your child can use his imagination to drive cars over a road of cards with pictures that start with a certain letter on them. When the car stops, ask him to tell you what object is on the card.

Continue to talk about the days' events to improve your child's memory skills. He may be counting to two or three by now. He can match colors, and he can name some of the primary colors even though he may not always be correct. If your child isn't quite ready to name colors, keep modeling the names of the colors for him. The better his comprehension becomes, the more accurate his expression will be.

Continue to take advantage of situations that can teach your child about cause and effect. For example, while washing hands together, say, "If the water is too hot, it will burn you." Continue to model the opposites you've been working on, and add some new ones. Try to find books that reinforce the concepts he's learning. Your child is beginning to grasp many of the grammatical forms of language now, so read a variety of books together often.

Reading Suggestions

- Let your child choose longer books with more difficult vocabulary.
- Choose books that reinforce customs, holidays, and topics that interest your child.
- Interrupt your reading occasionally, and ask your child various "wh" questions (who, what, where) about what you've read.
- Ask your child what he thinks will happen next in the story.
- Ask your child to tell you the story in his own words.
- If your child has memorized all the words in a book, change a word or two and see if he catches the change.

Age Three to Four Years

At this age, your child begins to enjoy group activities more and more. Make a toy camera out of a cardboard box and go on a safari in your neighborhood. Take a winter adventure walk in the snow to find icicles or snow rainbows (branches bent over from the weight of the snow). Your child loves to go outside and collect objects, play in the sand, take walks, or just roam. While you're out and about, talk about what you see and what you're doing. Computers and electronic gadgets can make daily life physically and mentally undemanding, so make time for the exploration that's so important for your child's physical and cognitive development.

Take time for artistic endeavors, too. Sit down and make a collage together. Color or paint pictures, count the crayons or paints, and label the colors. Ask your child what his artwork is about rather than describing what you see. Play dough and clay are fun materials to play with at this age, and they can be used to teach prepositions: "The snake is *inside* the cave." Make up stories about what you create. Museums provide a wonderful introduction to art and art history. If you live near an art museum, check to see if it offers fun arts-and-crafts activities for kids. Some museums offer free admission for children who accompany a paying parent.

Parenting author John Rosemond recommends that children play with toys that let them create and construct things. Examples of such toys are crayons, scissors, clay, Lincoln Logs, Legos, blocks, gear toys, and cardboard bricks. You can turn any large cardboard box into a playhouse, rocket ship, or cave, and provide great language stimulation. Adding toy people to boxes and blocks can be a wonderful way to inspire imaginative fun and conversation. If your child has too many one-dimensional toys that don't allow for creative transformations, he may become bored. Help your child's imagination grow by taking a common household object, like a shoebox or kitchen container, and encouraging him to imagine all the different things it could be.[25]

At this age, your child likely engages in lots of imaginary play. He's also old enough to share his toys, take turns, and play in a group. He often punctuates his play with sounds and words as he explains his actions, makes noises, or assumes various roles. Give your child some of your old clothes, and let him play dress-up. Show him how to put on a play or a puppet show. Take time to explore and rediscover your world through the eyes of your child.

Reinforce familiar prepositions, and begin modeling more complex ones like *to, from, beside,* and *between.* This stage is a good time to begin talking about letters. Many children learn letter sounds through musical activities. (See Appendix A.) Other fun musical ideas include recording your child singing a modified Simon Says game. He'll think it's funny to hear his voice played back, and it'll be fun for both of you to follow his commands.

At this age, your child asks lots of questions. He still needs help with "why" and "how" questions, so model these often. He's typically mastered the other "wh" questions by now (who, what, where, when). He continues to work on grammatical forms. A good activity for learning possessive noun forms is sorting laundry. Ask your child, "Whose is this?" Reading books also reinforces grammatical rules.

If he makes a grammatical error, don't correct him and make him say it again. Instead, use the techniques described in Chapter 1. (See pages 24–26.) If your child makes a grammatical mistake with verb tense or word order, simply recast the sentence using the correct order or verb form. Recasting your child's sentences is an excellent way to model correct grammatical forms without calling attention to what you're doing.[26] Your child will pick up on the proper order and form without feeling he's been corrected.

When you hear your child attach regular endings to irregular verbs (*eated* instead of *ate,* or *knowed* instead of *knew*), model the correct form by using it in a sentence. To help your child learn irregular past tense forms, play the following game:[27]

Today I am riding. Yesterday I . . . . . . rode.
Today I am driving. Yesterday I . . . . . . drove.
Today I am sleeping. Yesterday I . . . . . . slept.
Yesterday I rode. Tomorrow I will . . . . . . ride.

Provide the last word of each sentence until your child learns them. Then, leave off the last words and see if he can provide them.

Also work on past tense forms by asking your child what he did today. Work on future tense forms by asking your child what he'd like to do tomorrow. To help your child understand temporal sequences, cut out the frames of a favorite comic strip, mix them up, and have your child put them in the right order. Try to find a comic strip whose story is told more by the pictures than the words. You can also read the words to your child and help him use the language to put the frames in order. Talk about what happened first, second, third, and so on.

Because language games don't require props, they're excellent for car trips—especially long ones. You can play I Spy to encourage your child to guess an object you have in mind. Car trips are also great times to address important questions like, "Why is Big Bird called *Big* Bird?"

Rhyming games are fun for four-year-olds who can understand and manipulate rhyming words. At this age, my son loved to change the endings of familiar nursery rhymes to different rhyming words (or nonsense words). For example, he'd say, "Humpty Dumpty sat on a *track*. Humpty Dumpty had a big *back*. All the king's horses were *black*, and all the kings' men said *quack*." Don't be afraid to read new rhymes with more complex vocabulary to help your child learn new words.

When your child is this age, you begin to hear the hilarious quips that children are famous for and that parents love to tell stories about. Jot down some of his quotes in a journal so you can enjoy them later.

Reading Suggestions

- Give your child his own library bag and let him pick out his library books.
- Stop reading when you encounter a difficult word, and talk about its meaning.
- Choose books that reinforce concepts you're working on.
- Choose rebus books (ones in which small pictures occasionally appear in place of words), so your child can "read" part of the story.
- Point to the words as you read them to show your child that a story is read from left to right and top to bottom.
- Choose books that contain special auditory or visual effects, and let your child push the buttons, act something out, or follow the directions at the right place in the story.
- Reward your child's good behavior with books instead of toys or candy.

Age Four to Five Years

By now your four-year-old has become an avid explorer. He wants to share increasingly complex books and continues to soak up new experiences. He probably asks numerous questions every day. ("Why don't I fall out of bed when the earth moves?") He's curious and eager to show off his knowledge and abilities.

A four-year-old's sentences contain four to five words on average. He can use negative forms and construct questions correctly. If your child still has problems with question forms, have him play games like Twenty Questions and Who-Stole-the-Cookies-from-the-Cookie-Jar? Memory games, which can help teach new vocabulary, also teach your child how to use the conjunction *and* to combine phrases and sentences. "I went to the toy store *and* bought a ball." Challenge your child's memory by adding more and more words. "I went to the toy store *and* bought a ball *and* a marble." Here are some more word games for car trips or anytime:

- *Word classification games.* See how many items in a particular category your child can name in one minute. Choose categories that interest your child (tools, games, books, movies, toys, animals, vegetables, sports, clothing items, flowers, colors, and so on).
- *Name the category.* Name several items in a particular category, and have your child identify the category. For example, "Penguins, zebras, horses, and foxes are all...animals."
- *Pick the word that doesn't belong.* Tell your child a list of items that are closely related, except for one. For example, "Cookie, Popsicle, horse, candy bar. Which one doesn't belong?"
- *Which two words go together?* Tell your child a list of words that contains two items with a special relationship. For example, "Hammer, orange, nail, bird. Which two go together?"
- *Complete the sentence.* Have your child complete your sentence. For example, "A playground is a place to...play."
- *Synonyms.* Have your child answer your question. For example, "Can you think of another word that means *big*?"
- *Antonyms.* Have your child complete your sentence. For example, "The opposite of cold is...hot." "The opposite of tall is...short."
- *Similarities.* Ask your child, "How is a car the same as a truck?"
- *Differences.* Ask your child, "How is an apple different from an orange?"[28]

At this age, your child probably uses conjunctions in simple sentences quite well. He may, however, continue to need help using conjunctions to combine and embed phrases within sentences. He may also use long run-on sentences to tell a story. He still doesn't fully understand the concept of time, and he relies on word order to understand a sentence. Passive sentences and sentences joined by a conjunction may confuse him. Sentences that contain the words *before* and *after* often have confusing word order. ("Before we go to baseball practice, we need to stop at the store.") Sentences that use specific time-constraint words like *yesterday, today,* and *tomorrow* often don't disturb the word order. ("We need to stop by the store today, then we'll go to baseball practice.")

By age four, your child may understand some kinship terms. The concept of family develops in three stages. A child first understands the terms *mother, father, sister,* and *brother.* At the second stage, he understands the terms *son, daughter, grandfather, grandmother,* and *parent.* At the third stage, he understands the terms *uncle, aunt, cousin, nephew,* and *niece.*[29] Work with him on verbs like *was, were, would, should, could, must,* and *might.* Also model comparative forms like *big, bigger, biggest,* and *more than;* possessive nouns like *John's* and *your sister's;* and possessive pronouns like *his, her,* and *your.*

By age five, your child can tell stories and has a growing sense of humor. He begins to realize when nonsense words don't fit. He understands knock-knock jokes and can use silly words in familiar rhymes. For example, "Baa-baa black sheep, have you any…hot dogs?" or, "Little Bo-Peep has lost her…elephant!" Children this age can also tease and talk about their emotions. They also love magic, make-believe, and group games, and will be ready for new experiences when they start school.

Reading Suggestions

- Choose library books that expand your child's comprehension and vocabulary.
- Talk about abstract ideas in a story, like problems that are solved and emotions that are felt.
- Be willing to repeat your child's favorite story umpteen times. Repetition not only reinforces the experience, but also allows him to direct his learning.
- Reinforce the connection between books and reality. For example, "He has a kitten just like your friend Abby's!"

Age Five to Six Years

When your child begins school at this age, he enters a new phase of language development. His thirst for knowledge and his ability to absorb information amaze you. He begins to refine his conversational skills to consider the listener's perspective. While you may find it difficult to make enough time to talk with your child, remember that he still needs your attention and verbal stimulation. Try not to tune out his nonstop chatter when you're tired and trying to get dinner on the table.

Your child needs to hear you use longer sentences and more challenging vocabulary. Don't underestimate his ability to understand what you say. It's fun to explain abstract concepts to a child this age. Your child is learning the grammatical rules for suffixes, and he benefits from hearing you use the passive construction occasionally. For example, when returning home from soccer practice, you might say, "How well the ball was caught by the goalie," or, "The game was won by someone's clever moves."

Remember to follow your child's lead. Allow him to initiate and control the conversation by letting him change the subject. He's learning to tune into his listener's comprehension and clarify points that weren't understood. He's also learning to build on another's statements to make the conversation flow. When you focus on your child's topic of interest, he probably takes more turns in the conversation because the topic interests him.

Your child is probably eager to apply new reading and writing skills he's learning at school to situations at home. Help him reinforce these skills. Here's one way: When eating pretzels, bite strategically so the remaining pretzel shapes resemble different letters. Point out the letter shapes to your child and have him trace each letter with his finger. The tactile sensation will enhance his memory of the letter's shape. See Chapter 6 for more ideas to help reinforce literacy skills.

Your child also is learning the names of coins and basic concepts about money. He's now more interested in stories, especially in making up his own. Help him create stories and songs by writing down his words as he narrates. Have him illustrate each story or song, then staple or clip the pages together so he can read the story often. Encourage your child to act out his stories by dressing up or using puppets. Also encourage him to use different voices to represent different characters. This activity is a great alternative to watching TV.

Your child is becoming skilled at word games, so play them whenever you're waiting in line or driving in the car. Rhyming is a skill that helps your child learn to read. Children who enter school knowing many rhymes have greater success learning to read. Have fun with rhymes by occasionally changing the endings. Also change some of the common rhyming words in your child's favorite songs. Children think these changes are hilarious!

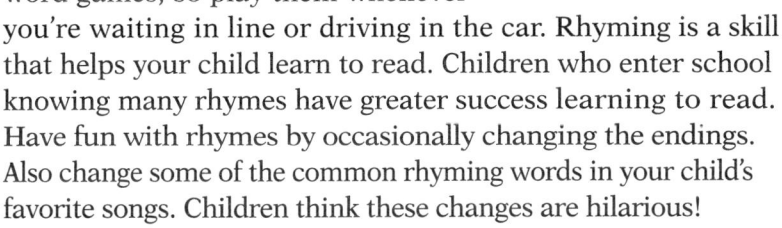

At this age, your child is curious about customs, human anatomy, and how things work. He still understands more than he can express, so don't be afraid to read more difficult books with him. Reading is essential to building vocabulary and learning about the world.

Reading Suggestions

- Subscribe to a children's magazine like *Ladybug* or *Spider*. Your child will look forward to receiving a copy every month.
- Do plenty of reading yourself so your child can see that reading is enjoyable.
- Occasionally share with your child nonfiction books filled with fun facts and challenging vocabulary.
- Choose a few rebus books from the library. When you get to a picture, point to it and wait for your child to name it.
- If your child has a good attention span, try reading some short chapter books like *Charlotte's Web* or *Mrs. Piggle-Wiggle*. These books help your child learn to comprehend the words without illustrations. Try reading a chapter a night.

Age Six to Seven Years

I can't stress enough the importance of creating a solid foundation for your child's language and literacy development. As he progresses through the grade levels, your child's verbal and writing skills face greater challenges. Every new subject added to your child's curriculum requires language skills. His ability to manipulate the smallest parts of language during rhyming and syllable exercises is linked to his ability to read. If your child has difficulty with these skills, get early intervention. Don't assume a language problem is just a phase your child will outgrow. Many children with early language delays show signs of later language delays as they advance through middle school and high school. If your child has a language delay, make it a priority to give him the help he needs to build strong language skills.

A child this age enjoys telling stories, acting out events, and solving problems. He can follow complex directions such as, "Please give the dogs food and water. Then bring in their chew toys because it's going to rain." The words *tell, ask,* and *promise* might cause sentence structure problems at this age, because they tend to break the normal rules about where to place nouns, verbs, and objects in a sentence. For example, in the sentence "Brent promised Phillip he'd come to the soccer game," the person coming to the soccer game is different than in the sentence "Brent told Phillip to come to the soccer game." Your child will still work on mastering passive sentences until he's about ten. The more he hears you model the correct forms, the quicker he learns the rules—and the exceptions.

Talk about how words can have more than one meaning. For example, when you're reading a book together about a boy who saw a bat, take the opportunity to talk about how the context determines whether the boy saw a baseball bat or the nocturnal animal. As always, the best way to build your child's language skills is to read, read, talk about what you've read, and read some more! As difficult as it may be at times, try to limit your child's screen time—that includes TVs, computers, and electronic games. Encourage him to think of reading as his primary form of entertainment.

Reading Suggestions

- Continue reading to your child even when he begins to read on his own.
- Help your child choose age-appropriate books that won't frustrate his reading attempts.
- Encourage your child to read silently if he wants to, but also make time for reading aloud so you can help him with new words.
- If your child struggles with a word that can be sounded out, teach him strategies for pronunciation, like figuring out what the first letter sounds like.
- If your child struggles with a word that can't be sounded out, tell him what it is rather than letting him guess randomly.
- Let your child use his finger or a marker to keep his place while reading a story.
- Don't frustrate your child by correcting his mistakes in the middle of a sentence. Wait until the end of the sentence, then model the appropriate reading. When you become bogged down with corrections, you lose track of the story.
- Take turns reading aloud with more challenging books.[30]

Chapter 6

Nurturing Pre-literacy Skills

Beyond the ABCs

Imagine that your child is three years old and talking up a storm. She enjoys listening to you read books and has been singing her ABCs for several months. She's excited about starting preschool, too. The first day at preschool you notice that signs are everywhere in her classroom: above the door, next to the clock, near the books, at the sink. You ask yourself, "Why have the teachers done this? Is my child ready to read?" This chapter addresses these and other questions that may come up as you wonder how and when to help your child learn to read.

There are two facts about how reading skills develop that you should know. First, having excellent verbal skills doesn't necessarily mean your child will learn to read easily. Reading isn't something children acquire naturally (like language); it needs to be taught. Second, there are several pre-literacy skills your child must develop before she starts to read. These skills extend far beyond singing the ABCs and having a good attention span for listening to stories.

The Parent's Role

Reading to your child is the most important activity you can do to help your child build the knowledge required for eventual reading success.[1] Parents support their children's pre-literacy skills by selecting age-appropriate books and making sure the books are readily available. Exposure to books and other reading materials in the home is the best predictor of your child's reading success.[2] You can also keep books in your car and your bag for times when you and your child have to wait in line or are otherwise delayed.

While listening to you read stories filled with laughter, suspense, and excitement, your child learns that reading is fun. Develop a habit of reading to your child every day. Make it a cherished time you both look forward to during which you curl up together and escape to another world. Some of your best memories will come from sharing books with your child.

Reading with your child promotes a rich language environment because your child hears and learns new vocabulary, sentence structure, and background knowledge about her world. Background knowledge is a general sense of people, places, and how things work in the world. Your child needs to develop basic background knowledge so she can make sense of what she reads independently. When a child reads about a topic with which she isn't at least somewhat familiar, she may have trouble figuring out unknown words and comprehending what she's reading.

The easiest way to help your child acquire background knowledge is to read lots of books on various topics, including nonfiction books about science, history, geography, and so on, together. Children can learn background knowledge through everyday experiences and from listening to someone explain how things work and why events occur. Children can also acquire this knowledge by overhearing adult conversations and by interacting with other children and adults. For example, your child can learn a lot about cause and effect, measurements, and following directions simply by helping you prepare dinner.

Try to schedule reading times when you're not feeling rushed so you can enjoy the story. If you have time for only one story, make it one that leads to further discussion. If your child wants to choose a book, let her. Toddlers may choose the same books over and over. The repetition allows them to predict the plot and direct some of their own learning. Try not to let a tiring day affect how you read a story to your child, and try to read aloud in a natural, relaxed style. Trust that you'll know when to use an animated or excited voice, when to pause or speed up, and when to emphasize the suspenseful parts.

Children need to experience literature not only as listeners but also as participants. While reading aloud, stop and ask questions about the characters, events, and words: "Where do you think the mouse will go next?"[3] Don't ask questions so often that they distract your child from the story. Some children naturally ask questions during a story. If your child asks you a question, stop reading and answer it, then continue reading.

If your child can answer simple questions (and doesn't feel intimidated by them), ask her to predict what might happen next in the story. If she says, "I don't know," make some predictions and ask her if she agrees. Your predictions might encourage her to come up with her own ideas. Also ask her how she might solve a problem that comes up in a book, or what she thinks a character might be feeling in a certain situation. Expand on her responses as you did when developing her early verbal skills. (See page 25.)

Illustrations usually help a child comprehend a story, but sometimes they draw a child's attention away from the story. Children tend to rely on illustrations to help them understand a book. Whenever possible, try to help your child understand the meaning of the words themselves by encouraging her to listen closely to what's happening in the story.[4] Ask her questions about information gleaned from the words that can't be gleaned from the illustrations.

When you've finished a story, take time to chat about the pictures, the new words you've discovered, and the feelings and morals in the story. Make sure to talk about these issues on a level your child can understand. Also ask her to retell the story in her own words so she can use the new words she's learned and put events in the right order. Retelling the story develops her ability to concentrate and express herself. Studies show that retelling helps increase a child's verbal expression and vocabulary tremendously, and nurtures her appreciation for books.[5]

Developing Pre-literacy Skills

Susan L. Hall and Louisa C. Moats, researchers in the field of literacy, have written a great book on the subject called *Straight Talk About Reading: How Parents Can Make a Difference During the Early Years*. In the book the authors refer to another excellent researcher, Marilyn Jager Adams, author of *Beginning to*

Read: Thinking and Learning about Print. Together they describe the three basic skills your child must learn in order to read:

1. Print awareness: knowledge of the basic conventions and characteristics of written language
2. Alphabet awareness: the ability to recognize and name the letters of the alphabet
3. Phonemic (sound) awareness: the ability to hear, identify, and manipulate individual sounds (phonemes) in words[6]

Children naturally develop print awareness from their reading experiences with parents and others.[7] They learn that books are read from left to right, top to bottom, and front to back. They also learn what to do at the end of a line and at the bottom of a page. They eventually learn that the words tell the story, not the pictures. They learn that words are associated with concepts and that many words make up a story. They also learn about the structural elements in books (title, characters, setting, plot, climax, and ending). In addition, they learn some of the phrases frequently used in stories, like *once upon a time*.

One of the most important ideas your child learns from her reading experiences is that print makes sense. When she's exposed to lots of different books, she understands that even the nonsense words in Dr. Seuss's books make sense in Dr. Seuss's world. Good readers read nonsense words the same way as new words: by sounding them out using the same rules that apply to sounding out real words.

The rhyme and repetition of books like Dr. Seuss's let children make sense of the stories, and let them know to expect the same patterns as seen in "real" books. For example, children who've had many reading experiences know that a story has a beginning, middle, and end. They understand that a story has a title, characters, and a setting. They also understand that the characters usually have a problem to solve. The action revolves around solving the problem, and there's a climax or resolution at the end.[8]

Reading stories to your child isn't the only way she learns how stories make sense. Your child may ask you to make up a story or recite a familiar story from memory. She might pick one of her favorite characters and say, "Tell me a story about [so and so] tonight." Even though you're not reading, telling impromptu, made-up stories is a wonderful way to enhance your child's literacy. As you tell the story, your child must focus exclusively on the words, which allows her to imagine illustrations that correspond to the words. The stories don't have to be long or creative. When you can't think of a new twist, ask your child what she'd like the character to do. Take turns adding new elements to the story to enhance your child's creativity and problem-solving skills. Together you reinforce the values that are important to you.

Or try this storytelling idea: Let your child flip through your photo albums, and tell her stories from your childhood. When she's having a rough day, tell her a story about how you felt when something similar happened to you as a child. She'll appreciate that you understand what she's going through.

Another way to help your child develop print awareness is to let her see all the ways you use written language. Let her watch you write checks, shopping lists, invitations, thank-you notes, and memos to family members. Draw her attention to signs and bulletins when you're out and about. Encourage her to recognize her name on cards, signs, and in books. Incorporate reading and writing into make-believe play. For example, when you help your child make an imaginary cake in her toy kitchen, you can make a grocery list of the ingredients you need. Exposing your child to various printed materials helps her see how important reading and writing are in everyday life.[9]

Making Your Home Print Friendly

- Make sure your child has a comfortable place to curl up and look at books. A beanbag chair or oversize pillow with a blanket and a basket of books next to it invites reading time.
- Display magazines, newspapers, and photo albums prominently so your child can see them and handle them. (Make sure the content is age appropriate.)
- Let your child see you make shopping lists. Show her how to cross off items as you put them in the cart. If she likes

special foods or needs a few things of her own, help her make a list of those items.

- As you shop, have your child look at coupons and try to match them to the products. If she wants, let her sort the coupons into categories like cereals, fruits, vegetables, and snacks.
- Instead of throwing away expired coupons, let your child use them in her toy kitchen. Let her play with empty food containers that have the labels intact (oatmeal canisters, cake mix boxes, yogurt cups).
- When you clean out your office or car, give your child old takeout menus to play with in her toy kitchen.
- Let your child help you write invitations.
- Show your child any mail she receives, and read the words together. Explain to her that the purpose of a letter is to send a message to someone.
- Help your child notice written language on things around your home, like toothpaste tubes, shampoo bottles, cereal boxes, milk cartons, and so on.
- Encourage your child to collect items printed with words, like bubblegum wrappers, baseball cards, coins, stamps, and so on.
- Label items in your child's room to help reinforce the letters and words she's learning and to help her recognize how words can be used in different situations.
- Have your child tell a story, and write it down while she dictates. This activity helps her see the connection between spoken and written words. Also have her dictate thank-you notes and birthday greetings to family members and friends.
- Have your child help you make books about topics that interest her. Children love to read handmade books that they've helped create, even if they've only pasted some pictures or stickers onto a sheet of paper.
- Let your child see you reading instead of watching TV.
- When you read to your child, insert silly words and see if she notices. Teach her that some words don't make sense

and that she must come up with the right words to make sense of conversations, stories, and songs.

- If you leave your child with a family member or caregiver who doesn't read regularly or has a reading problem, make a cassette tape of you reading to your child. Have her take the book with her so she can follow along while the tape plays. Remember to include a signal in the tape (like a bell) to let her know when to turn the pages.

Ideas for Learning the Letters of the Alphabet

The second pre-literacy skill is knowledge of the alphabet.[10] Rapid recognition of alphabet letters is an important precursor to reading success.[11] By the time she starts kindergarten, your child needs to recognize each letter, both upper- and lowercase. She also must build her phonemic (sound) awareness of each letter. Let her get familiar with the names of the letters before she learns the corresponding sounds.

When your child is age two, begin singing ABC songs and reading ABC books with her. When she turns three, begin teaching her the names of the letters. Here are some ways to help your child learn her letters:

- Make learning fun; don't make it a drill or a chore. For example, as you make spaghetti, talk about the letter *s* and make the shape with a spaghetti noodle.

- Don't worry about having your child learn the letters in any particular order. She first learns the ones that are most important to her, like the letters of her name or the first letters of her favorite characters' names.

- Buy a set of magnetic letters and put them on the refrigerator (low enough for your child to reach). Let her play with them whenever she wants. Make words together and name the letters as you go.

- Make your own ABC book with one letter on each page. Glue on a magazine picture of an object that begins with the letter.

- Pick a letter and focus on it for an entire day. For example, when you're at the park, pick the letter *b* and look for all the birds, bikes, balls, and babies.
- If your child is learning how to write alphabet letters, draw an outline of each letter on a sheet of paper, and have her glue macaroni onto the outline. Feeling the shape of the letter helps her learn how to recognize it and write it. As you cook or play in the kitchen, use your finger to write letters in different materials like sugar, flour, or cornmeal. Then have your child use her finger to trace the letters.
- Let your child use sidewalk chalk to trace letters outside.
- Let your child use finger paints or a wet paintbrush to trace letters you've drawn on construction paper.
- Let your child form letters using clay, play dough, or a similar material.
- Make an alphabet quilt by writing different letters on separate square pieces of paper. On each square glue a magazine picture of an item that starts with the letter.
- If your child can write some letters, have her practice on a sheet of paper. Show her how to make a rainbow design by tracing each letter repeatedly with markers or crayons in different colors.[12]
- When your child can identify individual letters, reinforce the proper alphabet order by putting magnetic letters in a bag, shaking them up, and dumping them on the floor. Sing the ABC song while you put the letters in order together.
- Use the American Sign Language (ASL) alphabet to give your child motor and visual links to help her remember the names of letters. Show her the sign for each letter (or for the letters that seem difficult for her) as she learns them. For example, children sometimes mix up the letters *u* and *v* because they look similar. Show your child the

signs for these letters to help her realize they're different and to help her remember their names.[13]

When your child is age four, she's ready to begin concentrating more on the shapes of letters.[14] Make sure she learns both upper- and lowercase forms. She'll see lowercase letters most often when reading. Your child's sense of touch can enhance this learning process. Let her play with letter cutouts, trace letters in sand, trace them with finger paint, and so on. Let her glue buttons, cotton balls, beads, or sandpaper strips onto the outline of a letter so she can feel its shape while naming it.

Once your child knows the shapes of letters, she's ready for more sophisticated games like matching uppercase letters to lowercase ones. There are many puzzles and games available to enhance this skill. When your child is familiar with the shapes, she's also ready to learn the sounds associated with each letter. Phonemic (sound) awareness is the most difficult pre-literacy skill to master, and it's a key predictor of late developing readers.

Building Specific Phonemic (Sound) Awareness

Phonemic awareness is the ability to hear, identify, and manipulate the individual phonemes (sounds) associated with the letters of words.[15] The ability to sound out unfamiliar words by looking at the letters is crucial to a child's reading success. While many workbooks designed to systematically teach each sound are available, the National Association for the Education of Young Children (NAEYC) claims that workbooks aren't appropriate for typically developing preschoolers. Some children don't have the small motor skills necessary to hold a pencil before kindergarten, and many work on this skill throughout the kindergarten year. In preschool, learning should occur naturally through active play. If you want to work with letters and sounds systematically, look for stories and books that focus on a particular letter. For example, if you want to work on the hard *c* sound, choose books about farms (cows, cats, corn, carts) and point out the hard *c* sounds. Here are other phonemic-awareness activities:

- Use songs to emphasize the sound of a letter, like "Do You Hear the Way Sounds Ring?" (See Appendix A.)

- Model short vowel sounds first (*a*nt, *e*gg, *i*tch, *o*tter, *u*mpire). People use short vowels more often than long vowels in their speech, and short vowels appear earlier than long vowels in a child's development. Many parents use songs, actions, or pictures to model short vowels. For example, model the short *e* sound by having your child swing her arm like an *e*lephant's swinging trunk. Then move on to modeling long vowels (*a*pron, *e*at, *i*ce, *o*ver).
- If you have an alphabet chart, go through it every day and say all the sounds associated with the letters. Start with the most common sounds for each consonant, and remember to first choose short pronunciations for vowels. To make this activity more fun, let your child act out some of the animals or toys featured with the letters on the chart (for example, "Bear, *b*. Can you make a bear sound? *Grrrrr!*" or, "Top, *t*. Can you spin like a top? *Whirr! Whirr!*").
- Children love to hear the sounds from their environment that are similar to letter sounds. For example, a bee makes a *z* sound, a train makes a *ch* sound, a snake makes an *s* sound, a monkey makes an *oo* sound, and so on. Call attention to these sounds when you hear them or when you read a story that features them.
- Gather alphabet flashcards and pictures of different objects. Have your child match a picture of an object with the flashcard that shows the first letter of the object's name. For example, if she looks at a picture of a dog, see if she can point to the *d* flashcard. She has to say the object's name, think of the letter that's associated with the first sound of the name, and point to the letter on the flashcard.
- When pronouncing consonants for your child, try to avoid adding *uh* at the end. For example, when pronouncing *s*, try to say "sss" instead of "suh." ("Suh," "aaa," and "tuh" put together don't sound like *sat*.) You may find it tricky to pronounce a consonant without a vowel, but try your best.
- Play games in which you give your child a few sounds and ask her to put them together. For example, ask your child to be a word detective. Say, "I'll give you three clues and

140   Chapter 6

see if you can figure out the right word. If I said 'd-ah-g,' you might guess 'dog.' Let's try a different one now."
- Play games that help your child break up a word into its separate sounds. For example, *cat* is made up of the sounds *c*, *a*, and *t*.
- Play games in which you isolate the first or last sound in a word. For example, the beginning sound of *big* is *b*. The ending sound of *big* is *g*.

Building Overall Sound Awareness (Phonological Awareness)

Children learn certain parts of phonological awareness earlier than the specific phonemic awareness concepts discussed in the previous section. For example, children learn rhyming, word, and syllable awareness earlier than phonemic awareness. Here are some ways to enhance your child's overall phonological awareness:

- Help your child realize that a sentence is made up of smaller units (words, syllables, and sounds). For example, have your child count the words in a sentence by having her select a penny for each word. Then have her count the pennies. Help her count syllables by clapping your hands and counting as she sounds out each syllable in a word.[16]
- Read books that contain lots of rhyming words. Books by Dr. Seuss are great for rhymes featuring real and nonsense words. Talk about how words rhyme based on their final sounds. Sing songs that contain rhyming lyrics. Play word games that replace the regular words with fun rhyming words. For example, "Mary had a little lamb whose fleece was *pink as ham.*"
- Change the words in familiar songs to make them alliterative (having the same first sound). Don't be afraid to use nonsense words; kids think they're hilarious! For example, "Little boy blue come blow your *b*orn; the *b*eep's in the *b*eadow, the *b*ow's in the *b*orn."
- Play games like Odd-Man-Out in which you look at several pictures or objects and decide which one doesn't belong.

You can play this game with rhyming words (*mat, cat, sat, horse*) or with words that begin or end with the same sound (*hog, pig, dog, cat* or *doll, door, day, sun*).

- Play word games that help your child recognize the beginnings and endings of words. Jokes that play on compound words are fun and help children realize the separate meanings. For example, "Why did Sarah throw the butter out the window? Because she wanted to see butter fly. Get it? Butterfly!" or "What has arms but no hands? An armchair!"

- Play other compound word games such as, "I've got pop and you've got corn. Put them together and what do we have? Popcorn!" Practice dividing compound words, too. Give your child a compound word, and have her try to figure out the smaller words that make up the big word.

- Play games in which you manipulate words by changing the beginning or ending sounds to create new words. For example, "Run...fun!" "Dig...dip!"

- Talk about how the length of a word has nothing to do with the size of the object it represents—a concept that can be difficult for children to understand. For example, "Look at the teeny caterpillar! How did such a small animal end up with such a big name?"

- Allow your child to spell words as they sound. Phonetic spelling helps refine phonemic awareness and increases knowledge of spelling patterns. Children with good phonemic awareness can figure out spellings that are close to the actual spellings.[17] Children with poor phonemic awareness more often guess spellings randomly.

- Encourage your child to watch TV programs that promote overall phonological skills. Programs like *Between the Lions* encourage literacy by showing and manipulating letters and words on the screen while the characters say rhymes and tell stories.

Make Time to Rhyme

Good rhymers make good readers. A child's ability to recognize and produce rhymes is one of the most powerful predictors of her later reading achievement.[18] Sharing poetry and nursery rhymes with your child nurtures her awareness of sounds and words. Many children's poems are humorous, which makes them even more entertaining to children and parents alike.

If your child doesn't develop an awareness for rhyming words, she may face greater challenges during her early reading attempts. Many books, songs, and poems include rhyme patterns. Your child's ability to recognize words that belong to the same word family (for example, *and, hand, sand*) will help her when she first tries to read. For example, a child who's familiar with rhymes should have no problem recognizing the rhyming patterns among the final words of each line in "Humpty Dumpty":

Humpty Dumpty sat on a *wall*.
Humpty Dumpty had a great *fall*.
All the king's horses and all the king's *men*
Couldn't put Humpty together *again*.

Between ages three and five, children quickly learn about the nature of written language.[19] They need essential skills like print awareness, letter awareness, and phonemic awareness before they can read their first books.[20] Enhance your child's print awareness by encouraging her to focus on printed words.[21] Prompt her to recognize letters, to make the corresponding sounds for letters, to listen for sounds that are similar, to notice certain characteristics of words (rhyming, alliteration, opposites), and to look for matching letters or words.[22]

It's easy to enhance these skills during everyday activities, and it's important to keep the process fun. Children are more apt to learn to read when parents use a light touch to help them learn letters and words.[23] Drilling your child or demanding correct answers could slow her learning. Pick some of the listed activities your child will enjoy, and you'll be amazed by how quickly she'll be ready to read.

When Is My Child Ready to Read?

When your child grasps print awareness, letter awareness, and phonemic awareness, she has a solid foundation for literacy. Before your child can begin to read, she must also be able to sound out unfamiliar words. If your child doesn't know how to sound out unfamiliar words, she can't tackle more difficult words later on. Some words, however, can't be sounded out and must be recognized by sight (sight words). For example, the word *was*, if sounded out, might rhyme with *gas*. Many sight words appear frequently in books, so it's best for your child to memorize them.

Learning Sight Words

Of all words that appear in books, newspapers, and magazines, 50 to 75 percent belong to the Dolch Basic Sight Vocabulary of "service" words, a list that includes 220 pronouns, adjectives, adverbs, prepositions, conjunctions, and verbs.[24] Because children can't learn these words by associating them with pictures or by sounding them out, they must learn to recognize them at a glance. Some examples of these sight words are *a*, *are*, *away*, *go*, *has*, *here*, *to*, and *was*.

Children generally learn sight words in kindergarten through third grade. These words can be introduced earlier, however, like when a child is learning overall phonological awareness skills (see pages 141–143). For this reason, parents may find it helpful to know some techniques for teaching children sight words. One technique is presenting a sight word on a flashcard. The child can focus on the length, shape, and letters of the word, which help her recall it later. Once a child becomes familiar with a sight word, she can use it in simple sentences. Eventually she can include it in games and other contexts.

Another strategy is introducing sight words in timely and relevant contexts—while playing games, for example. To teach the word *big*, you might find a book about something big, like a big dog or a big hat. You may find a combination of these techniques works best.

Sight Word Soup

This method involves working with your child on selected words from the Dolch Basic Sight Vocabulary.[25] Choose up to ten sight words to work on during the week, and write each one on a separate three-by-five-inch index card. Teach your child the words, have her practice them, then have her apply them in a meaningful context (like in a phrase or sentence). To teach the words, show the cards to your child one by one saying, "This is the word ___." Point out special characteristics of the word, like the fact that it begins with the same letter as your child's name or that it contains only two letters. Ask your child questions such as, "What letter appears at the beginning of this word?" or, "Does this word have a smaller word inside it?" Have your child repeat each letter of the word as you spell it aloud.

You can also write the word in sand, or use glue and glitter, cereal letters, letter cutouts, sandpaper letters, shaving cream on a baking sheet, chalk on a sidewalk, magnetic letters, and so on. Let your child take a turn writing the word using these materials, and compare spellings. Have your child spell the word aloud while you print it on a sheet of paper. She can post the paper on her bedroom wall. Repeat the same procedure for each word.

Once your child is familiar with the words, have her practice them by using the index cards in a hands-on activity like a memory game or bingo. You can use the cards while playing board games by having her read a card before she takes her turn. Have her read the cards to her favorite doll or teddy bear, or make a second set of cards and play a matching game.

After your child has practiced the sight words, have her read them in a meaningful context (in a sentence, paragraph, poem, or riddle). The length of the reading depends on your child's reading level. Some children may need to read the sight words in simple phrases or three word sentences along with words they already know (for example, "*her* room," "*his* car," or "*our* bed"). You can use more than one sight word per sentence. Print the reading neatly on lined paper and double space the lines of text so she can easily see the sight words in the context of printed text.

Other Ideas for Learning Sight Words

- Have your child write a sight word on a card (or do it for her). Have her listen for the word as you read a story that features it. Tell her to raise the card every time she hears the word.

- Play a game in which you put the index cards in a box or bag. Add a wild card that features a funny word like *oops*. Have your child select and read the cards one by one. If she draws the wild card, she must put all the cards back in the box. The object of the game is to collect the most cards before drawing the wild card.
- Arrange the index cards on the floor like steppingstones, and play a game in which your child follows your commands. For example, have her hop on *and*, step on *a*, put her hand on *away*, and so on.
- Use American Sign Language (ASL) to provide visual cues for sight words. ASL can help children who are having trouble remembering these words.[26]

Tips for Successful Early Reading Attempts

Your child may hesitate often when she begins to read aloud. Hesitation is normal, so try not to rush her. Here are a few tips to enhance her skills for reading aloud:

- At first, choose predictable books that use lots of repetition, have only a few new words on each page, and provide illustrations to help your child figure out the words.
- Use rebus books that substitute small pictures for some words. Children enjoy giving the words that represent the pictures.
- Choose reading material that matches your child's skills. If she has to sound out almost every word, have her read an easier book.
- If your child becomes frustrated when sounding out a word, help her figure it out.
- Wait until your child finishes reading a sentence before correcting a word she's read incorrectly. Waiting to correct your child allows her to read the sentence completely and decide whether it makes sense. If she doesn't catch her error and correct it herself, ask her if the sentence makes sense or point to the misread word and ask her to reread it.[27]

- Your child will more likely respond to your specific questions about what she's read than to general comments about it.[28]
- If she wishes, let your child reread aloud the same story several times. The repetition bolsters her confidence and allows her to feel she's mastered an important skill.
- Watch for signs that your child is growing tired of reading aloud. If she is, read to her for a while and let her resume when she's ready.
- Praise helps your child want to continue reading aloud, so praise her reading efforts regularly.

An Overview of Whole Language Methods versus Phonics

For several decades, scholars and teachers have been debating the merits of using whole language methods versus phonics to teach children how to read. Whole language methods teach a child to use the story's context to figure out unknown words. Instead of breaking down unfamiliar words into component sounds, children are encouraged to look at the story as a whole and to share ideas about its content.[29] Phonics teaches children to decode unknown words by sounding them out. Children are encouraged to learn the phonemes (sounds) before they start to read.[30] Phonics supporters maintain that the ability to sound out words is crucial to reading success.

Studies by the National Research Council and the National Academy of Sciences concluded that a reading program that balances both methods best teaches a child to read. The National Institute of Literacy stresses the importance of phonemic awareness, phonics, fluency, vocabulary, and text comprehension for successful reading instruction.[31] As discussed on page 139, phonemic awareness is the ability to hear, identify, and manipulate individual phonemes within words. Phonics is the ability to understand the relationship between letters and sounds. Fluency is the ability to read words quickly and accurately. Vocabulary is the repertoire of words one must know to read and speak. Text comprehension is the ability to understand what's been read. Good readers think actively as they read, and they compare their experiences and knowledge of the world with what they're reading.[32]

Researchers seem to agree that teaching children direct, systematic phonics is necessary for successful reading instruction, which should focus both on comprehension and appreciation of literature. This means that teachers should teach children how to read for understanding, enjoyment, and enrichment *and* teach them phonics. If a child isn't taught phonics, she must rely on illustrations or the other words in the sentence to figure out an unfamiliar word. When she's ready for more difficult books, she won't have the skills necessary to break down harder words. It's also important that she enjoys reading and finds it meaningful as she develops her reading skills. Children who develop their reading skills are the ones who read often and are highly motivated to read.[33]

About one-third of children in reading programs can't learn to read without systematic phonics instruction, which requires identifying the sounds in words and matching them with letters. These children also need structured practice applying the sound-letter links to reading and spelling.[34] A report by the National Reading Panel concluded that systematic phonics programs better contributed to children's reading growth than other programs that provided unsystematic or no phonics. Phonics especially helped low-achieving students, students with learning disabilities, and children from low-income families.

Literacy Performance Levels

During your child's toddler and preschool years, focus on enhancing her reading comprehension. Choose books for your child that are appealing and age appropriate. When she reaches school age, her reading development benefits from strategies other than your asking her "wh" questions (who, what, where, when, and why). For example, before you begin reading, you might review new vocabulary found in the book, provide background information your child isn't familiar with, and encourage your child to predict what the story will be about. While your child is reading, you might direct her attention to the circumstances of the story, point out difficult words and ideas, and ask her to identify problems and suggest solutions. You might also encourage her to monitor her reading to make sure it makes sense. When she's finished reading, you might ask her to summarize the story.

According to the Learning First Alliance, a partnership of twelve leading national education associations, the best approach to handling reading disabilities is *prevention*. Make sure that your child's reading development is assessed frequently and that her teachers use that information to help prevent her development from falling behind her peers' and staying behind. Long-term studies of reading development clearly showed that most children who were poor readers in the third grade and beyond had had difficulty with phonological skills right from the start. These studies also showed that instruction targeting children's weaknesses often prevented later reading problems and facilitated the reading development of most children. The Learning First Alliance recommends that children demonstrate the following skills in the first few years of school.[35]

Kindergarten Goals

By the end of kindergarten, children typically have well-established language skills that allow them to describe their experiences. They're familiar with the alphabet and can identify the sounds that make up words. Some children develop reading competence more slowly than others, but these children still go on to become fluent readers. Testing to identify children at risk for reading problems usually begins during this year. Teachers should pay close attention to any child who may show signs of a reading problem. By the end of the kindergarten year, your child typically can do the following:[36]

- Know the parts of a story and their functions
- Notice when simple sentences don't make sense
- Listen attentively to a story, retell it, and act it out
- Answer questions about a story
- Predict what's going to happen in a story
- Know the sounds of all the letters

- Recognize and name upper- and lowercase letters, and write many of them without help
- Recognize common sight words
- Engage in listening and sound-awareness games
- Recognize subtle differences between words
- Try to spell words phonetically (based on their sounds)

First Grade Goals

When it comes to your child's developing reading skills, first grade is crucial. At this age, children typically start reading beginning-reader books and gradually progress to simple chapter books. Parents notice the exciting change as their children become better at sounding out words and recognizing sight words. *All* children this age should learn phonics as part of their reading instruction. Encourage your child to read new books so she can practice sounding out new words. Make sure to choose books that are interesting and meaningful to your child, and continue to stress reading comprehension. A child finishing the first grade typically can do the following:

- Read aloud accurately and demonstrate comprehension of a story
- Notice and correct her reading errors
- Sound out unknown or nonsense words
- Have a reading vocabulary of 300 to 500 words
- Read and understand both simple fiction and nonfiction books
- Answer questions about stories and predict what's going to happen in them
- Read and answer simple written questions about a book to show comprehension
- Correctly spell three- to four-letter words
- Count the number of syllables in a word
- Recognize sentences that are incomplete or don't make sense
- Separate phonemes and blend them together in a one-syllable word
- Write simple stories using correct punctuation and capitalization

Second Grade Goals

In second grade, children typically can sound out short, phonetically regular words. They know many sight words and have good reading comprehension skills. A child who doesn't demonstrate these skills needs immediate attention. At this age, your child continues to master phonics and can read literature that includes some nonfiction. Her instruction focuses on enhancing reading comprehension, building vocabulary, and developing writing skills.

Continue reading to your child even after she's started reading on her own. A child can understand more difficult vocabulary and sentence structure when it's read to her than she can when she reads it herself. (You might recall that when your child was first acquiring language, her receptive skills far outpaced her expressive skills—that is, she understood more than she could say.) Occasionally choose challenging books, including short chapter books, to improve your child's vocabulary and increase her background knowledge. A child completing the second grade typically can do the following:

- Read more difficult words, including multisyllabic and longer nonsense words
- Automatically reread sentences that don't make sense
- Use phonics to sound out multisyllabic and nonsense words
- Read independently for entertainment and learning
- Begin to understand information in charts and tables
- Remember details about specific parts of books
- Act out stories
- Compare characters and events from different stories
- Answer more complex "how," "why," and "what if" questions about stories
- Correctly spell words that she's previously studied in school or at home
- Show more refined writing skills

What to Do If You Suspect Your Child Has a Reading Problem

Reading problems can often be resolved if a child receives early intervention. If you think your child struggles with reading, consider the following:

- First talk to your child's teacher. Find out if she thinks your child has a reading problem. Make sure your child is receiving phonics instruction. Discuss the ways you can reinforce your child's reading skills at home.
- If your child struggles with spelling quizzes, ask if she's been taught to sound out words.
- Consider having your child screened for vision or hearing problems. Both can cause reading problems.
- Consider enabling closed-captioned TV to enhance reading skills.
- If reading easily frustrates your child, make sure she's reading books she can handle. Small reading successes go a long way toward promoting self-confidence.
- It's normal for young children to reverse letters and numbers occasionally up to age eight (for example, like when they first learn the shapes of letters).[37] Be aware, however, that one of the symptoms of dyslexia (a learning disorder marked by impairment of the ability to recognize and comprehend written words) is seeing or writing letters or words backward or upside down. If you suspect your child has dyslexia, have her tested by the school reading consultant, or find another qualified professional to test your child and make recommendations.
- Don't wait too long to ask for help. If you feel your child's reading problems affect her self-esteem or make her apprehensive about school, get help promptly. Research shows that most reading problems don't get better on their own, and that children generally don't catch up once they fall behind unless they receive help.[38]

A Few Words on Writing and Spelling Skills

Writing and spelling activities are important because they bolster your child's overall reading ability.[39] Parents should participate in such activities to help guide their children's development. These activities include sounding out letters, realizing what letter goes with what sound, remembering the distinctive shape of a letter, and printing letters.[40]

Some researchers claim that writing is easier to learn than reading for some children. When you read, the message is unknown; when you write, the message is known.[41] In reading, you start with letters, figure out the sounds, and eventually interpret the meaning. In writing, you start with a message and translate the sounds into letters.

Your child's writing skills begin to develop with scribbling. Your toddler spends several months scribbling "meaningless" figures and shapes. This activity strengthens her hand and finger muscles and helps her learn that she can start, stop, and control the lines. Eventually she names her scribbles and shows them off to you. Even though her scribbles might not look like the family dog or her favorite toy to you, *your child* realizes that her scribbles stand for real things. This realization is a major step toward understanding language's symbolic nature.

Respond encouragingly to all your child's writing attempts. Feel free to ask open-ended questions about her writing, such as, "What have you written? That's nice! What about this part?" Eventually her scribbling progresses to writing letters, her name, other words, and finally invented spellings in which she consciously tries to match sounds to letters. Don't teach her to write in uppercase letters only. She sees more lowercase letters when she reads, so she should learn to write them, too. To reinforce the shapes of letters, have your child trace them with a highlighter.

By the end of kindergarten, your child can recognize, name, and print letters, and know which sounds they represent. Many children initially try to "invent" spellings that may not match the actual spellings of words. Research shows that invented spellings help a child internalize phonemic awareness and alphabet awareness.[42] When children invent spellings, they use their letter knowledge to recognize the first and last letters of a word, which helps them see the boundaries between words. By this age, children can sound out pronunciations, which is good practice for reading words in a story. They also can use letter awareness to recognize words by sight.[43]

It may seem counterproductive to encourage your child to do something "incorrectly," but research shows that invented spellings don't prevent your child from eventually learning correct spellings. In fact, invented spellings are excellent for learning the relationship between sounds and letters. With this said, however, the National Academy of Sciences encourages parents to model correct spellings whenever children use invented spellings. The Academy further suggests that parents should expect children in elementary school to spell previously studied words correctly.[44] Expect your child's spelling skills to go through a series of stages that gradually progress toward the correct spelling of words.

Fun Pre-writing Activities

Learning to write is much more enjoyable when you incorporate the task into a meaningful daily activity. Don't ask your child to practice out-of-context words that she doesn't understand and can't read. Furthermore, don't require her to print letters to fit between lines. These requirements may create a negative association between reading and writing. Instead, try some of the following fun, creative approaches to developing your child's writing skills.

Treasure Hunt

Fill a box with some of your child's favorite toys and knickknacks, hide it somewhere it your home, and have your child look for it. When she finds it, have her make a list of all of the treasures inside. Enhance the adventure by first giving her a map that features a dotted line leading to the treasure. Your child will have so much fun with this activity, she won't even realize she's working on pre-writing skills!

Magazine Search

Search through junk mail and magazines, and let your child pick out some pictures she likes. Help her cut them out and paste them onto construction paper or into a handmade book. Ask her to describe each picture, and write the description below it. Let an older child write her own description, if she can.

Handwritten Notes
Faraway relatives love receiving notes from children. The next time your child hands you a stack of scribbles and you can't find enough room on the refrigerator to display them, fold up a few and send them to loved ones. Let your child sign her name on the scribbles however she can.

Creative Play
Figure out ways to incorporate writing into your child's favorite games and activities. If she enjoys playing school, let her pretend to be the teacher and write on a chalkboard. If she loves trains, let her write some "words" on handmade tickets to board the train. Let her create her own menus when she plays with her toy kitchen.

One Last Word on Language and Literacy

This chapter takes early language skills (speaking and understanding) to the next level (reading and writing). Whether primarily you or a teacher helps your child's pre-literacy and literacy development, this chapter shows you the developmental process your child goes through as she becomes literate. Some children will face literacy challenges. Recognizing these challenges early allows you and your child's teacher to create a plan that helps your child's development in whatever way she needs. Encouraging and nourishing your child's literacy are the most long-lasting contributions you can make toward her overall development.

Chapter 7

Gestural Communication (Sign Language)

Why Sign with My Child Who Hears Perfectly Well?

For centuries the deaf community has used sign language to communicate. Hearing parents of deaf children and deaf parents of hearing children have long known that babies can learn to sign before they can learn to talk. In fact, some babies can learn several signs by the time they're 9 months old, whereas an early talker this age might speak only one word.[1]

Over the past several years, public awareness of sign language's benefits has increased. Many preschool programs, library programs, and children's TV programs now teach sign language to *hearing* children. These programs aren't designed to help hearing children communicate with the deaf community (though that's one benefit); they're designed to help hearing children learn language concepts, help language-delayed children communicate without frustration, and help preschoolers develop letter awareness and other pre-literacy skills. Parents are also discovering that sign language can facilitate multiple language learning, and can bridge gaps between parents and adopted children who don't speak the same language. Research suggests that parents can understand their babies' thoughts and feelings by using sign language to communicate with them.

During the past fifteen to twenty years, researchers have realized that children naturally use their own invented sign language during the preverbal stages. Gestures are integral to the communicative act (see pages 16–17), and many infants use simple gestures to express themselves. Many of these gestures resemble what they represent, and they help children progress from babbling to using proto-words to using real words. (See the buzzing-bee example on page 17.)

By age 9 months, a child has learned how to communicate intentionally by using eye contact, gestures, vocalizations, or simple combinations of these three methods. He's grasped concepts about the world around him like object permanence, means to an end, and so on (see page 68). He's also learned to use gestures or vocalizations to represent objects around him. Typically developing children ages 8 to 22 months benefit from learning sign language because these children can use signs to represent words that are too difficult for them to say. In fact, introducing your baby to signs regularly and consistently at age 7 months may help him begin communicating expressively at age 9 months. That's several months earlier than a typically developing child might otherwise verbally communicate!

Will Sign Language Delay Spoken Language?

Research shows that signing does *not* delay or interfere with a child's speech development.[2] In fact, signing not only leads to better and earlier communication, but it also stimulates cognitive development, speeds up language development, builds vocabulary, reduces frustration, enhances self-esteem, and strengthens the bond between parents and children.[3] Sign language connects the visual areas of the brain to motor and language areas.[4] People who learn sign language starting at birth seem to activate a specific part of the right brain devoted to visual-spatial processing more fully than those who learn the language later in life.[5]

A ten-year study at the University of California at Davis found that seven-year-olds who signed as babies scored an average of twelve points higher on standard IQ tests than members of a control group who didn't sign as babies.[6] Supporters of signing claim that sign language stimulates the brain processes of babies who learn to sign before age three, because these early years are when the majority of neural synapses (connections) form.

Modeling signs while saying the corresponding words enhances a child's later language development.[7] When you combine signs with words, you stimulate your child's auditory, visual, and kinesthetic senses. He hears the spoken word (auditory), observes your gestures and facial expressions (visual), and imitates your physical movements to produce a sign (kinesthetic). Early in a child's development, there's a big gap between comprehension and verbal expression. Children who sign show that they understand what certain objects are because they can sign the names of the objects before they can say them. Signing reinforces and helps build a child's vocabulary. When children sign a word, they show that they understand the word and that they're ready to learn more about the object or person the word represents. For example, if your child shows that he understands what an airplane is because he uses the sign to draw your attention to one, you can expand his language skills by saying, "The airplane is loud." Such expansions also provide good opportunities for you to introduce new signs, like those for adjectives.

Signing also gives children an emotional advantage because it allows them to express what they can't say, which reduces frustration and builds self-esteem. For example, hearing impaired children who sign experience milder stages of the "terrible twos" than their nonsigning peers, because they can better express themselves. Likewise, hearing children who use signs to communicate are less frustrated and have fewer tantrums than children who don't use signs. Teaching your child some basic signs before he can speak could minimize his (and your) frustration by enabling better communication.

Signing helps you and your child bond. When you model signs for your child, you play into his natural tendency to

Signing for Expression

Jessica's parents became concerned when their daughter was still not talking at age 20 months. She was hitting others and biting herself to express her frustration when she couldn't communicate. Her only forms of communication were grunting, squealing, and pointing. Her parents began to use sign language at home to communicate on a basic level with her. Soon Jessica began smiling more than she had in months. She learned the signs more *and* milk *immediately. She grunted less often as she learned more signs. She seemed less frustrated and could focus better on learning the words to speak. After only two months of signing, Jessica could put two words together regularly (signed and spoken), and she stopped her biting and hitting altogether.*

communicate with gestures. Signing while speaking allows you to have a dialogue with your child much earlier than you could if you relied on speech alone. Imagine going to the zoo and teaching your child the signs for *elephant* and *flamingo*. Such multisyllabic words are difficult for young children to say. Then imagine your delight when your child sees an elephant and uses the sign to show you that he knows what it is!

Where Do You Start?

To learn about signing, I encourage parents to consult an American Sign Language (ASL) dictionary or another signing resource like the book *Sign with Your Baby* by Joseph Garcia. While some parents create their own gestures or follow their children's made-up gestures, using ASL signs has advantages. First, ASL is well known and widely used, which means caregivers and others can likely understand a child's ASL gestures better than non-ASL gestures. Second, it's easy to forget invented signs, and parents who haven't kept careful notes must replace forgotten signs with new ones, confusing the child. Finally, ASL is a real language, and research shows that hearing infants prefer ASL over an invented sign language.[8] A child who uses ASL is bilingual and can use this second language to communicate with the deaf community and others who use ASL as their primary language.

At first, show your child a few signs that he's most likely to use every day. These signs might include *eat*, *drink*, *more*, *milk*, *pain/hurt*, *scared*, *hot*, *all done*, and *help*. Research shows that even if you were to sign everything you say, your baby would still focus mostly on these signs. In *Sign with Your Baby*, Garcia recommends sticking with a few basic signs until your baby begins to use them, at which time you can model new signs for him.

Learning signs requires your child's concentration and memory, so introduce signs when you have his full attention. It's also best to introduce signs in a natural setting, like when you're feeding or playing with him. Children learn signs more readily if you use them in real situations. For example, children learn at an early age how to wave bye-bye and blow kisses because they see these gestures used frequently. Make eye contact with your baby as you model signs. Eye contact demonstrates that signing is a social act and a way to direct a request. Try to sign close to your face while your baby looks at you, so he sees the gesture clearly.

You can use a sign to represent any person, object, or activity that interests your baby. Be sure to say the corresponding word whenever you use a sign so your child hears the name for what the sign represents. Once your child says the word, you don't have to continuing using the sign. Some parents, however, continue to use signs because they want their children to be fluent in ASL.

Signing also requires coordinated motor skills. When babies first learn to sign, their small motor skills may not be fully developed, and they often can't reproduce a sign exactly as it's modeled. Continue modeling the sign correctly even if your child makes it imperfectly. Just as you avoid modeling baby talk (see page 9), avoid simplifying signs if your child can't make them perfectly. Eventually he'll make the signs properly. If you can't make the sign correctly in certain situations (like when you're holding your child), it's okay to modify it slightly (for example, by making it one-handed). But be sure to model the sign correctly for your child when you next have the chance.

Steps for Successful Signing

Because many of the techniques that enhance your child's acquisition of words can also help him learn signs, please review the section on being a good language model. (See pages 6–10.)

At first, babies can't understand abstract concepts; they understand the emotions they're feeling or the events that are happening *right now*. For example, introducing the sign for *pain* when your baby is happy and content wouldn't be as effective as introducing it when he's cutting his first tooth. At that time, his pain is immediate, and he's more likely to connect the sign to the feeling it represents.

When you begin signing with your baby, model signs for his favorite animals, toys, and foods, and incorporate the signs into your day together. Assemble a photo album of his favorite people, places, and things. When he looks at the photos, he'll initially communicate by smiling or cooing, then he'll use gestures and signs, and eventually he'll say the words.

While signing with your child, don't anticipate his needs. Whenever possible, give your child a chance to use a sign to make a request. Consider giving him a choice between two objects, and let him sign a response before giving him the desired object. As when children learn spoken language, repetition is crucial when they learn signs. When you introduce a new sign, point out the object whenever you make the sign. For example, when you model the sign *bear*, show your child his teddy bear whenever you make the sign. You can also show him pictures of bears in books.

Remember that it's important to say the word whenever you make the sign. For example, as you model the sign *bear*, you might say, "Look at your bear," or, "Give your bear a big hug!" or, "Your bear is *sooooo* soft!" The verbal repetition helps your baby identify and remember the sign for *bear*. You can also reinforce a sign by helping your child make it with his hand after you've made it. Some children like the physical interaction. Whenever your child attempts to sign or after you've helped him make a sign, praise him immediately or reward him by giving him the requested object.

Build on your child's understanding of signs by using them in different situations. Children sometimes undergeneralize signs when they first learn them, just as they sometimes undergeneralize words. Show your child that the sign *bear* includes all bears, not just his favorite teddy bear, by using the sign when you see bears at the zoo or in books. You can use the signs *up*, *more*, and *all gone* in various situations. *More* can mean "play with me some more," "more juice," "more snack," or even "more bubbles in the bath."

When your child is around age 18 months, you can begin showing him combinations of signs. For example, you can sign both *food* and *hot* when there's steam rising from your child's plate and he has to wait for his food to cool. You can also reinforce the signs you use during reading times. Have your child sit at your side or across from you so he can see both the pictures and your signs. Find picture books, puzzles, or storybooks with sign language diagrams, like *Winnie-the-Pooh's ABC: Sign Language Edition*, *Simple Signs*, and the Early Sign Language series. It's also a good idea to have a sign language dictionary handy. (See Appendix C for additional signing resources.)

Make sure all your family members and caregivers know some of the basic signs you and your child use. Having these people know the signs gives your child more opportunities to communicate by signing. Plus, knowing the signs makes it easier for your babysitter or daycare provider to satisfy your child's needs.

Signing classes designed for children are cropping up in cities around the country. One example is Little Signers, Inc., a company cofounded by Debbie Lesser and Sarah Preston. At Little Signers, parents learn how to incorporate over three hundred signs, games, and activities into their babies' everyday activities. Programs like these have helped parents enhance communication skills in language-delayed children and have bridged gaps between parents and adopted children who don't speak the same language.

Sign language can help people learn a second verbal language.[9] Some signing programs encourage parents raising bilingual children to use signs for words in both languages. The signs can represent the words of both languages and help the children visualize the concepts. For example, in one bilingual family a father speaking Spanish to his child could model the sign *water* while saying, "*Agua.*" The mother speaking English to the child could also model this sign while saying, "Water." Hearing different words while seeing the same gesture helps the child grasp the meaning of the same concept in different contexts with different speakers. Some families are even raising trilingual children, with one of the languages being ASL. Whatever languages you want to teach your child, signs can reinforce the fact that certain words in different languages have the same meaning.

Other signing programs incorporate music into the lessons. The beat of the music motivates children to learn and builds

Signing and Singing

Mai was a 4-month-old infant adopted from Vietnam. An early intervention therapist predicted that she would be unlikely to speak before age two. Her parents exposed her to sign language at home and at classes to help her overall language development and to motivate her to communicate. When Mai was 10 months old, they took her to a music-mediated sign language class. Although Mai had some challenges with overstimulation, hearing simple songs and seeing accompanying signs helped her. Initially she was only a watchful listener, but eventually she signed her name during the hello song. She also enjoyed signing action words like jump, stand, *and* dance.

During a song about feelings, her parents were thrilled to see her sign many emotions, including the sign hope. *Mai progressed quickly through the single-word stage, speaking and using signs. She began using two-word combinations at age 18 months and spoke in short sentences at age 22 months, well within normal limits for language acquisition.*

their social skills. When learning the sign *more*, the class might sing "The More We Get Together" and practice making the sign. Teaching sign language through music helps parents follow their children's lead, and studies show that combining songs with gestures helps a child's language development more than using gestures alone.[10]

Research also suggests a possible connection between keeping a steady beat and acquiring basic reading skills.[11] This connection may be due to the rhythmic nature of music and language. If your child can keep a beat, he may have an easier time learning to read because he can feel the rhythm of the language as he reads it. Researchers have noted that early exposure to signing (in or before preschool) encourages keeping a steady beat.[12] If children can learn to feel the rhythm of music and/or signing, their reading skills could be enhanced. Some library and preschool programs teach songs in sign language. Videos of signed songs are also fun to watch with your child, or you can videotape you and your child signing songs to enjoy later.

Go with the Flow

A child's age, the number of signs he already knows, and his interest level influence how quickly he'll understand a sign and begin using it himself. Don't be surprised or worried if your child takes several weeks or months to learn the signs you've introduced. If you start showing your child signs when he's 9 or 10 months old, his comprehension and motor skills may not be as developed as when he's 12 months old. Be patient if your child doesn't respond quickly to a sign, and don't stop modeling it because you think he's not understanding it. Keep using it naturally, and don't show any frustration. Sensing your frustration or disappointment may curb his enthusiasm for learning. Also, don't pressure your child to acquire a lot of signs. Sometimes just a few signs can enhance communication enormously.

If your child seems reluctant to sign, don't push him. Signing should be an option your child chooses not a necessity or an obligation. Demanding that your child learn to sign may impede his signing success. Create a rich environment that stimulates your child's development, and let him do the rest. Use the words along with the signs, and let your child respond as he wishes. In his book *Sign with Your Baby* Joseph Garcia emphasizes the importance of not *teaching* signs to your child. Instead, he suggests that you include them naturally in your everyday life. Allow your child to discover signs and use them on his own. Think of signing as a way to enhance communication—not as a sure-fire way to make your child a genius.

Transition to Verbal Communication

For some children, the period between starting to use signs and starting to use words may last only a few months. For other children, this period can last a few years. As

"I Need Help"

I remember my 14-month-old daughter struggling to move her doll's carriage into the garden. She was getting very frustrated and started to sign help *over and over. It was wonderful to be able to understand exactly what she wanted. I think this sign is particularly useful for toddlers, since they desperately want to be independent but sometimes lack the ability to handle things on their own. When your toddler uses this sign, you can be sure she really wants you to intervene. I feel I've really gotten to know my daughters' personalities and have learned a great deal about their intelligence and memory skills as a result of signing.*

—Adele Marshall, Signing Babes (a signing organization in the U.K.)

Signing and Speaking

Mr. and Mrs. Meyer decided to begin using a few signs with their 9-month-old twins, Trey and Paige. They modeled the signs *more, please,* and *thank you* in various situations. The twins began signing back to their parents within a few months, using the sign *more* most often. At age 15 months, the twins weren't using words yet, so the Meyers sought speech services to promote their children's language skills with additional signs and to aid in the transition to verbal communication. Trey and Paige spoke their first words at age 17 months and were in the mid-range of development at age 21 months. Although their verbal skills were flourishing, they continued to use signs until they were age two and a half.

your child grows, he needs more sophisticated ways to communicate. When your child's verbal skills first emerge, he may use a simple version of a word and its sign simultaneously. Next he may use a more intelligible version of the word along with the sign. Eventually he phases out the sign and uses only the word.

Joseph Garcia recommends that during a child's transition to verbal communication, parents add spoken adjectives to signs to motivate children to use signs *and* speech to describe a situation more precisely. For example, when you're out walking with your child, you might see someone playing with a dog. When your child uses the sign *dog,* you might say, "Oh yes, I see the big white dog." When your child sees the dog running and uses the sign *run,* you might say, "Yes, the dog is running after the blue Frisbee."

At this stage, children often use the same word or proto-word to represent several different objects or people. To my son, *ba* meant ball, bath, *Barney,* and Bandit (our dog). If your child knows the distinct sign for each item, you can understand his meaning more quickly.

After your child stops using signs expressively, he still understands them. This knowledge may come in handy when you want to communicate silently with him. For example, you may want your child to communicate the need to use the restroom by signing instead of speaking in public. Or you may want to silently prompt your child to share, wait, or be patient as you talk on the phone.

Sign language may augment other skills. Debbie Lesser, owner of the company Little

Signers, Inc., uses signs to help her daughter differentiate colors. She shows her daughter the sign without saying the word, and the visual cue helps her daughter remember the color.

Marilyn Daniels, author of *Dancing with Words: Signing for Hearing Children's Literacy*, suggests that parents can use signing to promote children's self-esteem, pre-literacy skills, reading ability, vocabulary, language concepts, and spelling proficiency. She uses alphabet signs to help children learn the names of letters. For example, to help children learn the letter *r*, she shows the sign for the letter and then a sign for a keyword to help children remember the letter, like *rabbit*.

Daniels suggests that sign language can enhance memory skills. She encourages teachers to use finger spelling to teach children how to spell, because the small motor skills necessary for writing and printing take longer to develop than the motor skills for finger spelling.[13] Also, the movement involved in finger spelling helps children remember how to spell words. Daniels also encourages teachers to show students how to construct stories using ASL, because children can sign stories before they can write them. She recommends using signs to help children express emotions and to help teachers manage their classrooms.[14]

One Last Word on Signing

Signing gives your child more ways to express himself, and it's a fun, rewarding experience for both of you. With this said, however, it's best to use signing from the earliest stages of your child's language development rather than using it when a language problem arises. Sign language won't prevent or solve all language problems, but it's a valuable resource, and parents should take advantage of all that it offers.

Quiet Time

My daughter was lying in bed with a pacifier in her mouth, and I was kneeling beside the bed singing her a song. When I finished, she signed the word more *without saying anything, even though she knew the word. Apparently she understood that bedtime was quiet time, so it was natural for her not to use her voice. I was delighted and sang the song one more time.*

—Debbie Lesser, Little Signers, Inc.

Chapter 8

Bilingualism and Second-Language Learning

This chapter introduces the benefits of bilingualism and discusses how families can successfully raise bilingual (and even trilingual!) children. In it, I talk about language concerns stemming from international adoptions and from children who are learning English as a second language. I also discuss education, assessment, and treatment options for bilingual children who are language delayed.

Why Should My Child Learn a Second Language?

As bilingual children grow up, they discover that knowing a second language has many benefits and few drawbacks. Bilingualism gives children insight into two cultures. Many parents encourage their children to learn a second language while speaking a native language at home and preserving their family's culture. In many cases, monolingual parents take advantage of their children's opportunities to learn a second language and become bilingual themselves.[1] Bilingual children may travel with their families to countries where the second language is spoken to visit relatives or to experience the culture firsthand, and they may benefit more from these visits because they understand the language.

Learning two languages helps a child's cognitive development.[2] Bilingualism strengthens concept formation, creativity, conversation skills, visual-social abilities, logical reasoning, classification skills, and cognitive flexibility.[3] Bilingualism doesn't hinder a child's education or limit his choice of careers.[4] In fact, bilingual children may augment their education by attending afterschool or weekend classes conducted in the second language. Knowing two languages and understanding two cultures can open doors to careers like international business and diplomacy, to name just two.[5]

In some studies, bilingual children seemed to have better pre-literacy skills than monolingual children of the same age. Some bilingual children have stronger phonological awareness skills (like the ability to count syllables, to omit the first part of a word, or to identify words that start with the same sounds) than their monolingual peers. Bilingual children are used to listening closely because they must distinguish among the sounds in two languages.[6] Some typically developing bilingual children understand abstract differences between the written word and meaning (for example, they understand that the word *ice* on the page doesn't feel cold) earlier than monolingual children—more than a year earlier in some studies.[7]

At the pre-literacy stage, bilingual children may also better understand that the length of a word doesn't reflect the size of the thing it represents, a difficult idea for children to grasp.[8] For example, if a monolingual child looks at a picture of a car and another of a chameleon and then tries to match the pictures to the words *car* and *chameleon*, she may choose the shorter word (*car*) to represent the smaller object (chameleon). If the child is bilingual, she may not make this choice because she better understands the concept of a word as a symbol.

These findings don't mean that bilingual children always learn to read more easily than monolingual children. Other abstract language structures, like reading a map that has symbols, are difficult for both monolingual and bilingual children to grasp. Some bilingual adults who are otherwise equally fluent in both languages find reading in one language slower and more difficult than reading in the other.[9]

Most bilingual children aren't equally proficient or fluent in both languages. Usually, a stronger language emerges.[10] Although learning two languages delays vocabulary growth in at least one of the languages at first, bilingual children learn to use words from both languages to express themselves.[11] Eventually, they become fluent in both languages, if they use both consistently. Bilingual children acquire other skills in both languages, like sounds and sentence structure, in the same way and at the same rate as monolingual children.[12]

They can also achieve sophisticated language abilities, like the complex ability to translate.[13] All these skills depend on the amount of social stimulation the child receives and the experiences she has in both languages.[14]

Bilingual speakers experience social differences when they switch languages. For example, some languages seem more tactful than others, and a person who speaks both types of languages must know how to interact with others when speaking them. Because languages reflect cultures with different values and morals, bilingual speakers often report feeling different when communicating in different languages. The language affects the speaker's style of communicating, personality, and perception by others. Some of these effects are negative. For example, some bilingual adults report feeling frustrated and restricted while trying to express their thoughts and opinions in a second language. They feel that the language makes it difficult to express their individuality.[15]

For these reasons, it's important for parents to know the facts about language acquisition as they consider the options for raising bilingual children. Teaching your child a second language is a gift, but you must consider your child's self-identity, self-esteem, schooling options, and other social factors for the gift to be well used and appreciated.[16] Whether you and your child learn a second language together, or you help your child learn a language you already know, you'll enjoy experiencing another culture together.

How Do Children Become Bilingual?

Starting at birth, babies can detect differences in speech sounds of all languages. This ability fades between ages 6 and 12 months, when babies pay closer attention to the language they hear most often.[17] Young bilingual children can develop two separate sets of sounds,[18] which means that you could introduce two languages to your baby during the first year and promote her acquisition of both.

Researchers have found that the earlier you introduce a language to your child, the more native-like her pronunciation will tend to be. They disagree, however, on the age at which a child can no longer learn a second language with a native-like pronunciation, or whether a cutoff age actually exists.[19] (Some studies suggest the cutoff age is five years, others eight, and others puberty.[20]) Researchers seem to agree that the ability to successfully acquire a second language declines with age.

There are two ways for a child to become bilingual: simultaneous bilingualism and successive bilingualism.

Simultaneous Bilingualism

Simultaneous bilingualism occurs when a child learns two languages at the same time before age three.[21] If, for example, you speak a second language, your child has an opportunity to learn the second language while she learns her first. Some parents even hire a bilingual nanny to read and talk to the child in the second language. When a child simultaneously learns two languages, she goes through the same developmental stages as a child learning one language. For example, whether a child learns one language or two, her first words emerge between ages 9 and 18 months, and word combinations appear between ages 18 and 24 months.

When children begin to acquire words from both languages simultaneously, it may seem as though they lump the words into one mixed language. At this early stage, children don't know enough words to separate the languages. Researchers have noticed that by about age two, some bilingual children begin to code-switch, or separate their languages and switch between them to address different listeners and different situations.[22] Some parents worry that when the children mix languages while trying to code-switch, they're becoming confused. Mixing languages initially is normal for bilingual children and shows that they're learning to code-switch. Language-mixing doesn't necessarily suggest a language disorder; instead, it may show a proficiency in learning the two languages.[23]

Bilingual toddlers might not comment on their bilingualism until age three, but they might be aware that they can speak two languages.[24] During this stage, bilingual children may blend words according to concepts. For example, a child who speaks Spanish and English may ask for *"agua*-water." Others might blend words phonetically. For example, a child who speaks French and English might say *"tati,"* a mixture of "thank you" and *"merci."*[25]

A bilingual child begins to use two different grammatical systems from the time she starts using multiword combinations (around age 18 months).[26] As she learns the rules of grammar, she becomes more confident speaking the second language because she can better understand the parts of the language. She might continue to borrow vocabulary from one language to express ideas in the other, sometimes within the same sentence. She may also borrow vocabulary to emphasize meaning or accommodate the language of the listener. Some children may mix languages, even though the parents try to keep the languages separate (for example, the family speaks one language at home and the other outside the home).[27]

Some researchers believe that language-mixing and code-switching prove that parents don't *need* to separate languages in order for children to learn how to separate the languages themselves.[28] I believe, however, that separating languages helps children's bilingual development. (See pages 175–76.) When bilingual children hear a lot of language-mixing from others, they'll naturally mix their languages. Plus, children tend to mix languages more when using their second language.[29] Eventually, a bilingual child's language-mixing tapers. She'll continue to use one language in certain situations and use the second language in other situations.

Successive Bilingualism

Successive bilingualism occurs when a child learns a second language after age three, usually after the first language is well established.[30] If you took foreign language classes in school, you were learning to be bilingual successively. Learning a second language this way tends to be more complicated and less natural than becoming simultaneously bilingual. Research suggests that the younger the child, the easier it is for her to acquire a second language. But this finding doesn't mean older children can't learn a second language. In fact, older children seem to comprehend the rules of grammar better than younger children, especially when the second language is similar to the first.[31]

Developing a Language Plan

Experts suggest that families who wish to raise their children bilingually first develop language plans. Families who carefully plan exactly how their children will develop two languages, and who commit to bilingual language development, tend to raise bilingual children more successfully than families without language plans.[32]

To make a language plan, first define what bilingualism means to your family. Do you want your child to become completely fluent in two languages? Do you want her to be literate in both languages? What parts of the languages will she need to master so she can function in your community and culture?

Next, plan how you'll provide opportunities for your child's bilingual development. Will she learn the second language simultaneously with the first or successively? If she'll learn the second language successively, how will you introduce it to her? When deciding whether your child should become bilingual simultaneously or successively, keep this in mind: Learning a second language isn't as important as becoming proficient in at least one language by the time she starts school.[33]

Introducing a Second Language

TV shows and CDs often introduce children to a second language. Although these media might stimulate second language development, to learn the language properly your child must learn it interactively. The more she can speak the language and try to understand it in conversation, the better she'll learn it.

Even if you don't know the second language, you can help your child develop it, especially during the first few years of her life. You know what motivates your child and what helps her learn. Knowing just a few words can help you successfully introduce your child to the second language. Encourage her to listen to a simple story that you read in the language. Have her point to the pictures and repeat the words to practice pronunciation. Try teaching her the phrase *I feel* in the second language, then give her a choice of emotion words, like *angry* or *glad*, in the second language. Knowing how to complete a sentence in the second language helps your child build vocabulary.

Opal Dunn, an expert on bilingual education, suggests that children like to learn key phrases, chants, and rhymes in the beginning stages. These phrases, chants, and rhymes help children feel as though they're quickly learning the language.[34] When a child can complete thoughts in a second language and see others react to what she's said, she's more willing to use the second language.

Find creative, interactive ways to introduce the second language to your child. For example, in her book *Help Your Child with a Foreign Language*, Dunn suggests introducing a puppet friend who speaks only the second language to your child. Or visit a restaurant with servers who speak the second language, and teach your child a greeting or two in the second language to use with them. Become friends with a neighborhood family who speaks the language. A child can quickly pick up the language during regular playground or home visits.

After the introduction of a second language, further immersion can frustrate children, especially if they aren't ready or willing to learn at the next level. You know your child best. Guide and support her as she learns a second language, but don't pressure her to advance to the next level if she's not ready.

Providing Rich Bilingual Experiences

To successfully develop their children's bilingualism, parents must provide rich experiences in both languages.[35] There are several methods you can use to encourage your child's second language development, but most experts agree that separating the languages makes acquisition a little easier. If parents mix the languages in the same conversation, young children may have trouble separating the vocabulary and grammar of each language. Devise some strategies for your family that emphasize boundaries between the languages, and remember that consistency is key.[36] Here are some examples:

- You and another family member speak only your native languages to the child. (For example, you speak only English and your spouse speaks only Spanish.)
- You and your child use one language at home and your child uses the second language at school.

- You and your child use one language at home and at work and school, and use the other language in the community.
- You alternate speaking one language to your child one day, then the second language the next day. Or you speak one language during one activity, and the second language during another. (For example, you speak Spanish to your child during meals, but speak English at bedtime.)

Language interaction is important for successful bilingualism. Studies suggest that the size of a child's vocabulary depends on the number of words addressed to her.[37] Encourage your child to use the second language whenever you can to help her develop that language.[38]

When choosing a method, keep in mind where and with whom your child spends the most time and how much she concentrates on learning language in that environment. She'll probably pick up more language from that environment. How consistently a bilingual child hears a second language affects how well she develops it. If your child hears less of the second language than she does the first, you may need to compensate for the difference.[39] For example, if your child uses one language all day in school and uses the other language at home in the evenings and on weekends, she'll likely develop the school language more proficiently than the home language. In this case, plan times to use the home language with your child in various situations and with various speakers.

Many parents find that the best way to reinforce a second language is to find opportunities for their children to talk with other people in the language.[40] Some families even reinforce a second language by living abroad. If your family moves away from a community in which your child had many opportunities to converse in the second language, she'll have difficulty retaining it unless you find ways for her to converse in it with people in the new community.

To encourage bilingualism at home, you and your child can read books, write stories, sing songs, play games, use computer programs, watch closed-captioned TV shows, or converse in the second language. If your child can't yet read, she can participate in active listening and speaking activities. For example, try playing number games in the second language.

As your child's vocabulary in the second language grows, play language games you've played in the first language or try some language games with your child that use the alphabet in the second language. Ask friends and relatives to talk with your child on the telephone in the second language. Some parents encourage their children to translate family conversations from one language into the other.

Check your local library for story hours conducted in both languages (for example, your child hears the same story first in one language, then in the other). Some libraries play music from the two cultures between stories, which is a great way to keep the children's attention while teaching vocabulary through song. At your library, you can find bilingual books as well as interactive music CDs and movies in the second language.

If you want your child to be literate in both languages, she'll most likely use her first language to learn how to read and write in the second language. Make sure your child knows how to read sufficiently in the first language—and knows the names of the letters in the second language—before you introduce reading activities in the second language. If both languages use the same alphabet, your child may be able to transfer literacy skills from the first language to the second. She may still need help with phonics (connecting sounds to written letters) and spelling. If the languages use different writing systems (for example, the Roman alphabet and Chinese characters), your child most likely will need additional resources (workbooks, classes, and so on) to become literate in the second language.

Depending on the languages spoken in your area, your community center may offer classes for children in the second language. These classes are a fun way for children to learn the language. Many classes last six to ten weeks, and some are geared toward children as young as three. Some instructors use workbooks, and others rely on interactive activities. Still others might use music to teach basic concepts like colors, numbers, and the alphabet. Music can reinforce a second language by helping children practice vocabulary, idioms, sentence patterns, pronunciation, stress, rhythm, and intonation, as well as providing background cultural information.[41]

Give both languages equal importance in all parts of your child's life, but don't force bilingualism, especially if your child feels that communicating in either language is more work than fun or if bilingualism makes her feel so "different" that she becomes isolated. During the school years, a child is very aware of any differences that separate her from her peers, and her use of both languages may feel like a liability, not an asset, if her peers aren't bilingual. Support your child's bilingualism by using the method that helps her succeed in most environments. Remember to be a good language model (see pages 6–10), whether your child is acquiring one language or two. She'll develop the languages at her own pace and in her own style.

To successfully raise your child bilingually, remember that your attitude counts. The more you make bilingualism a natural part of family life, the more likely your child will enjoy being bilingual and you'll keep both languages active in your home.[42] Keep language models simple, and build and expand on your child's attempts while giving encouragement and praise naturally.

Trilingualism

If you think bilingualism requires a lot of thought and planning, adding another language to your family's language plan may seem impossible. Many families, however, have managed to raise trilingual children successfully.

Trilingual speakers don't usually have the opportunity to use their three languages equally.[43] A trilingual child tends to use one language more than the other two.[44] The dominant language isn't always the one that's first introduced to the child. Sometimes she prefers to use the language that was introduced last. In most cases, the trilingual child chooses the language that works in most situations.[45] Amazingly, trilingual children seem to recognize the language boundaries among the three languages. The child learns which person speaks what language, and she can switch languages easily to match listeners.

Few studies have analyzed simultaneous trilingualism (a child's ability to learn three languages at the same time by age three). Here's one account of a couple raising their son trilingually from birth:

> Liya is originally from Russia, and her husband, Jens, is from Germany. They both speak English fluently. When their son, Coby, was born, they decided to speak to him in their native languages. Liya and Jens spoke English to each other but not to Coby. He heard only Russian from Liya and only German from Jens. By age two, Coby could comprehend and speak all three languages. He picked up additional English by listening to the radio and interacting with playgroup friends who spoke English. When Coby began preschool, he was fluent enough in English to fully communicate with his teachers and peers. Now age five, Coby prefers speaking English to his parents. Although Liya and Jens wish Coby would speak only Russian and German to them, they've modified their language plan. They continue to speak Russian and German to Coby and hope the exposure to the different languages will increase his fluency and make visits with Russian- and German-speaking relatives easier and more rewarding.

This story shows that children can simultaneously learn multiple languages naturally when families from different backgrounds devise a language plan that cultivates trilingualism.

In most cases of trilingualism, a child learns two languages simultaneously at home before starting school, where she then picks up the third language successively. A child often acquires a third language more easily than the second, especially if she learns it in the same way as she learned the second. She can draw on her ability to think in different languages as she learns a new language. Generally, a third language that shares qualities with the other two languages, like a Latin origin, is easier to learn than one that doesn't. If your child consistently interacts in all three languages, she'll successfully maintain them. To help her, provide lots of fun, interesting opportunities to interact in the languages, especially the nondominant ones.

When Your Child Is Adopted Internationally

In the United States, the number of international adoptions has grown substantially since the early 1990s.[46] More than 19,000 children each year are adopted from other countries, and 46 percent of the children are younger than a year old. Almost 90 percent of internationally adopted children are younger than age five.[47] Research in speech-language pathology on internationally adopted children is just beginning. I gathered much of my research by talking with international adoption agencies and adoptive parents, and by observing internationally adopted children.

In most international adoptions, the children come from orphanages. Some countries have hundreds of thousands of orphans; for example, in 2000 the Ministry of Education in Russia estimated that their country had 700,000 orphans.[48] These countries face extraordinary challenges to clothe and feed orphans, and most of these children don't receive adequate language stimulation in their first (birth) language, much less learn the language of a potential adoptive country. International adoption is often these countries' last option for solving orphan overpopulation problems.

Challenges Facing Internationally Adopted Children and Adoptive Families

International adoptions require families to complete myriad tasks. Families must process a lot of paperwork, resolve legal and financial concerns, arrange meetings with social workers, and take stressful trips to another country. After adoption, a family focuses on meeting the child's emotional and physical needs. They must also encourage the child to attach to her new family, which may change household arrangements and routines.

Children adopted from international orphanages can face complex developmental problems. Many of these children have histories of ear infections and other illnesses. One study of 56 children adopted from orphanages in Eastern Europe found that the majority had some type of large motor, small motor, language, or social-emotional developmental delay.[49] Other studies found that some delays were long-lasting and required rehabilitation to overcome.[50]

Researchers suggest that children lose one month of developmental growth for every three months spent in an orphanage, and language delays are the most commonly diagnosed problems with these children.[51] Some may be language delayed simply because they didn't have the one-on-one adult interaction necessary for proper language development. In some cases, inadequate care and stimulation may have prevented the children's neurological systems from developing correctly, causing sensory problems. Children might be overly sensitive or insensitive to touch, textures, food, lights, and sounds.[52]

Once adopted, these children may show a combination of symptoms called the post-institutional response.[53] Because many have had little high-quality adult interaction, they may show self-stimulating behaviors like those seen in autistic children (rocking back and forth, for example). They also may distance themselves from others when feeling stressed out. Some have trouble controlling their emotions, don't tolerate frustration well, and react severely to perceived threats. They may be aggressive and independent when fulfilling basic needs. For example, they may be overly possessive of their food at mealtimes. Depending on the severity of these symptoms, these children's developmental delays may be prolonged.[54]

Many internationally adopted children have difficulty processing what information to act on and what to filter out (symptoms that resemble attention deficit disorder), even when the information is in their birth languages.[55] This condition usually improves with time, but because many may have had difficulty understanding and expressing themselves in a birth language, they often have trouble learning an adopted language. I encourage families internationally adopting children of *any* age to learn as much about ESL as possible (see pages 191-95).

Language Development and Internationally Adopted Children

Families with internationally adopted children have unique communication challenges. If a child is language delayed in a birth language, she may also be delayed in other areas of development, which may hinder her ability to learn a new language. In many cases, an internationally adopted child must first catch up on a lot of physical and emotional growth. Many factors influence the growth rate, like a history of poor nutrition, developmental delays, health problems, environmental conditions, and the ability to handle stress.

With all the challenges families of internationally adopted children face, many find it difficult to include birth languages in their language plans. Most internationally adopted children quickly lose their birth languages because they don't converse and interact in them. One study showed that children adopted internationally between ages four and eight lost most of their expressive birth language three to six months after adoption, and lost all functional use of the language within a year. Infants and toddlers lost birth languages even more rapidly.[56]

Don't push your child to use a new language initially. Using unnatural methods (like flashcards) to teach the new language can strain an already stressful situation. For the first few weeks in a new home, an internationally adopted child may grieve for her life in the birth country. If she tries to express her grief in the birth language, her adoptive family may not understand her, and she may try to communicate by hurting herself, showing aggression, and crying.[57] When a family can't communicate with a child, it's hard to comfort her. Sign language can facilitate communication before the child learns the new language. (See Chapter 7.) When appropriate, use words in the new language naturally and in context along with the signs. When your child is emotionally ready, research suggests that she'll rapidly acquire vocabulary in the new language. An adoptive family's attention and care seem to make a child flourish.

Despite poor language stimulation in orphanages, children adopted internationally at age three and younger without other health or developmental complications should have few problems learning a new language.[58] Through a parent survey study conducted at Towson University in Baltimore, Maryland, Sharon Glennen and M. Gay Masters found that infants and toddlers adopted from Eastern Europe developed English language skills in the same patterns as nonadopted English-speaking children. In fact, most toddlers in the study started learning English soon after adoption, and their language skills progressed quickly. Most children in the study had conditions that might have slowed language development, like premature birth, weight and height below the tenth percentile, large motor delays, developmental delays, and a history of chronic otitis media (chronic ear infections). Despite this fact, the study concluded that while it's important for adoptive parents to know a child's medical history, especially any conditions that may slow growth, the presence (or absence) of these conditions doesn't necessarily dictate language development.

In most cases, an internationally adopted child's language development lags behind her nonadopted peers'. How much it lags depends on her age at adoption. The older a child is when adopted, the more time she needs to develop language skills and catch up to her nonadopted peers. Once she's continuously exposed to a language, her language skills usually catch up quickly. Any adopted child who's not progressing needs immediate speech and language services.[59]

Some parents mistakenly think that adopting a baby internationally before she begins talking (that is, adopting her during the first year) means that she won't have any trouble acquiring an adopted language. It's true that the younger a child is when she's adopted, the more likely she'll learn a second language quickly. During the first six months, a child hears and can distinguish among all the phonemes in her birth language (the language she hears the most) and among those in another language, even though she hasn't spoken her first word yet. But this ability begins to decline after age 6 months, which affects future language development. A baby adjusts to hearing only her birth language between ages 6 and 12 months, when she begins to babble using sounds from her birth language, thereby laying the foundation for saying first words in her birth language.

If a child is adopted internationally when she's older than 6 months, she has more trouble acquiring an adopted language for two reasons. First, like anyone learning a new language, a child who's used to hearing her birth language and babbling in it initially has trouble perceiving and producing phonemes that aren't used in the birth language. Second, the child stops developing the birth language (unless the language is part of the family's language plan) and restarts language development, relearning all the sounds she knows so they work with the adopted language. For these reasons, speech-language pathologists usually consider internationally adopted children at high risk for speech and language delays. These children require direct evaluation and long-term follow-up to help determine which ones will need intervention to overcome delays.

Based on Glennen and Masters's study, the following is a list of typical language-development lags parents can expect with children adopted internationally at specific ages. Keep in mind that this survey studied children only through age 40 months, and it didn't rule out other language delays that might continue past this age. Expect variations in catch-up growth.[60]

- **Adopted before age 12 months:** Most children this age begin talking at the same time as typically developing nonadopted children. If by age 18 to 24 months, your child doesn't reach typical milestones (see Chapter 4), like acquiring fifty words in the adopted language and using some two-word phrases, seek evaluation. Children should be close to reaching typical norms by age 24 months and should reach typical language milestones by age 30 to 36 months.

- **Adopted between ages 13 and 18 months:** Children this age rapidly acquire vocabulary in the adopted language. While many of these children acquire fifty words and use two-word phrases by age 24 months, some of the children's development may still be two to four months behind their nonadopted peers' at age 37 to 40 months. If your child doesn't acquire fifty words and doesn't use some two-word phrases by age 24 months, seek evaluation.

- **Adopted between ages 19 and 24 months:** Children this age rapidly acquire vocabulary in the adopted language, and their development catches up to their nonadopted peers' remarkably well. If your child isn't using any words in the adopted language by age 24 months and hasn't acquired fifty words by age 28 months and two-word phrases by age 28 to 30 months, she may be language delayed and needs evaluation. At age 37 to 40 months, expect some expressive and receptive language skills to be two to four months behind the norm.

- **Adopted between ages 25 and 30 months:** Expect a child this age to use words in the adopted language within the first few weeks at her adopted home. If she isn't adding words in the adopted language immediately and hasn't acquired fifty words in the adopted language and some two-word phrases by age 31 months, seek evaluation. Expect some expressive and receptive language delays to continue. (In this study, the children were still delayed at age 40 months.)

In general, internationally adopted infants and toddlers match the language-development growth of nonadopted children. Children adopted at age three and older began speaking an adopted language immediately and caught up in development soon after adoption. Still, there may be a period during which your adopted child seems language delayed in both the birth and adopted languages. Until she fully acquires the adopted language, expect her to have limited proficiency in all languages. (An assessment of your child's language development doesn't always consider this factor.) In the meantime, make sure her adopted language skills are continually progressing.[61]

Facilitating Communication with Your Internationally Adopted Child

In this section, I suggest ways that you can facilitate communication after you adopt your child so you can make your family's language plan easier to follow. First, before adoption gather all available information about your child's medical/developmental history, including any native (or birth) language skills. Be familiar with the stages of normal language development (see Chapter 4) so you can gauge her development and make sure her language skills are continually progressing.

During the first few weeks at home, communicating with a child in her birth language can comfort her when the new environment overwhelms her. Learn a few common expressions in your child's birth language, like "Yes," "No," "I love you," "Are you hungry?" "Are you thirsty?" "Do you have to go potty?" "Are you tired?" "What do you want?" "Let's play," "Come here," and "Stop." Don't worry if you can't pronounce the words perfectly. Hearing familiar words—no matter how simple or mispronounced—can comfort a child more than hearing eloquent adopted language she can't understand.[62] To make a child feel comfortable before adoption, some families send a "family book" that includes photos of the family and pets. Some also send recorded oral "letters" in the child's birth language.

I strongly urge families to learn some simple signs (see Chapter 7) to help bridge the language gap. Some sign language classes are just for parents; others are for parents and children. Keep in mind that acquiring sign language takes time and patience, but the effort can be worthwhile, as the following account shows:

> *Mai was adopted at age 4 months from Vietnam. Early intervention therapists worked with her to overcome several challenges. Her parents exposed her to sign language at home and in classes to help her communicate basic needs and desires. At age 10 months, the first—and one of the most important—signs Mai learned was* full. *In Vietnam, her bottles had been propped up against the rails of her crib so she couldn't turn her head away and refuse food. As a result, she'd eat until she was sick because she hadn't learned to express that she was satiated. It took only a month of signing and the model of moving the spoon away for Mai to express that she was full.*

In this case, sign language helped the child catch up on development that had been stymied, and helped her acquire language at the same rate as her typically developing nonadopted peers.

If your family's language plan includes bilingualism, know that despite the challenges of maintaining two languages, bilingualism *is* possible, especially if you adopt your child before age one. Learning and developing two languages simultaneously is often the simplest way to become bilingual. If you'd like your child to be bilingual, start by consistently maintaining the birth language soon after adoption.

Whether you decide to incorporate your child's birth language into your family's language plan or replace her birth language with an adopted language, the decisions you make about her language development may influence her sense of identity more than any other factor, as the next section discusses.

Language, Culture, and Identity

While gathering data for this book, I met Jan King, founder of the Inter-National Adoption Alliance, a nonprofit organization that provides educational and cultural resources to adopted children and their families. Jan adopted a boy and a girl from Korea. She wasn't Korean, but she'd chosen to raise the children bilingually, teaching them to speak English and Korean and including American and Korean cultures in their daily lives. She wanted the children to grow up comfortable speaking, listening, reading, and writing in both languages, and interacting in both cultures. Jan showed me that language is strongly connected to a child's sense of identity. Language helps create a sense of belonging, and a child can connect to her birth culture by knowing some of the language.[63]

In 1999, the Evan B. Donaldson Adoption Institute, a national research foundation on adoption, surveyed adults adopted as children from Korea and Vietnam by families of a different race. When asked about their views on transracial adoption, the majority of participants reported pervasive racial discrimination and confusion about identity while growing up. Some felt they hadn't belonged to any culture, especially when they'd had no experiences in their birth cultures. This survey's results showed that it's important for adoptive families to expose their children to diverse cultures, especially birth cultures. The results also emphasized the need for families to help children handle discrimination and identity issues.[64] Introducing adopted children to others who've had the same experiences growing up helps strengthen the children's sense of identity.

If an adopted child doesn't talk about her birth culture, her family might think it doesn't interest her. It's natural for an adopted child to wonder about her past. Many young children realize that they look different from their adoptive families at very early ages,[65] but they often can't formulate questions about the differences they see and sense. The children may wish to learn more about their birth cultures, but won't act on this wish if they feel their adoptive families would disapprove or become upset. For this reason, a family's attitude is crucial to helping an adopted child develop an interest in her birth culture.

When families provide birth culture experiences, adopted children may go through phases during which they set the cultures aside. Many participants in the 1999 survey said that they appreciated their families' desire to expose them to a birth culture, but almost all agreed that it was more beneficial when their families allowed them to "move in and out of that [interest in the culture] without feeling pressured." About 75 percent of participants explored their birth cultures when they were grown.[66]

Some adult adoptees return to birth countries to experience birth cultures and to find birth families. These experiences tend to go more smoothly if the adoptees had been exposed to the culture and the language while growing up. About 25 percent of participants in the 1999 survey who returned to birth countries reported feeling that the population discriminated against them because they didn't speak the birth language. About 20 percent of participants reported having mixed experiences. These participants found that once the population realized that they couldn't speak the language, they were ignored or treated rudely.[67] Adoptees who found birth families discovered that knowing the birth language let them communicate with family members without a translator, which made the reunions more comfortable for everyone.

Families expose adopted children to birth cultures in different ways. Some start the exposure when the child is very young (birth to age five). They might invite a neighbor or a friend from the child's birth country to speak to her. While some young children seem to enjoy this experience, other children may perceive people who speak the birth language as a threat.[68] In some cases, the children scream and clap their hands over their ears when hearing the birth language. Some families conclude from this reaction that the children are rejecting the birth language and culture, and they decide not to further expose the children to them. The children's reaction, however, may show that they fear being removed from yet another home or being sent back to the birth country. Constant reassurance and patience should eventually make these children comfortable enough to use the birth language and interact in the birth culture.

When the child is older, the family might take her to a restaurant that serves food from the birth country, buy dolls or toys from that culture, and teach her a few phrases in the birth language. They might enroll her in a camp that immerses her in the culture. They might even take her to visit her birth country. Some families feel that these experiences give the children enough information about the birth culture. Other families feel that these experiences may not be enough, because the children tend to still feel isolated from their birth cultures.[69] To build the children's self-esteem and confidence, these families may arrange to have their children interact with communities that speak the birth language.[70] Some groups of families with adopted children or support groups organized by adoption agencies offer language and culture classes. Some communities let adopted children of the same culture participate in their schools, play programs, or church services.

Some families, like the one I mention at the beginning of this section, choose to immerse their children in both the adopted and birth languages and cultures right from the start. This option certainly takes the most time and effort (especially if you don't speak your child's birth language), but it lets her develop so she's comfortable in both cultures. Plus, becoming bilingual is easier when a child learns the languages simultaneously. If this is your language plan, arrange for language modeling to begin in both languages as soon as your child seems comfortable with you. Provide opportunities for her to interact in the birth culture. Enroll her in a school that teaches in her birth language (exclusively or with the adopted language). Some families hire people to tutor their children in the birth languages or invite exchange students from the children's birth countries to live in their homes. These families claim that their children learn more about a birth culture from these arrangements than they could in less intensive situations.

Depending on the country from which you plan to adopt your child, there may be many resources to help alleviate adoption anxieties. Ask your adoption agency what resources are available locally. Knowing your options helps you plan for your child's language and cultural development. If one plan doesn't work for whatever reason, don't give up—find another plan. Associations like the Inter-National Adoption Alliance offer practical suggestions for preventing and solving everyday problems of families with adopted children. For example, Jan King suggests that a typical adoptive family get to know one family from the child's culture at a time. Even before a family adopts a child, they can seek out other families who've adopted children from the same country or culture so they can prepare for life after adoption.

While the challenges of exposing your adopted child to both her adopted and birth languages and cultures may seem overwhelming at times, doing so can help find her place in a multicultural, multilingual society.

Adopting an Older Child Who Doesn't Speak the Adopted Language

In international adoptions, 46 percent of children are adopted younger than age one, 43 percent between ages one and four, 8 percent between ages five and nine, and 3 percent older than age nine.[71] Children ages four and older are likely fluent in their birth languages and suffer from post-institutional response (see page 181) longer. Very few of these children have received proper education or been given opportunities to learn to read and write in a second language. If the children have become literate in a second language, they've seldom had opportunities to become fluent speaking it.

Some adoptive families choose to home-school their children until the kids are comfortable using the adopted language and can function in school. To help learn language concepts used in schools (for example, abstract language, sentence construction, and new vocabulary), internationally adopted children age four to eight seem to benefit especially from speech therapy and English as a Second Language (ESL) classes. Some families supplement a child's schooling with tutoring. Some use adoption agencies to find tutors to work with their children several times a week. If your language plan calls for it, you may choose to find a teacher who can teach in your child's birth language. It's often difficult to find and pay for such a teacher, so many families pool resources with other families and conduct classes for their children.

The number of learning disabilities among adopted children seems to be unusually high.[72] The effects of institutionalization can leave an adopted child with symptoms that professionals may misdiagnose as caused by a learning disability or even attention deficit disorder. To help differentiate between disabilities caused by post-institutional response and those caused by a learning disorder, have a school psychologist observe your child at different times and in various situations.[73]

If possible, let your child help decide if bilingualism is right for her. Some children eagerly pursue both languages, and others show their excitement for adopted cultures by setting their birth languages aside for a while. Whatever your decision about bilingualism, support your child by showing respect for both cultures and languages and by giving her opportunities to experience both cultures. When questions arise about your child's heritage, she needs to know enough about it to answer them with pride.

ESL and Bilingual Education

In 2000, the U.S. Census Bureau found that almost 47 million people spoke a language other than English in their homes.[74] This number increased from 31.8 million people in 1990.[75] Demographers predict that by the 2030s about 40 percent of the school-age population in the United States will speak a language other than English as their primary language.[76] In some areas of the United States, that percentage has already been surpassed; for example, 60 to 70 percent of school-age children in parts of California don't speak English as their primary language.

To function in a new culture, a child often must learn a second language. Second-language learning is typically similar to first-language learning: Children first learn single words or common short expressions, then learn longer and more complex sentences. When learning a second language, children often make mistakes because they incorrectly translate the first language into the second. For example, they'll translate a sentence word for word and in the same order from the first language to the second, jumbling the message in the second language.

A child may pick up a second language at school or by interacting with peers. If she learns the language from peers, she may go through the following stages.[77] First, she forms a relationship with the speaker of the second language. She might then go through a period of silence during which she focuses on listening to and understanding her new friend. (The younger the child, the longer this silent period tends to last. Older kids may be silent for only a couple of weeks or months, but preschoolers may be silent for a year or longer.) Once she's ready, the child first learns basic greetings and expressions, like "Good morning," "How are you?" and "Fine, thank you." Then she begins to express herself with simple words. Finally, she learns correct verb forms and other language constructs, and can successfully communicate in the second language.

It's rare for someone to be equally fluent in two languages.[78] One usually becomes the dominant language, and it's usually the one that's used most often. For example, when non–English-speaking children acquire English as a second language at school, sometimes English replaces a first language as the dominant one.[79] When this shift happens, it's important that families remind children that the first language (and the culture it's connected to) is *not* inferior to the second language and culture.

To promote successful bilingualism, families must make sure children continue to learn skills in both languages. If families don't reinforce and maintain a first language, children learning a new language may lose some skills and fluency in the first language.[80] Language loss can occur at any age, even in adulthood. If a second language becomes dominant and the first language isn't nurtured, it's possible that a child could lose the ability to communicate with her family in the first language.[81]

Bilingual Education for Children Who Don't Speak English at Home

Children who speak a language other than English at home must steadily improve their comprehension of what they hear and read because comprehension of all academic subjects depends on these skills. State government authorities—and many parents—disagree on the best way to educate such children. Some promote total immersion, believing that children learn a language quicker in sink-or-swim situations. Others advocate bilingual schooling (instructing the child in two languages), claiming that a child who's gradually introduced to the English language acquires English language skills—and math and science skills—better than a child who's totally immersed in English from the start.

In bilingual schooling, kindergartners and first-graders ideally are taught in their first language 90 percent of the time and in English 10 percent of the time. As they progress through the grades and learn more English, teaching in the two languages equals out.[82] Children who learn English this way tend to outperform those who must sink or swim, because they can understand more of what they hear.

Most public schools don't offer bilingual schooling. Instead, these schools must quickly bring children's English language skills up to speed so they can function in the classroom. To accomplish this goal, schools usually assess the children's English proficiency, then provide ESL classrooms so the children can receive help when needed. Typically, children have one to three years to become proficient in English. After three years, they're often tested and treated like native English speakers. Keep in mind that most ESL children need two to five years to become proficient enough in English to benefit fully from classroom learning.

When children are taught in their nondominant language, they must learn the subject material and the language at the same time. Until they're literate in English, they struggle to understand what they read. As a result, it can take several years for these children to perform well on standardized tests.

The abstractness of the English language can further complicate learning. Idioms, slang, jokes, similes, metaphors, and other confusing constructions can make comprehension difficult for some ESL children. Consider the following passage:

> The teacher says, "Maria, could you **lend me a hand**? Please **run down** to the cafeteria and **pick up** the onion they have **set aside** for us. That will **take care** of our specimen for science today. **Run along** and why don't you **stop by** the other seventh-grade classroom and **see if** Ms. Barnes would let us borrow a box of slides. We're missing more than I realized and I don't see how we can **make do** without them. Meanwhile, we'll **look over** the fifth chapter. I know you're **up to date** on that information."

This passage shows how abstract language, particularly idioms, may cause comprehension problems among ESL students. Children who try to interpret abstract language literally are sure to get confused.

ESL students may also have trouble mastering pronunciation. The older the child and the longer she's spoken her native language, the more likely she is to have difficulty learning to speak English with a standard accent, especially after adolescence.[83] Depending on her native language, certain sounds may be difficult for a child to make. (Some of the most commonly mispronounced sounds are *l* and *r*.) Abstract language and accent are areas that can be improved with time, effort, and help from speech therapists.

The rate at which a child acquires English depends on her level of development in the native language. For general educational success, knowing two languages equally well is less important than knowing one of the languages well enough for effective schooling.[84] A child who has strong native language skills can learn English quickly.[85] One study concluded that by the end of fourth grade (after five years of schooling), over 90 percent of limited English proficiency (LEP) students had achieved oral English proficiency. But the students didn't achieve academic proficiency until the end of sixth grade (after seven years of schooling). In general, there's rapid growth in language skills during the first two to three years of learning the language, then learning slows gradually.[86]

How families support literacy in the home strongly influences how fast a child learns. Developing literacy skills in a native language can help a child learn to speak English, and when she's ready, she can extend those literacy skills to reading and writing in English. This is why families shouldn't stop using a native language with a child at home. If families speak to their children in the native language but don't help maintain reading and writing skills in that language, most children will fall behind in the those skills.[87]

Also, language is linked to emotion, temperament, and identity.[88] If families abruptly stop using a native language, it can lead not only to language loss or language shift (that is, shifting from using primarily the native language to using only English), but it also can cause emotional and psychological problems for both parents and children.

Despite the obstacles, many ESL students successfully learn English with the help and support of family and teachers.

How Varying Cultures Affect Language

Throughout this book, I advocate teaching children to express their thoughts, desires, and feelings—no matter how insignificant they might be. Some cultures, however, don't support this way of teaching. While I was the international student coordinator for Auburn University, I learned that culture can strongly influence communication, and when different cultures interact, miscommunication or lack of communication can result.

In the United States, for example, teachers expect direct eye contact from their students. Some Asian children, however, have been taught that making eye contact is inappropriate and disrespectful when they're communicating with adults.[89] I've observed that views on eye contact vary among Asian cultures and depend on factors like gender, personality, age, and length of residence in the United States. I believe that American teachers can require eye contact from these students, but teachers should be aware that a child's unwillingness to establish eye contact may stem from cultural teaching, not from shyness, dishonesty, or another negative factor.

Several studies show that the amount of time children spend talking with others varies significantly among cultures. Some cultures consider talkative children unintelligent, impolite, self-centered, and undisciplined.[90] These cultures value a child's ability to listen, which may mean very few of the child's requests are fulfilled.[91] In some families, parents may not allow their children to talk at the dinner table, and they teach the children not to control the topic of conversation.[92] Other families encourage boys to talk and girls to listen. Some gestures have different meanings in different cultures; for example, the same thumbs-up gesture that means "good" in North America is an extremely rude gesture in other parts of the world. Even the kinds of words children learn differ among cultures. For example, Mandarin-speaking children acquire mostly verbs.[93]

Despite the many cultural differences, children around the globe learn language with or without direct instruction from adults. In cultures that don't often provide children with direct instruction, children learn language by overhearing others.[94] Because different cultures teach children language in different ways, parents, caregivers, and teachers need to respect the differences as parts of the children's cultural identities—and adjust how they communicate with them accordingly.

Bilingual Testing and Intervention for Speech and Language Delays

One bilingual child out of ten may experience a speech, language, or hearing delay in one or both languages that's *not* related to the fact that she knows two languages.[95] If you're concerned about the speech-language development of your bilingual child, find a bilingual speech-language pathologist (SLP) to conduct tests in both languages. These tests must consider the specific circumstances in which a child learned each language.

An SLP might ask you how long your child has spoken each language, when and how she acquired the second language, how both languages are maintained, and whether there's a language loss or language shift occurring. The SLP should assess your child's proficiency in speaking, understanding, reading, and writing both languages, as well as assess her academic performance. Because children may initially learn certain words in one language and not in the other, SLPs can measure children's bilingual vocabularies by determining the total conceptual vocabulary for each child (that is, all words in one language that denote different concepts plus the words in the second language that denote concepts not already counted in the first).[96]

When a speech-language pathologist concludes that a bilingual child needs language intervention, the SLP typically provides therapy in the language that best helps the child learn. When the child has special needs, a bilingual approach to intervention may best facilitate language development. There's no evidence that a bilingual approach "confuses" or taxes the learning abilities of children with disabilities.[97] Furthermore, forcing families to "choose" the language of intervention (typically the dominant language) isn't ideal when the children live in a bilingual environment.[98]

Bilingual language therapy may involve families working with children on skills in the native language and therapists working with the children in the second language. Other approaches involve therapists working with children in the native language and the children continuing to acquire the second language in school.[99] Unfortunately, state laws and the lack of bilingual speech-language pathologists often limit treatment options. Nevertheless, taking the time to have your bilingual child properly assessed and treated will help her language development greatly.

One Last Word on Bilingualism and Second-Language Learning

This chapter condenses an enormous amount of information and can only begin to answer your questions about bilingualism and second-language learning. It should give you a foundation upon which you can add research. Whatever your family's circumstances, design a language plan that best uses the bilingual opportunities available. Remember that you can modify your family's language plan as needed. Promoting bilingualism and second-language learning as naturally as possible will benefit your child now and in the future.

Chapter 9

Using Musical Activities and Imaginary Play to Enhance Language Skills

What's the Magic behind Music and Learning?

Music is a natural part of children's lives. Children enjoy singing, moving, dancing, playing instruments, and making musical sounds. These activities lay the foundation for learning because they promote language development, creativity, coordination, and social interaction.[1] Playing or listening to music is a fun, exciting way for a child to learn new words and challenge his listening and perceptive skills.

Many studies show that music education and making music enhance general thinking skills, abstract thinking skills, reasoning skills, language development, pre-literacy and literacy skills, verbal abilities, creativity, and originality. Additional benefits include enhanced memory skills, ability to improvise during play, motor development, coordination, positive attitudes toward school, improved personal and social adjustment, as well as stress reduction. Music and science researcher Norman Weinberger believes that these benefits result from a lot of time spent listening to, studying, and enjoying music.[2]

In one study, six- to nine-year-olds with reading difficulties participated in a program that involved listening to music. The act of listening to music helped the children learn to read new words. This result suggests that music may help language development, especially for children with reading problems.[3] This finding also suggests that we're beginning to understand how music influences mental processes and behavior.

Parents and caregivers don't have to sing or play an instrument well to incorporate music into children's lives.

For young children, it's important that parents emphasize the enjoyment that music can bring. Share the kinds of music you enjoy with your child, and expose him to diverse musical styles.[4] Play music from other countries and cultures. Take time to learn the words to songs your child loves. Children develop preferences for music at an early age. (One of my sons enjoyed imitating Elvis Presley at age five). As children grow, they should continue to sing songs with their parents and caregivers. Singing songs, especially those that let children contribute their own verses, helps children develop a sense of belonging and control.[5] Singing with your child and showing approval for different kinds of music facilitates his growing appreciation of music.[6]

If children learn to appreciate music early on, they may later learn to play a musical instrument, which can provide all kinds of cognitive benefits. Weinberger reports that learning to play an instrument engages the brain and uses the auditory, visual, tactile, and kinesthetic senses. Reading music and planning how to play it uses cognitive and memory skills, and requires both large and small motor skills. The cognitive cycle of music production—reading music, planning how to play it, hearing and evaluating the music you produce, and adjusting your playing for improvement—repeats every few seconds while you're playing the instrument.[7]

Remember to follow your child's lead when it comes to musical pursuits.[8] Early music training may not interest every child. If your child dislikes practicing the piano and taking lessons, forcing him to do these activities won't encourage his appreciation of music. Encourage your child to take music lessons only if he expresses an earnest interest in them.

Music, Babies, and Development

Exposing infants to music may help develop their memory skills.[9] Infants' brains try to determine whether the sounds they hear are musical or linguistic. Studies show that a 5-month-old infant can discriminate small changes in pitches.[10] And infants age 8 to 11 months can remember melodies. They can detect changes as notes move up and down the scale and can categorize them by pitch.[11]

Playing music in the background provides an early musical experience for an infant's developing brain. Turn on some background music when your baby goes to sleep and for short periods when he's awake. Classical music is a great choice because its rhythm is similar to the human heartbeat, which relaxes us and helps our alertness and ability to learn.[12] Never play background music too loudly, and turn off the music if your child shows signs of fatigue and overstimulation.

Just as infants seem to prefer child-directed speech or CDS (see pages 10–12), they also seem to prefer child-directed singing.[13] While singing to their infants, some mothers slow the tempo of songs, pause between the phrases, and slightly raise the pitch of their voices.[14] Infants prefer a mother's voice to any recorded music because the live sound gives the music a nurturing quality that's absent in recorded music.[15] Music, especially lullabies, calms babies and can foster good parent-infant interactions.[16] You, too, might feel calmed and soothed after singing to your baby.

Music and Movement

Movement facilitates learning, thinking, and all mental processing.[17] When your baby is alert enough to enjoy brief stimulation (age 6 to 8 weeks), you can move and massage his body while singing or saying rhymes. The interaction may interest him for only a short time, but the physical contact can help him learn. Here's one activity to try: Lay your baby on the floor with his head elevated on a pillow. Sing a song or say a rhyme while stroking his arms or legs. While massaging your baby, name the parts of his body ("Right leg, left leg,…")

While you listen to songs with your baby, gently clap his hands or feet together to the beat. Children learn to keep a steady beat before they learn the rhythm of a song or rhyme. They take awhile to demonstrate the difference between beat patterns, but you can teach your child the difference early on. The following example illustrates the difference:

The steady beat

♩ ♩ ♩ ♩

Hump-ty dump-ty sat on a wall (four claps equally spaced)

The rhythm of the rhyme

♩ ♩ ♩ ♩ ♩ ♩ ♩

Hump-ty dump-ty sat on a wall (eight claps, one for each syllable)

Starting when your child is age 5 months, you can nurture his appreciation for music by rocking and patting him to the beat, and by chanting and imitating the sounds he makes. Babies as young as age 5 to 8 months may even initiate rhythmic movement as they respond to music.[18] You can also act out large locomotor motions (motions that involve moving from place to place, like stepping or jumping) or non-locomotor motions (motions that occur while standing in one place, like clapping, swaying, singing, bouncing, or rocking) to the music with your child.[19]

Here are other ways you can use music and movement to help your child's development:

- **Action rhymes**: Action rhymes like "Ride a Little Horsie" promote face-to-face interaction and help teach the first rule of conversation: turn taking. Your child watches and listens to you as you say the rhyme, then responds with a smile or a coo. Anticipating an action develops your child's memory skills. As your baby gets older, he'll enjoy more complex action rhymes. Action rhymes provide opportunities to teach your child new words because the accompanying motions help him recall the words.[20]

- **Dancing**: Put on some music and let your baby dance. Dancing in front of a mirror is great if your child enjoys seeing his reflection. Or dance around in a circle with your baby, bouncing him to the beat of the music. Some libraries and other organizations incorporate music and folk dances into children's activities. These are fun ways for your child to interact with others and hear new music.

- **Personalized songs and rhymes**: Instead of singing "B-I-N-G-O," sing the letters of your child's name. Replace *Humpty Dumpty* with your child's name in the rhyme ("Little Tyler sat on a wall..."). Personalized songs and rhymes help develop your child's self-awareness.

- **Crossover activities**: Some researchers suggest that crossover activities might help coordinate the right and left sides of the brain and help promote better development.[21] While singing songs, take your baby's right hand and tap it to his left knee or foot, then tap his left hand to his right knee or foot. Or gently cross his arms in front of his body so his hands reach toward his shoulders. For fun, use colorful scarves while doing crossover activities.
- **Change in position**: Babies love to be raised up and lowered down as if they were flying. While singing songs, make your child "fly" near a friend or sibling, and see what kind of reaction you get from your little one! (I always heard lots of giggles.) Some children enjoy sitting up for more complicated rhymes so they're more involved in the movements.

Singing, Music Play, and Musical Instruments for Toddlers and Preschoolers

Some children begin to sing songs on their own around age two to three. Many kids this age simply have no idea whether they're speaking or singing at any given moment.[22] To show your child the range of his voice, try these activities. Together make rising and falling sounds like the wind, a siren, or a passenger on a roller coaster. Listen to music together and touch your head when you hear high notes and touch your toes when you hear low notes. (This activity also helps develop your child's spatial orientation.) Lora Heller, a music therapist, suggests telling a story about a fire station, lowering and raising your voice as the firefighters go down the fire pole and up the ladder. Teach your child about volume and tempo by having him sing to his toy animals. He can sing them softly to sleep, then wake them up with a loud song. He can also sing slow and fast songs to his animals. Make sure you and your child don't overuse or abuse your voices (see pages 64–65).

Children can learn lots of language skills through creative music play. Encourage your child to make up verses to a song. He'll have fun even if he changes just the last word. Once in a while, turn on a radio station or play a CD that features music your child doesn't hear often. Whether it's classical, bluegrass, country, or jazz, it's fun to imagine what the music represents. When I do this activity with my sons, I start by saying, "What does this music sound like to you? What do you think is happening?" We've come up with some intriguing stories about cowboys and horses chasing other animals through the desert or the mountains, crossing a stream, then settling down by a nice campfire.

You can use musical instruments to act out stories and role-play. You can make toy instruments from common household items. Always supervise your child while he plays with the instruments. Some of the instruments contain items that can be choking hazards.

- *Maracas*: Fill 16- to 20-ounce plastic bottles with dry beans or rice.
- *Drum set*: Use pots, pans, and wooden spoons. Use an aluminum pie pan as a cymbal. Blocks, empty margarine tubs, water bottles, and coffee cans also make great drums.
- *Tambourine*: Cover a paper plate with dry beans or rice, squeeze glue around the edge of the plate, then set another paper plate upside down on top of the first.
- *Shakers*: Fill plastic film containers or plastic Easter eggs with dry rice.
- *Guitar*: Wrap rubber bands around a lidless shoebox.
- *Bells*: Sew bells onto the fingers of a pair of child's gloves.

Let your child decorate the instruments however he likes. While playing with the instruments, imagine what the sounds they make could be. For example, shaking maracas could be bacon frying in a pan. To keep your child's interest, use the instruments to sing about his favorite foods, animals, and characters. Take turns being the performer and the audience.

When you sing songs or do musical activities with your child, think how best to incorporate language skills. For example, if you're singing a song about elbows and knees, have him point to those body parts as you sing the names. Even if you're just talking with your child, try to include an occasional rhyme or song. Leave out the last word of a phrase for him to supply. When singing together or singing to your child, always remember to sing the songs he requests.

Music's Role in Reading Readiness

Music can foster a lifelong love of reading.[23] Children's natural affinity for rhythm and melody makes music ideal to reinforce listening, speaking, reading, and writing skills.[24] In one study, music therapists found that music significantly enhanced four-year-old children's print awareness and pre-writing skills.[25]

On page 102, I mention the connection between keeping a steady beat and basic reading skills. When you read text or listen to music, you hear cadences, phrases, and rhythm. Starting between ages four and six, most children can keep a steady beat. Your child might move his whole body or just his arms or legs to the beat. By age six, he's more physically coordinated and can clap to the beat.[26]

Studies suggest a connection between a child's difficulty keeping a beat and his difficulty learning to read.[27] Keeping a beat, however, also depends on physical maturation and coordination, so if your child can't keep a beat, it doesn't automatically mean he'll have trouble reading.[28]

If your child can't hear a steady beat, help him by tapping lightly on his shoulder to the beat while he claps. Or teach him to tap different parts of his body to the beat. Make up phrases, such as, "I like chocolate ice cream," and tap sticks to the beat. You can also tap out a rhythm and see if your child can name the song that uses it. Lora Heller, a music therapist, suggests teaching your child to do a "finger dance" (tap his index fingers together to a beat). Some music teachers use rhythm sticks to help children learn a steady beat. The teacher holds one end of the stick, and the student holds the other end. Then they take turns pulling the stick back and forth to the beat.[29]

Research suggests a connection between how well children can discriminate pitch and how well they can read.[30] When learning to read, children must be able to hear the differences among phonemes so they can sound out the words. Musical activities, especially those involving pitch discrimination, facilitate reading by training the ear to hear the differences among sounds.[31]

Parents can promote reading readiness as soon as their children can hear the difference between low-pitched notes and high-pitched notes. (This ability typically emerges in the toddler stage.) Play two notes on an instrument or sing two notes and ask your child whether the notes are the same or different. Then talk about which ones are high and low. Use different-pitched voices when reading stories together. Have your child imitate the characters by moving his voice up and down. To visually reinforce the concept of pitch, pretend you're doing "the wave" at a football game, standing when the pitch is high and sitting when the pitch is low.

Matching pitch is a skill that develops after a child can distinguish between two sounds. This skill develops at different rates in different children, and it requires the ability to hear and remember a note as well as to reproduce it.[32] Lynn Kleiner, music teacher and creator of the Babies Make Music series, plays a game in which she stops singing a song to give the children an opportunity to repeat a word with a simple melody consisting of two or three notes. The children try to sing the notes the same way she did. (Kleiner: "hel-LO-oh"..., Children: "hel-LO-oh").[33] This game also improves children's listening skills.

You can use many songs to enhance pre-literacy by substituting sounds in the songs with other sounds. For example, you can use "Willoughby, Wallaby, Woo" (Dennis Lee's poem that's sung by Raffi) to teach phonological awareness by incorporating your child's name: "Willoughby, Wallaby, Willip. An elephant sat on Phillip." The "Name Game" song is also great for manipulating sounds: "Robin, Robin, Bo Bobin, Banana Fana Fo Fobin, Fe Fi Fo Mobin, Robin!"

You can use any song with nonsense lyrics to play a game called Change-That-Sound. For example, "I've Been Working on the Railroad" includes the nonsense words:

Fe-fi-fiddly-i-o
Fe-fi-fiddly-i-o-o-o-o
Fe-fi-fiddly-i-o...

Now replace the *f* sound with the *s* sound.

Se-si-siddly-i-o
Se-si-siddly-i-o-o-o-o
Se-si-siddly-i-o...

Now try it with the *d* sound.[34]

Young children quickly realize that music communicates feelings and generates ideas. Help your child express his feelings and ideas by incorporating other activities while doing musical activities. For example, have him draw pictures that illustrate the story of the song. Encourage him to use hand gestures, finger plays, or sign language to demonstrate the directions or actions in the songs. Or have him draw what he hears. Children older than age three pick up on the music's patterns and can make representational drawings. Your child might draw shapes or different-size lines or squiggles to differentiate between loud and soft notes, short and long notes, and fast and slow tempos. He might draw a solo differently than a chorus. Changing the type of music added a lot of variety to my sons' representational drawings.

The Importance of Imaginary Play

When your child is age three or four, his imaginary play helps him develop both mentally and physically. When a child plays make-believe, he practices the kind of conceptual thinking he'll do while reading and solving math problems. When your child plays make-believe with other children, they must cooperate and agree on what the props symbolize and what the characters should say and do. Participating in imaginary play can help your child develop his symbolic language skills (see page 17), add to his vocabulary, develop his interpersonal skills, and broaden his view of the world. Plus, the imaginary adventures you have with your child can make the best memories!

Imaginary play doesn't require expensive dress-up clothes and props. A child's creativity grows by using everyday items to invent adventures. My oldest son loves to blast off to "outer space." He pretends to launch off the couch or the beanbag chair. While traveling in space, we visit the pizza planet and order our own choices of toppings. We take turns making up the next adventure and never use the same prop twice. Imaginary play doesn't have to be extraordinary; you and your child can reenact everyday events, like feeding and caring for a baby or talking on the phone. When you initiate a simple, everyday action, your child can think of new, creative ideas.

Puppets make wonderful props for imaginary play. You can also use them to retell a favorite story or make up a new one. You don't need to buy expensive puppets; you can turn socks and paper bags into simple puppets that your child can decorate. If your child has lots of plush animals, you can turn some of them into puppets by cutting a seam in the back or bottom of the animal and removing some of the stuffing. Finger puppets can make car trips fun for your child, and taking in a puppet show is always an enriching experience.

Encourage your child to play dress-up with whatever old or used items you can find. Save old pairs of boots, scarves, hats, and Halloween costumes. Let your child dress up to act out his favorite fairy tale or song. After I bought two firefighter hats from a dollar store for my sons, my house has been saved from multiple arson attempts.

Many preschoolers include make-believe friends in their imaginary play. Children with make-believe friends engage in a sophisticated level of imaginary play (because they converse with their make-believe friends) and show that they can separate reality from fantasy. They also tend to interact and form relationships well with real people because they're aware of another "person's" point of view. Research shows that having an imaginary friend can foster your child's language skills because he's talking to the friend.

For a while my son's imaginary friends seemed to be multiplying in his room at night. Each morning he'd wake up with two or three new ones. Norman was his steadfast pal who always had every new toy a boy could wish for. Alice, Norman's baby sister, was sick for months at a time and needed my son's care and attention. There was also Too Tall and Stanley, who were great at sports and really strong. On a tour of a fire station, a firefighter showed my son the Jaws of Life and said that they were very heavy, to which my son replied, "My imaginary friend Stanley is very strong, and he has his own set of those!"

Researchers suggest that parents strike a balance between accommodating the imaginary friend and letting him become overly intrusive (for example, allowing your child to use his imaginary friend as an excuse for poor behavior).[35] My son has used imaginary friends as an excuse, but I use the excuse to my advantage. For example, while taking his time to get into the car my son might say, "Jessica doesn't want to go to the doctor." I reply, "What do you mean? Jessica's already in the car and buckled in her seat. You'd better buckle in next to her—quickly." Although he tends to argue about some things, he's never argued about what I've seen his "friends" doing. He thinks it's fun that I play along.

Parents shouldn't worry about a child's preference for imaginary friends. Eventually, he outgrows the need for them. Now that my son plays with children at school every day, his need for imaginary friends is waning. Although an imaginary friend may still sleep over or ride to school with us, the friend isn't present when my son plays with a real child. He seems to separate fantasy from reality just fine.

Dramatic Play

If your community offers drama programs for children, consider enrolling your child in one. Genevieve Aichele, an artistic director who helps teachers and parents use creative drama, says, "Drama is not something you sit down and do; it's simply having a sense of play." Participating in drama programs helps children learn creativity as they use their imaginations to act out stories. The Wolf Trap Institute, for example, emphasizes the importance of using music, drama, and dance to help preschoolers learn concentration skills, social skills, memory skills, large and small motor skills, and language basics. The institute connects performing artists with children and their families for programs often sponsored by a community library or performing arts center.

My sons participated in a Wolf Trap program developed by an artist and sponsored by our local library. The artist combined pre-literacy skills with music and dance to help the children learn the names of letters, letter sounds, and new words. They also formed the letters and other shapes with their bodies. The children learned self-confidence as they acted out familiar stories for one another. This fun program showed that using music, dance, and drama can help children reach many developmental goals naturally.

One Last Word on Musical Activities and Imaginary Play

Giving your child opportunities to participate in musical activities and imaginary play can be fun and worthwhile. When you expose your child to different musical styles and instruments, it helps him become well rounded and gives him a healthy appreciation for different cultures. Engaging in imaginary play further adds to his symbolic language skills, vocabulary development, and interpersonal skills. Music and imaginary play can fit into any family's busy life, even if it's just while riding in the car with your child as you run errands. Memories are tied closely to songs, and words can't describe how sweet it is to hear your child sing his first song!

Afterword

Watching a child develop language skills brings joy to any parent. This book has provided you with comprehensive information about speech and language development. You now know how babies communicate before speaking words, and you've learned how children simplify speech while learning to articulate words. You also know the typical progression of speech and language development—and you may have been surprised by the wide range of normal development.

Be the best language model you can and don't overanticipate your child's needs. Give your child opportunities to communicate however he can, whether by sign language, spoken language, augmentative communication (using a computer or some other device to communicate), musical methods, or combinations of these. Your child will learn to communicate if you take advantage of natural opportunities that encourage language skills every day.

There are many reasons for speech and language delays, and you now know when and how to seek professional help. Take advantage of community programs that help your child develop better language skills. Be proactive with your child's health care and choose childcare that best benefits his language development. Select activities and media that provide a rich language environment for your child. Remember that you can refer to the charts and lists of norms to monitor your child's development.

Helping your child develop pre-literacy and literacy skills is an exciting experience. The suggestions I've given will help you facilitate his reading skills and check his progress at each stage of development. The information will also help you talk with a teacher confidently if your child has trouble reading.

You now know that gestural communication can enhance speech and language development. You can introduce sign language to your baby so you can communicate preverbally. You can also use it to support multiple language learning and literacy, and to help the transition period from a birth language to an adopted language.

Successfully raising children bilingually can be challenging. If you decide to go this route, design a language plan that systematically uses the bilingual opportunities available at home and in your community. Remember to stay flexible; you might need to modify your language plan to meet your child's needs, especially if your child is learning more than two languages or is internationally adopted. Understanding your child's language needs will help further his overall development.

No matter what your family's needs are, take the time to have fun with your child. Make musical activities and imaginary play part of your busy day. Childhood is fleeting, and I hope that the strategies for promoting language development I've suggested will encourage you to interact with your child in fun, natural ways so you can enrich your lives to the fullest.

Appendix A

Little Language Song Lyrics

My husband and I developed *Little Language Songs for Little Ones* to help you stimulate speech and language skills while you sing the songs or read the lyrics with your child. (For sample melodies and pictures to go with the songs, visit www.littlelanguage.com.) Help your child learn the vocabulary words and concepts by talking about the song lyrics before or after you sing the songs. Several of the songs concentrate on specific sounds. You can use them to help your child hear the difference between correct and incorrect sound production.

Many of the songs feature minimal pairs (rhyming words like *mice/ice*, *fish/wish*, or *air/hair*). Therapists use minimal pairs to teach the difference between two words that differ by only one phonemic character. Teachers use songs with rhyming words to reinforce pre-literacy skills. Using songs or stories with rhyming words helps children predict the words that end stanzas or sentences. The children retell the stories or sequence of events after playing the songs to work on short-term memory and sequencing skills.

Do You Hear the Way Sounds Ring?

This phonetic alphabet song focuses on the sound of each alphabet letter, not just its name. It helps your child's pre-literacy skills because it lets her practice the sound connected to each alphabet letter and provides a vocabulary word that matches each letter sound. You can easily make this song into a game. Have your child point to or name an object, then sing the name of the object and the sound that starts the name (for example, your child points to a table, and you sing, "Table, table, *t t t*.").

> Do you know your ABCs?
> Can you sing along with me?
> Once you know these letter sounds,
> You can learn by leaps and bounds.

Apple, apple, *a a a*
Baseball, baseball, *b b b*
Cowboy, cowboy, *c c c*
Doggie, doggie, *d d d*
Elephant, *e e e*
Fire, fire, *f f f*
Garden, garden, *g g g*
House, house, *h h h*
Inchworm, inchworm, *i i i*
Jack-o'-lantern, *j j j*
Kangaroo, *k k k*
Lion, lion, *l l l*
Mommy, mommy, *m m m*
Noodle, noodle, *n n n*
Otter, otter, *o o o*
Piglet, piglet, *p p p*
Quiet, quiet, *q q q*
Rabbit, rabbit, *r r r*
Scissors, scissors, *s s s*
Table, table, *t t t*
Under, under, *u u u*
Violet, violet, *v v v*
Wiggle, wiggle, *w w w*
Exit, exit, *x x x*
Yellow, yellow, *y y y*
Zebra, zebra, *z z z*
Do you hear the way sounds ring?
It just makes you want to sing.

Limericks

This fun song emphasizes specific sounds. It particularly focuses on the following sounds: *h*, *w*, *t*, and *l*. *H* and *w* are sounds children typically acquire by age three, and *t* and *l* are sounds they acquire later, sometimes as late as age four or five. The song also uses the regular past tense verb ending *-ed* (typically learned around age 26 to 48 months).

There once was a boy named Tommy
who tickled a tiger's tummy.
The tiger tasted Tommy's toes
and wrinkled up his whiskers and nose.

There once was a lion named Larry
whose mane was very hairy.
He leaped over a limb, and a bee stung him.
Then Larry the lion limped home.

There once was a horse named Horace
who loved to run in the forest.

He happened along a frog in a pond,
who hopped on his head, and they fled.

There once was a whale named Wally
who was always happy and jolly.
He would whistle a tune by the light of the moon
while the walrus would waltz in the wind.

An Undersea Adventure

Children age three and up will enjoy acting out this song. It features more difficult commands and many opportunities for crossover actions. The lyrics contain advanced vocabulary and promote fun imaginary play with sound effects.

We're going on an adventure, an undersea adventure.
Underneath the deep blue sea, fun for you and me.

Let's put on our flippers, left foot, right.
[reach right hand across to left foot, then left hand to right foot]

Jump out of the boat, let's dive down deep.
[hands over head as if diving]

Now hold your breath, swim with the fish.
[arms swimming]

Reach to your left, get your flashlight.
[right hand to left side of waist]

Reach to your right, get your camera.
[left hand to right side of waist]

Shine your flashlight in a dark cave.
[arm sweep in front]

What do you see? A treasure chest!
Take a picture of the treasure chest.
[pretend to take a picture]

Tap on the left, tap on the right.
[cross right arm over to left side of body and switch]

Open the box, what's inside?
[pretend to open lid]

Oh, wow! It's gold coins, filled to the brim!
Let's grab some, let's go!
[pretend to grab an armful of coins]

We'll swim with the fish, we'll have fun.
[arms swimming]

We'll swim for the top, we'll see the sun.
[arms reaching up]

Appendix A

Let's climb the ladder into the boat.
[climbing]

Back to the beach, we'll motor the boat.
[pretend to steer]

Jump to the beach and crawl like a crab.
[jump then walk sideways on all fours]

Then jump up, dust off your feet.
[cross right hand to dust left foot and switch]

Oh, we went on an adventure, an undersea adventure.
Underneath the deep blue sea, fun for you and me.

What a Colorful World!

Children typically learn primary colors by age three. This song covers color concepts, and it includes lots of nature vocabulary and the consonant cluster sounds *sk*, *tr*, *str*, *gl*, *gr*, *br*, *bl*, and *dr*. (Children typically produce these sounds correctly sometime between ages three and nine.) The song also uses copulas, which are verbs that identify the predicate of a sentence with the subject (for example, *is*). Children usually learn this concept at age 27 to 39 months.

Yellow is the sun that's bright to your eyes,
and blue is the color of the sky.
Green is the color of grass and leaves,
while red is the apple in the trees.

Orange is a pumpkin we see in the fall,
while purple is a grape that's round like a ball.
Brown is the deer who drinks from the stream,
and white is the snow that in winter gleams.

Pink is a pig in the mud having fun.
Black is the night when the day is done.
Learning your colors is lots of fun,
and now we will sing them one by one.

Red, orange, yellow, green,
blue, purple, pink, and brown.
Black and white, you know it sounds right
'cause everything has color that's bright.

Do You Know What It Means to Be a Shape?

This song talks about circle, square, triangle, and star shapes. The lyrics use spatial relationship vocabulary like *under*, *far*, and *everywhere*. They also use a contraction form of the being verb *is* (for example, *that's*, *tangle's*, and *car's*), a concept children typically learn around age 29 to 49 months.

Do you know what it means to be a shape?
A circle or a star that's so far?
Triangles and squares are right under our chairs.
If we look, we will find them everywhere.

Do you know what it means to be square?
Your hair isn't square, a dog isn't square.
But a box full of air, that's what's square.

Do you know what it means to be round?
A clown isn't round, a town isn't round.
But a circle or a ball, that's what's round.

Do you know what it means to be a triangle?
A rope in a tangle's not a triangle,
but the sail of a boat's a triangle.

Do you know what it means to be a star?
A truck or a car's not a star,
but a twinkle in the sky, that's a star.

Do you know what it means to be a shape?
A circle or a star that's so far?
Triangles and squares are right under our chairs.
If we look, we will find them everywhere.

Imagination

This song contains many English vowels and diphthongs, and it stimulates creativity as the child takes an exciting trip to several imaginative destinations. It includes vocabulary about outer space: *shooting stars*, *moon*, and *rocket ship*. It also uses the rhyming pairs *air/hair*, *ship/trip*, *crown/down*, and *hill/chill*.

One of my favorite things
Is to go to the park and swing.
I imagine myself up in the sky,
Like a bird in the air and the wind through my hair.

Then I'm suddenly a king with a crown,
High in a tower looking down.
In the distance, I see a big pirate ship
Hoisting up sails. Oh look, one just ripped.

I can ride a sled down a long, steep hill,
Fly by icy waters that give me a chill.
I've been to faraway places, seen wonderful things,
But I've never left the swings.

A magic carpet arrives, and I climb on for a ride.
I view dinosaurs and sandy shores
As I'm flying along
In the great outdoors.

Then I'm whizzing through space on a fast rocket ship.
Everything spins on an outer space trip.
I see shooting stars, and I land on the moon.
I feel like I'm floating in a balloon.

Then I slowly glide back down again.
My feet are on the ground, and I grin.
I've been to faraway places, seen wonderful things,
but I've never left the swings.

Garden Dance (The R Song)

Because it's hard to tell a child where to place her tongue to make an *r* sound, this sound tends to be a difficult one for many children to master (some children don't master it until age eight). This song provides many *r* sounds in the initial, medial, and final positions. If your child can say *er* and *r* in the final position but has trouble saying it in the initial position, this song's special word order may help. If a child can say *r* at the end of the word, then the tongue is in the correct position to say the initial *r*. So when saying pairs of words like *farmer Ray, riper radishes,* and *later raindrops,* a child can more easily say the *r* in the initial position of the second word. Before or after singing this song, talk about farmer Ray and his riper radishes. If you like, extend the story to include new characters, such as Ray's neighbors, farmer Roy and farmer Randall.

If your child can't produce the *r* sound at the end of the word, try to help her say the suffix *ler* (if she can say *l* correctly, of course). If she can say *ler,* then put this sound together with *r* initial words. This can be a fun way to learn the sound while you sing the song together (*ler-rain, ler-rob, ler-rug, ler-roy,* and *ler-ring*). This technique is advanced, so if your child seems to become frustrated, discontinue it. Or show your child how to lift the back of her tongue until it almost touches the roof of her mouth; this is the position for producing the *r* sound. If your child needs more help, seek a speech-language pathologist for treatment.

Farmer Ray liked growing stuff. In his garden was just enough.
Red, ripe raspberries on the vine, plump and juicy, looking fine.
Riper radishes down below; to dig them up, you use a hoe.
Rusty Rabbit took a bite of the farmer's fresh delight.

Chorus
Run, rabbit, run. You're having so much fun.
Twirling 'round and 'round the carrots you have found.

You pluck a cabbage from the row, and to the peas and beans you go.
Be careful not to hang around, or else your mischief will be found.

Repeat chorus

Later raindrops sprinkled down to feed the earth and wet the ground.
The big raccoon comes waddling over; he's spent his morning in the clover.
He sees the greener, fresher plants; with his woodland friends he'll do a dance.
The freshest ones they nibble on, with his friends, the deer and fawn.

Repeat chorus

The robin circles overhead; old grapevines make up her bed.
She sees some green leaves on the ground. Oh, what a treasure she has found!
See the animals scurry about; they feed their families with beans and sprouts.
The farmer isn't happy, though. He needs food, too, don't you know?

Repeat chorus

Can You Count to Ten?

This song helps with number concepts. Most children typically can count to five by age four and count to thirteen by age five. This song contains lots of repetition for easy learning, plus fun animal comparisons and vocabulary.

Can you count to ten?
Start off slow and then
Soon you'll be at the end.
Numbers will become your friends.
It's easy to count to ten.

One, two, three, and four
Five, six, seven, eight
Nine, ten, begin again.
See? It's easy to count to ten.
Can you do it again?

One, two, a cat says mew.
Three, four, a lion roars.
Five, six, a kangaroo kicks.
Seven, eight, aren't puppies great?
Nine, ten, bears live in a den.

One, two, three, and four
Five, six, seven, eight
Nine, ten, begin again.
See? It's easy to count to ten.
There you've done it, my friend.

Busy Days

This song includes the names of the days of the week. Children usually develop time concepts at age five to six. There are also a number of minimal pairs in the song: *mice/ice, frogs/logs, fish/wish, sheep/steep, otters/waters,* and *doves/gloves*. Sing this song with your child, then talk about the words that rhyme. See if your child can hear the differences. Use pictures of the objects to help talk about their different meanings.

> Did you know, did you know
> in this world below,
> things are very busy
> everywhere you go?
>
> Monday is for mice
> to go skating on the ice.
>
> Tuesday is for fish
> to play and make a wish.
>
> Wednesday is for otters
> to frolic in the waters, and
>
> Thursday is for reindeer
> to run from here to there.
>
> Friday is for frogs
> to hop and jump on logs.
>
> Saturday is for sheep
> to climb a hill so steep.
>
> Sunday is for doves
> to wear their white new gloves.
>
> See, animals play, too, and are busy
> just like you.

Changing Seasons

This song features more advanced time concepts, like the concept of a life cycle. At age four to five, your child most likely develops an understanding of *today* and *tomorrow* and may begin to understand the seasons as well. This song provides compound words, like *fireplace, countryside, bleary-eyed,* and *watermelon.*

> The year begins in winter cold,
> With fireplaces and stories of old.
> Children make snowmen with their friends.
> And drink hot chocolate when the day ends.
>
> In spring there are flowers, and everything's new.
> The sun is warm, and the sky is blue.

Baby animals are born and bleary-eyed,
And fields are green on the countryside.

Summertime is hot, and we swim at the pool.
Our friends come over, and we try to stay cool.
We eat watermelon and we drink lemonade.
The sun is bright, and we sit in the shade.

The fall brings rich colors to the land.
The trees are red, orange, gold, and grand.
The air cools down, we take a ride in the hay,
And before too long, another year flies away.

The Spider Shines Her Shoes

A central lisp is a mild speech problem that's common among children. When saying words that contain the sounds *s* or *z*, a child with a lisp instead produces a *th* sound. This song may help discrimination (hearing the difference between correct and incorrect sounds), the first step of treatment for a lisp. Before singing this song, help your child hear the difference between the correct and incorrect sounds. For example, you can say, "The sink sparkles in the *sun*, not the *thun*." Some children don't master the *s* and *z* sounds until age seven to nine. (Some children can say these sounds correctly at age four.)

Sing this song together, then talk about the story. Make up new silly stories about the spider. You might draw out the *s* sound so you sound like a snake (*hiss*). Tell your child to try to "keep the snake in the cage" (keep his tongue behind his teeth).

Another type of lisp, a lateral lisp, allows too much air around the sides of the tongue, and makes the child produce very slushy *s*, *ch*, and *sh* sounds. Talk with your child about how the sound needs to be "crisp," not "slushy" (*fuss*, not *fush*).

If your child continues to have difficulty hearing the difference between the correct and incorrect sounds or shows any frustration, seek professional help.

In a shack by the seashore,
Shelby the spider lived on a shelf.
There was a sink in the kitchen.
It shimmered and sparkled in the sun.

There was some soap and some water,
and Shelby was going to wash her shoes—all eight!
She shimmied down and shuffled over,
She lathered up and gave her shoes a scrub.

She used a brush, she used a washcloth,
She scrubbed and scrubbed and cleaned those shoes right up.

She dried them off, she shined them up.
She polished them until they shone like glass.

She laid them down, she put them on,
and she tied and tied and tied the many laces.
She climbed back out and sauntered over,
and prepared to climb back to her home, the shelf.

She saw a drop of apple cider. (She was thirsty!)
She simply had to go and take a sip.
She drank it down, she thought a moment.
She felt that she was ready for a nap.

There was a chair and a Chihuahua.
He barked as she ran up the china shelf.
She looked around and she was sleepy,
so she took a nap inside the sugar bowl.

All Aboard

Children normally go through a phonological process called velar fronting, in which they substitute the sounds *t* and *d* for *k* and *g* (for example, *doe* → *go*). This process should start disappearing somewhere around age three and a half. This song was created with this process in mind, and it features several minimal pairs that contain sounds typically made in the front of the mouth: *date/gate, coat/goat, time/dime, gap/cap, girls/curls*. Talk about the different meanings of each pair. Find pictures of the objects; for example, find a picture of curly-haired girls and talk about the girls and their curls.

> I made some fun plans to go on a train ride
> From one end of the country to the other side.
> I picked up my ticket; I looked at the date.
> I packed up my suitcase and went to the gate.
>
> *Chorus*
> Puff puff, chug chug, see the little train run
> Rolling down the train tracks, looks like lots of fun.
>
> I saw the colors of the passenger cars.
> They had many windows, like a night full of stars.
> I walked toward my favorite, the one that was red.
> It looked warm and comfy just like my own bed.
>
> *Repeat chorus*
>
> Inside it was warm, so I put on my coat.
> I looked out the window, and there was a goat.
> I glanced at my watch so I'd know the time.
> I looked on the floor, and there was a dime.
>
> *Repeat chorus*

We went up a mountain and went through a gap.
I saw the conductor was wearing his cap.
I sat by a lady who had two small girls.
They both had blue outfits and heads full of curls.

Repeat chorus

We went up and down hills, we crossed the Great Plains.
We even saw boats and a big airplane.
I saw the train station around the next bend
And knew that our journey had come to an end.

Repeat chorus

Celebrate the Holidays

This song lists all the months and includes holiday vocabulary. Children typically learn the names of the months around age five or six, and the concept of a monthly calendar is one that children need to comprehend for school readiness.

January starts a brand new year.
February brings our hearts so near.
In March, green leprechauns dance around.
April, the Easter Bunny comes to town.
May brings flowers to our mothers.
June brings summer to our fathers.
July celebrates our country's birth.
August is hot and dry on the earth.
September brings labor across the land.
October brings pumpkins carved by your hand.
November gives thanks for gifts from above.
In December there is cheer and children filled with love.

Good Manners Are the Key

This song provides respectful vocabulary: *please, thank you, you're welcome, yes sir, no sir, excuse me*. It also advocates the golden rule: *Treat others as you want to be treated*.

When you ask your mom for a cookie,
do you remember to say *please*?
Mothers like us to be polite.
It makes their day so bright.

Saying *thank you* and *you're welcome*
are ways to be polite.
Yes sir, no sir shows respect
and has a great effect.

Use *excuse me* when you need to,
and don't be a tattletale.
Share your toys and take good turns,
and remember not to yell.

Appendix A

Good manners is the key
to having lots of friends.
Treat others the way you would want to be treated,
and you might not disagree.

What Do We Eat?

This song includes meal vocabulary: *breakfast, lunch,* and *dinner.* It also contains food vocabulary, like *chocolate cake, eggs, toast, jam, ice cream, root beer, sandwich, soup du jour, cotton candy, rice,* and *grilled trout.*

> What shall you have for your breakfast, dear?
> "How 'bout chocolate cake right here?"
> That's not breakfast food, no ma'am.
> Have some eggs with toast and jam.
>
> What shall you have for your lunch, dear?
> "How 'bout ice cream and root beer?"
> That's not lunch food, no sir.
> Have a sandwich and soup du jour.
>
> What shall you have for your dinner, dear?
> "How 'bout cotton candy from the fair?"
> That's not dinner, without a doubt.
> Have some rice and some grilled trout.
>
> "But I want something good and sweet."
> You only get that as a treat.
> Remember you are what you eat,
> So eat healthy foods and be complete.

A Trip to the Fair

This song tells a story about a child's imaginary visit to the fair. The lyrics use some homonyms (*fare/fair* and *bear/bare*) and contain many irregular past tense verbs (*paid, saw, stood*), which usually emerge in a child's vocabulary between ages 25 and 46 months, and several regular past tense verb forms (*-ed*), which emerge between ages 26 and 48 months.

> Since it is fall and time for the fair,
> We asked Mom and Dad to take us there.
> We waited for the bus and paid the fare.
> We hopped on and rode without a care.
>
> Vroom, vroom bumpety bop bop fair,
> We hopped on and rode without a care.
>
> We jumped off the bus and walked to the gate.
> We paid for our tickets—the smells were great.
> Popcorn, hot dogs, sweet funnel cakes,
> And fresh, salty pretzels just starting to bake.

Pop, pop bumpety bop bop cake
And fresh, salty pretzels just starting to bake.

All of a sudden we saw a crowd.
With laughs and cheers, they sounded quite loud.
We ran to the tent, and what did we see?
A big brown bear was down on his knees!

Drop, drop bumpety bop bop see,
A big brown bear was down on his knees!

That big brown bear way down on his knees
Had a head that was bare, if you please.
He stood up in that tent so tall,
And we all stared, afraid he would fall.

Up, up bumpety bop bop tall
And we all stared, afraid he would fall.

Then he jumped and flipped up in the air.
He seemed to have taken quite a dare.
He caused that tent to tear into shreds,
And we looked on as we shook our heads.

Rip, rip bumpety bop bop shreds
And we looked on as we shook our heads.

He came back down, with never a doubt.
We all cheered for him and gave a shout.
The next time you go to the county fair,
You never know what you will see there.

Vroom, vroom bumpety bop bop fair,
You never know what you will see there, yeah.

Everybody on Your Feet

This is an interactive motion song. Its tempo is purposely slow so you can encourage a younger child to follow a one-step command. A typical 15- to 18-month-old child can follow a one-step direction and point to body parts. This song includes some body part vocabulary as well as verbs that describe motions (*clap, stomp, reach, turn around, touch, wave*).

Everybody on your feet.
Now clap your hands, 1, 2, 3.
Stomp your feet. Hey! That's neat!
Reach up high, touch the sky.
Reach down low, touch your toes.
Hands out straight, you're doing great.
Turn around, hear that sound.
Touch your nose, beep, beep, beep!
Wave good-bye. Now let's repeat.

Repeat the song twice: first time slowly; second time quickly
Last time
Wave good-bye, and take a bow!

Everybody Feels This Way

Between ages four and five, children learn to express their emotions. This song features vocabulary for emotion words, like *happy, glad, sad, mad, excited,* and *lonely*. It also uses the minimal pairs *glad/sad, mad/bad, way/day*.

> Some days I am happy and glad.
> Things go my way, so I'm not sad.
> But then there are days when nothing goes my way,
> And I can get real mad.
> Getting mad's not always bad.
> I just talk it out with Dad.
>
> There are times when I'm excited,
> When parties and games are so delighting.
> But then there are times when your friends leave,
> And you could get sort of lonely.
> Being by yourself's not always sad.
> You have time to think and be glad.
>
> Sometimes life is filled with surprises,
> Like to visit the zoo and eat ice cream.
> But other times we can get upset
> And not be very content.
> Things don't always go our way.
> There'll be joy in another day.
>
> *Chorus (sung after each verse)*
> Everybody feels this way.
> It's all right, it's okay.
> Talk about it; that's the way
> To deal with feelings every day.

Pets

The lyrics of this song contain sounds children typically acquire first: *p* (*pat, puppy, perks*), *b* (*bunny, button, ball*), and *h* (*happy, hops, he*). It also includes body part vocabulary: *eyes, nose, toes, ears, legs,* and *tail*. This is a good song for clapping to the beat.

> When I pat my puppy,
> It makes him very happy.
> He wrinkles up his button nose,
> And then he licks my little toes.

His eyes sparkle like the sand
When I pat him with my hand.
He perks up his ears when I call him near.

Chorus
Oh, how happy is my day
When with animals I play.
They need lots of love and care,
Food and water and fresh air.

Oh, how I love my bunny.
His ears look kind of funny.
He hops along on two hind legs.
Unlike a dog, he never begs.
He's soft and furry, warm and fun,
And I can catch him if I run.
His furry tail is like a cotton ball.

Repeat chorus

Things I Love

This is a relaxing, silly song about the end of the day and some simple pleasures. The lyrics contain the minimal pairs *hand/sand*, *nitty/gritty*, *feet/street*, *belly/jelly*, and *head/bed*.

Oh, I love to put my hand in the sand.
Oh, I love to put my hand in the sand.
Oh, I love to put my hand in the nitty gritty sand.
Oh, I love to put my hand in the sand.

Oh, I love to walk my feet down the street.
Oh, I love to walk my feet down the street.
Oh, I love to walk my feet down the straight and narrow street.
Oh, I love to walk my feet down the street.

Oh, I love to fill my belly with jelly.
Oh, I love to fill my belly with jelly.
Oh, I love to fill my belly with lots of purple jelly.
Oh, I love to fill my belly with jelly.

Oh, I love to put my head in the bed.
Oh, I love to put my head in the bed.
Oh, I love to put my head on the blanket that is red.
Oh, I love to put my head in the bed.

Appendix B

Organizations and Associations for Additional Information

Alexander Graham Bell Association for the Deaf and Hard of Hearing (AG Bell)
3417 Volta Place NW
Washington, DC 20007
202-337-5220
www.agbell.org

American Council on the Teaching of Foreign Languages
6 Executive Plaza
Yonkers, NY 10701
914-963-8830
www.actfl.org

American Speech-Language-Hearing Association (ASHA)
10801 Rockville Pike
Rockville, MD 20852
800-638-8255 (public)
800-498-2071 (professionals/students)
www.asha.org

Council for Exceptional Children (CEC) and the Division for Learning Disabilities (DLD)
1110 North Glebe Road, Suite 300
Arlington, VA 22201
888-CEC-SPED
www.cec.sped.org

Educational Resources Information Center (ERIC) Clearinghouse on Disabilities and Gifted Education
1110 North Glebe Road
Arlington, VA 22201-5704
800-328-0272
www.ericec.org

The Evan B. Donaldson Adoption Institute
120 Wall Street, 20th Floor
New York, NY 10005
212-269-5080
www.adoptioninstitute.org

Inter-National Adoption Alliance
Box 154, 2441-Q Old Fort Parkway
Murfreesboro, TN 37128
615-631-5660
www.i-a-a.org

The International Dyslexia Association
Chester Building, Suite 382
8600 LaSalle Road
Baltimore, MD 21286-2044
410-296-0232
800-ABCD-123 (voice message requests for information)
www.interdys.org

Joint Council on International Children's Services
1403 King Street, Suite 101
Alexandria, VA 22314
703-535-8045
www.jcics.org

Learning Disabilities Association of America (LDA)
4156 Library Road
Pittsburgh, PA 15234-1349
412-341-1515
www.ldanatl.org

National Adoption Center
1500 Walnut Street, Suite 701
Philadelphia, PA 19102
800-TO-ADOPT
www.adopt.org

The National Adoption Information Clearinghouse
330 C Street SW
Washington, DC 20447
888-251-0075
www.calib.com/naic

National Association for Family Child Care (NAFCC)
5202 Pinemont Drive
Salt Lake City, UT 84123
801–269–9338
www.nafcc.org

National Association for the Education of Young Children (NAEYC)
1509 16th Street NW
Washington, DC 20036
800–424–2460
www.naeyc.org

National Association of the Deaf (NAD)
814 Thayer Avenue
Silver Spring, MD 20910-4500
301–587–1788
www.nad.org

National Information Center for Children and Youth with Disabilities (NICHCY)
P.O. Box 1492
Washington, DC 20013
800–695–0285
www.nichcy.org

National Institute on Deafness and Other Communication Disorders (NIDCD)
National Institutes of Health
31 Center Drive, MSC 2320
Bethesda, MD 20892–2320
800–241–1044
www.nidcd.nih.gov

National Resource Center for Special Needs Adoption
16250 Northland Drive, Suite 120
Southfield, MI 48075
248–443–7080
www.spaulding.org/adoption/NRC-adoption.html

Stuttering Foundation of America
3100 Walnut Grove Road, Suite 603
Memphis, TN 38111–0749
800–992–9392
www.stuttersfa.org

Appendix C

Recommended Materials, Books, and On-line Resources

Music

Dyer, Laura. *Little Language Songs for Little Ones.* Twenty original educational songs, each specifically designed with a speech and/or language goal in mind. (See Appendix A for lyrics.) Also introduces your child to various musical styles. Visit the website to read national reviews, hear song samples, and view short video clips of songs. On-line ordering is available for CDs, cassettes, and animal castanet musical toys.

Language for Little Ones
P.O. Box 161
LaVergne, TN 37086
877-755-5402
www.littlelanguage.com

Kleiner, Lynn. *Babies Make Music!, Kids Make Music!, Kids Make Music Too!* videocassette series. Music Rhapsody.

Sumner, Rachel. *Join the Parade* CD or cassette. Rachel's Records.

Parenting

Rosemond, John. *John Rosemond's Six-Point Plan for Raising Happy, Healthy Children.* Andrews McMeel Publishing.

———. *Making the "Terrible" Twos Terrific!* Andrews McMeel Publishing.

Warner, Penny. *Baby Play and Learn.* Meadowbrook Press.

Warner, Penny. *Smart Start for Your Baby.* Meadowbrook Press.

Literacy

Adams, Marilyn Jager. *Beginning to Read: Thinking and Learning about Print.* MIT Press.

Hall, Susan L. and Louisa C. Moats. *Straight Talk About Reading: How Parents Can Make a Difference During the Early Years.* McGraw-Hill Trade.

Signing

Acredolo, Linda and Susan Goodwyn. *Baby Signs: The Complete Starter Kit.* Baby Signs, Inc.

Bahan, Ben and Joe Dannis. *Signs for Me: Basic Sign Vocabulary for Children, Parents & Teachers.* Dawn Sign Press.

Daniels, Marilyn. *Dancing with Words: Signing for Hearing Children's Literacy.* Bergin & Garvey.

Flodin, Mickey. *Signing for Kids.* Perigee.

Garcia, Joseph. *Sign with Your Baby: Complete Learning Kit.* Northlight Communications.

———. *Sign with Your Baby: How to Communicate with Infants Before They Can Speak.* Northlight Communications.

———. *Sign2Me* CD. Northlight Communications.

Holub, Joan. *My First Book of Sign Language.* Troll Association.

Sumner, Rachel. *Sign Language and Foreign Language Through Music.* Rachel's Records.

Tossing, Gaia. *Sing 'n Sign for Fun!* Heartsong Communications.

Multilingualism

Dunn, Opal. *Help Your Child with a Foreign Language.* Berlitz Publishing.

Harding-Esch, Edith and Philip Riley. *The Bilingual Family: A Handbook for Parents.* Cambridge University Press.

Adoption

Erichsen, Jean Nelson and Heino R. Erichsen. *How to Adopt Internationally: A Guide for Agency-Directed and Independent Adoptions.* Mesa House.

Steinberg, Gail and Beth Hall. *Inside Transracial Adoption.* Perspectives Press.

van Gulden, Holly and Lisa M. Bartels-Rabb. *Real Parents, Real Children: Parenting the Adopted Child.* Crossroad Publishing.

On-line Resources

Speech and Language
American Speech-Language-Hearing Association, www.asha.org
Caroline Bowen, Speech-Language Pathologist, www.slpsite.com
Ed Chapman's Speech and Developmental Delays, http://edchapman.tripod.com/ParentLinks.html
Hearing Resources, www.ibwebs.com/hearing.htm
Helping Hands School, www.helpinghands.org
Laura Dyer's Little Language, www.littlelanguage.com
Speech Delay.com, www.speechdelay.com
Speech Language Pathology Resources, www.herring.org/speech.html

Pre-literacy
Between the Lions, http://pbskids.org/lions
National Institute for Literacy (NIFL), www.nifl.gov
National Reading Panel (NRP), www.nationalreadingpanel.org
Rachel's Records/Emergent Literacy, www.rachelsumner.com
Reading Pathfinder, www.readingpath.org
ReadyWeb, http://readyweb.crc.uiuc.edu
Wolf Trap Foundation for the Performing Arts, www.wolftrap.org/institute

Signing
American Sign Language Browser, http://commtechlab.msu.edu/sites/aslweb/browser.htm
American Sign Language Sites, www.fcps.k12.va.us/DIS/OHSICS/forlang/amslan.htm
Baby Fingers, www.mybabyfingers.com
Joseph Garcia's Sign with Your Baby, www.sign2me.com
LittleSigners.com, www.littlesigners.com
Momagen's Speech & Language Stop, http://server2042.virtualave.net/momagen
Signing Babes, www.signingbabes.co.uk

Multilingual

Bilingual Education, http://esl.miningco.com/cs/bilingualed

Bilingual Parenting in a Foreign Language, www.byu.edu/~bilingua

Center for Applied Linguistics (CAL), www.cal.org

Center for Multilingual Multicultural Research, www.usc.cdu/dept/education/CMMR

Educational Clearinghouse: Bilingual and ESL Issues, http://www.ncela.gwu.edu/links/parenting.htm

Multilingual Site for Families, www.laukart.de/multisite/index.php

National Association for Bilingual Education (NABE), www.nabe.org

Adoption

The Adoption Web Ring, www.plumsite.com/adoptionring

Association for Research in International Adoption, www.adoption-research.org

Center for Cognitive-Developmental Assessment and Remediation, www.bgcenter.com/interAdoption.htm

International Adoption, www.internationaladoption.org

Inter-National Adoption Alliance (I-A-A), www.i-a-a.org

National Association of Ethical Adoption Professionals, www.naeap.com

Parent Network for the Post Institutionalized Child, www.pnpic.org

Practical Attachment, http://home.att.net/~PracticalAttachment/index.html

Transracial/Transcultural Adoption, http://adoption.about.com/cs/transracial/index.htm?once=true

U.S. Department of State/International Adoption, http://travel.state.gov/adopt.html

Notes

Introduction

1. A. Castrogiovanni, "National Strategic Research Plan for Language and Language Disorders, Balance and Balance Disorders, and Voice and Voice Disorders," *National Institute on Deafness and Other Communication Disorders*. NIH publication, No. 97-3217 (Bethesda, MD, 1995); National Institute on Deafness and Other Communication Disorders (N. D.), "Strategic Plan: Plain Language Version," http://www.nidcd.nih.gov/about/director/nsrp.htm. (accessed June 30, 2002).

Chapter 1

1. J. L. Elman and others, *Rethinking Innateness: A Connectionist Perspective on Development* (Cambridge, MA: MIT Press, 1996).
2. D. Paul-Brown, *Let's Talk: Inclusive Practices and Service Delivery Models for Preschool Children with Speech and Language Disorders* (Rockville, MD: ASHA, 1999), 53–54.
3. B. Hart and T. R. Risley, *Meaningful Differences in the Everyday Experience of Young American Children* (Baltimore: Brookes Publishing, 1995), 134.
4. E. H. Ginsberg, "Methodical and Social Concerns in the Study of Children's Language Learning Environments," *First Language* 12 (1992): 251–55.
5. L. Bloom, *The Transition from Infancy to Language* (New York: Cambridge University Press, 1993), 64.
6. R. Cooper and R. Aslin, "Preference for Child Directed Speech in the First Month after Birth," *Child Development* 61 (1990): 1584–95.
7. Ibid.
8. R. Cooper and R. Aslin, "Developmental Differences in Infant Attention to the Spectral Properties of Infant-Directed Speech," *Child Development* 65 (1994): 1663–77.
9. See note 6 above.
10. R. E. Owens, *Language Development: An Introduction*, 3rd ed. (Columbus, OH: Charles E. Merrill, 1995).
11. See note 6 above.
12. See note 6 above.
13. A. Fernand and others, "A Cross-Linguistic Study of Prosodic Modifications in Mothers' and Fathers' Speech to Pre-verbal Infants," *Journal of Child Language* 16 (1989): 477–501.
14. J. Morgan and K. Demuth, *Signal to Syntax: Bootstrapping from Speech to Grammar in Early Acquisition* (Mahwah, NJ: Lawrence Erlbaum, 1996).
15. L. J. Gogate, L. E. Bahrick, and J. D. Watson, "A Study of Multimodal Motherese: The Role of Temporal Synchrony between Verbal Labels and Gestures," *Child Development* 71 (2000): 878.
16. Ibid.
17. Ibid.
18. A. Fernald, "Human Maternal Vocalizations to Infants as Biologically Relevant Signals: An Evolutionary Perspective," in *The Adapted Mind: Evolutionary Psychology and the Generation of Culture*, ed. J. Barkow and others (Oxford. Oxford University Press, 1992), 391–428.

19. A. Wetherby, S. Warren, and J. Reichle, "Introduction to Transitions in Prelinguistic Communication," in *Transitions in Prelinguistic Communication*, ed. A. Wetherby, S. Warren, and J. Reichle (Baltimore: Brookes Publishing, 1998), 2.
20. P. J. Yoder and S. F. Warren, "Can Developmentally Delayed Children's Language Development Be Enhanced through Prelinguistic Intervention?" in *Enhancing Children's Communication: Research Foundations for Intervention*, ed. A. P. Kaiser and D. B. Gray (Baltimore: Brookes Publishing, 1993), 50.
21. E. Bates, *The Emergence of Symbols: Cognition and Communication in Infancy* (New York: Academic Press, 1979).
22. J. Bruner, "The Social Context of Language Acquisition," *Language and Communication* 1 (1981): 155–78.
23. A. Wetherby and G. P. Rodriguez, "Measurement of Communicative Intentions in Normally Developing Children During Structured and Unstructured Contexts," *Journal of Speech and Hearing Research* 35 (1992): 130–38.
24. A. Wetherby and B. Prizant, *Communication and Symbolic Behavior Scales-Normed Edition* (Baltimore: Brookes Publishing, 1993).
25. L. B. Adamson and S. E. Chance, "Coordinating Attention to People, Objects and Language," in *Transitions in Prelinguistic Communication* (see note 19), 3.
26. P. Yoder and S. Warren, "Maternal Responsivity Mediates the Relationship Between Prelinguistic Communication and Later Language," *Journal of Early Intervention* 22 (1999): 126–136.
27. A. Wetherby and others, "FIRST WORDS Project: Improving Early Identification of Young Children At-risk for Language and Reading Difficulties," Spotlight Forum handout presented at 2002 NAEYC Institute, 1. http://firstwords.fsu.edu (accessed March 22, 2003).
28. See note 21 above.
29. E. F. Masur, "Gestural Development, Dual-Directional Signaling, and the Transition to Words," in *From Gesture to Language in Hearing and Deaf Children*, ed. V. Volterra and C. J. Erting (New York: Springer-Verlag, 1990), 18–30.
30. J. M. Iverson and D. L. Thal, "Communicative Transitions: There's More to the Hand Than Meets the Eye," in *Transitions in Prelinguistic Communication* (see note 19), 68.
31. L. P. Acredolo and S. W. Goodwyn, "Sign Language in Babies: The Significance of Symbolic Gesturing for Understanding Language Development," in *Annals of Child Development*, ed. R. Vasta (London: Jessica Kingsley Publishers, Ltd., 1990), 1–42.
32. M. C. Caselli and V. Volterra, "From Communication to Language in Hearing and Deaf Children," in *From Gesture to Language in Hearing and Deaf Children* (see note 29), 263–77.
33. P. J. Yoder and S. F. Warren, "Can Developmentally Delayed Children's Language Development Be Enhanced through Prelinguistic Intervention?" in *Enhancing Children's Communication: Research Foundations for Intervention*, ed. A. P. Kaiser and D. B. Gray (Baltimore: Brookes Publishing, 1993), 45.
34. R. B. McCathren, S. F. Warren, and P. J. Yoder, "Prelinguistic Predictors of Later Language Development," in *Communication and Language Intervention Series*, vol. 6, *Advances in Assessment of Communication and Language*, ed. K.N. Cole and others (Baltimore: Brookes Publishing, 1996), 57–76.
35. A. Wetherby and others, "Validity and Reliability of the Communication and Symbolic Behavior Scales Developmental Profile with Very Young Children," *Journal of Speech, Language, and Hearing Research* 45 (2002): 1202–18.

36. N. Akhtar, F. Dunham, and P. Dunham, "Directive Interactions and Early Vocabulary Development: The Role of Joint Attentional Focus," *Journal of Child Language* 18 (1991): 41–49.
37. A. Wetherby and G. P. Rodriguez, "Measurement of Communicative Intentions in Normally Developing Children During Structured and Unstructured Contexts," *Journal of Speech and Hearing Research* 35 (1992): 130–38.
38. J. Reichle and S. S. Johnston, "Teaching the Conditional Use of Communicative Requests to Two School-Age Children with Severe Developmental Disabilities," *Language, Speech, and Hearing Services in Schools* 30 (1999): 324–34.
39. S. F. Warren and P. J. Yoder, "Facilitating the Transition from Preintentional to Intentional Communication," in *Transitions in Prelinguistic Communication* (see note 19), 375–76.
40. Ibid., 375.
41. See note 33 above.
42. C. A. Stone, "What Is Missing in the Metaphor of Scaffolding?" in *Contexts for Learning: Sociocultural Dynamics in Children's Development*, ed. E. A. Forman and others (New York: Oxford University Press, 1993), 169–83.
43. P. J. Yoder and S. F. Warren, "Can Developmentally Delayed Children's Language Development Be Enhanced through Prelinguistic Intervention?" in *Enhancing Children's Communication: Research Foundations for Intervention*, ed. A. P. Kaiser and D. B. Gray (Baltimore: Brookes Publishing, 1993), 41.
44. C. J. Dunst, L. W. Lowe, and P. C. Bartholomew, "Contingent Social Responsiveness, Family Ecology, and Infant Communication Competence," *National Student Speech-Language Hearing Association Journal* 17 (1990): 39–49.
45. J. MacDonald and J. Carroll, "Communicating with Young Children: An Ecological Model for Clinicians, Parents, and Collaborative Professionals," *American Journal of Speech-Language Pathology* 1 (1992): 39–48.
46. R. E. Owens, *Language Disorders: A Functional Approach to Assessment and Intervention*, 3rd ed. (Needham Heights: Allyn and Bacon, 1999), 262.
47. W. O. Haynes and B. B. Shulman *Communication Development: Foundations, Processes, and Clinical Applications* (Englewood Cliffs, NJ: Prentice Hall, 1994), 102.
48. Ibid.
49. Ibid.
50. Ibid.
51. K. Proctor-Williams, M. E. Fey, and D. F. Loeb, "Parental Recasts and Production of Copulas and Articles by Children with Specific Language Impairment and Typical Language," *American Journal of Speech-Language Pathology* 10 (2001): 155–68.
52. K. E. Nelson and others, "Effects of Imitative and Conversational Recasting Treatment on the Acquisition of Grammar in Children with Specific Language Impairment and Younger Language-Normal Children," *Journal of Speech and Hearing Research* 39 (1996): 850–59.
53. R. E. Owens, *Language Development: An Introduction*, 3rd ed. (Columbus, OH: Charles E. Merrill, 1995), 239.
54. E. Hoff-Ginsberg, "Maternal Speech and the Child's Development of Syntax: A Further Look," *Journal of Child Language* 17 (1990): 85–99.
55. S. M. Camarata, K. Nelson, and M. Camarata, "Comparison of Conversational-Recasting and Imitative Procedures for Training Grammatical Structures in Children with Specific Language Impairment," *Journal of Speech and Hearing Research* 37 (1994): 1414–23.
56. W. O. Haynes and B. B. Shulman *Communication Development: Foundations, Processes, and Clinical Applications* (Englewood Cliffs, NJ: Prentice Hall, 1994), 104.

57. S. McCleod, J. van Doorn, and V. Reed, "Normal Acquisition of Consonant Clusters," *American Journal of Speech-Language Pathology* 10 (2001): 99–110.
58. M. M. Watson and G.P. Scukanec, "Profiling the Phonological Abilities of 2-Year Olds: A Longitudinal Investigation," *Child Language Teaching and Therapy* 13 (1997): 3–14.
59. See note 57 above.
60. Ibid.
61. K. M. Kitchner and others, "Developmental Range of Reflective Judgment: The Effect of Contextual Support and Practice on Developmental Stage," *Developmental Psychology* 29 (1993): 893–906.

Chapter 2

1. L. Fenson and others, "Variability in Early Communicative Development," *Monographs of the Society for Research in Child Development* 59, no. 242 (1994).
2. Ibid.
3. D. Tannen, *You Just Don't Understand: Women and Men in Conversation* (New York: William E. Morrow and Company, 1990), 43–44.
4. R. E. Owens, *Language Development: An Introduction*, 3rd ed. (Columbus, OH: Charles E. Merrill, 1995), 373.
5. Ibid.
6. Y. Oshima-Takane, "The Learning of First- and Second-person Pronouns in English," in *Language, Logic, and Concept: Essays in Memory of John Macnamara*, ed. R. Jackendoff and others (Cambridge, MA: MIT Press, 1999), 373–409.
7. N. Akhtar, J. Jipson, and M. A. Callanan, "Learning Words through Overhearing," *Child Development* 72 (2001): 416.
8. B. Dodd and S. McEvoy. "Twin Language or Phonological Disorder?" *Journal of Child Language* 21 (1994): 273–89.
9. Ibid.
10. D. V. M. Bishop and S. J. Bishop, "Twin Language: A Risk Factor for Language Impairment?" *Journal of Speech, Language, and Hearing Research* 41 (1998): 150–60.
11. R. H. MacTurk and others, "Social Support, Motivation, Language, and Interaction," *American Annals of the Deaf* 138 (1993): 19–25; P. Yoder and others, "Does Adult Responsivity to Child Behavior Facilitate Communication Development?" in *Transitions in Prelinguistic Communication*, ed. A. Wetherby, S. Warren, and J. Reichle (Baltimore: Brookes Publishing, 1998), 41–42.
12. R. McCathern, P. J. Yoder, and S. F. Warren, "The Role of Directives in Early Language Intervention," *Journal of Early Intervention* 19 (1995): 91–101.
13. Ibid.
14. M. Tomasello and M. J. Farrar, "Joint Attention and Early Language." *Child Development* 57 (1986): 1454–63.
15. P. J. Yoder and others, "Facilitating Prelinguistic Communication in Very Young Children with Developmental Disabilities II: Systematic Replication and Extension," *Journal of Speech and Hearing Research* 37 (1994): 841–51.
16. B. Hart and T. R. Risley, *Meaningful Differences in the Everyday Experience of Young American Children* (Baltimore: Brookes Publishing, 1995), 134.
17. E. G. Conture, *Stuttering: Its Nature, Diagnosis and Treatment* (Needham Heights: Allyn and Bacon, 2001), 156.

18. A. M. Calandrella and M. J. Wilcox, "Predicting Language Outcomes for Young Pre-linguistic Children with Developmental Delay," *Journal of Speech, Language, and Hearing Research* 43 (2000): 1061–71.
19. S. B. Graves and others, *Young Children: An Introduction to Early Childhood Education* (St. Paul: West Publishing Company, 1996), 56.
20. W. S. Barnett, "Long-term Effects of Early Childhood Programs on Cognitive and School Outcomes," *The Future of Children* 5, no. 3 (1995): 25–50.
21. C. Howes, "Children's Experiences in Center-based Child-Care as a Function of Teacher Background and Adult:Child Ratio." *Merrill-Palmer Quarterly* 43 (1997): 404–25.
22. E. S. Peisner-Feinberg and others, "The Relation of Preschool Child-care Quality to Children's Cognitive and Social Developmental Trajectories through Second Grade," *Child Development* 72, no. 5 (2001): 1534.
23. National Institute of Child Health and Human Development Early Child Care Research Network, "The Relation of Child Care to Cognitive and Language Development," *Child Development* 71, no. 4 (2000): 960.
24. L. Berk and A. Winsler, *Scaffolding Children's Learning: Vygotsky and Early Childhood Education* (Washington, DC: NAEYC, 1995).
25. S. B. Graves and others, *Young Children: An Introduction to Early Childhood Education* (St. Paul: West Publishing Company, 1996), 60.
26. "Guidelines for Decisions About Developmentally Appropriate Practice in Early Childhood Programs Serving Children from Birth through Age 8" (Washington, DC: NAEYC, 1996), http://www.naeyc.org/resources/position_statements/dap4.htm (accessed May 31, 2002).
27. P. Warner, *Baby Play and Learn* (Minnetonka: Meadowbrook Press, 1999), viii.
28. S. Kim, "The Effects of Storytelling and Pretend Play on Cognitive Processes, Short-term and Long-term Narrative Recall," *Child Study Journal* 29, no. 3 (1999): 175.
29. L. Girolametto and others, "Directiveness in Teachers' Language Input to Toddlers and Preschoolers in Day Care," *Journal of Speech, Language, and Hearing Research* 45 (2000): 1101–14.
30. See note 22 above.
31. See note 29 above.
32. C. A. Marvin and A. J. Privratsky, "After-School Talk: The Effects of Materials Sent Home from Preschool," *American Journal of Speech-Language Pathology* 8 (1999): 231–40.
33. B. E. Dresher, "Child Phonology, Learnability, and Phonological Theory," in *Handbook of Child Language Acquisition*, ed. W. C. Ritchie and T. K. Bhatia (San Diego: Academic Press, 1999), 299–346.
34. Ibid.
35. American Academy of Pediatrics Committee on Public Education, "Children, Adolescents, and Television," RE0043, February 2001, http://www.aap.org/policy/re0043.html (accessed June 17, 2002).
36. L. K. Certain and R. S. Kahn, "Prevalence, Correlates, and Trajectory of Television Viewing Among Infants and Toddlers," *Pediatrics* 109, no. 4, (2002): 634.
37. "2001 Report on Television" (New York: Nielsen Media Research, 2001).
38. D. F. Roberts and others, *Kids and Media at the New Millennium: A Comprehensive National Analysis of Children's Media Use* (Menlo Park, CA: The Henry J. Kaiser Family Foundation Report, 1999).
39. N. Ahktar, F. Dunham, and P. Dunham, "Directive Interactions and Early Vocabulary Development: The Role of Joint Attention Focus," *Journal of Child Language* 18 (1991): 41–49.

40. L. R. Naigles and L. Mayeux, "Television as Incidental Language Teacher," in *Handbook of Children and the Media*, ed. D. G. Singer and J. L. Singer (Thousand Oaks, CA: Sage Publications, 2001), 138.
41. Ibid.
42. K. Martin, *Does My Child Have a Speech Problem?* (Chicago: Chicago Review Press, 1997), 54.
43. L. R. Naigles and L. Mayeux, "Television as Incidental Language Teacher," in *Handbook of Children and the Media*, ed. D. G. Singer and J. L. Singer (Thousand Oaks, CA: Sage Publications, 2001), 140.
44. J. L Singer and D. G. Singer. *"Barney and Friends* as Entertainment and Education: Evaluating the Quality and Effectiveness of a Television Series for Preschool Children," in *Research Paradigms, Television, and Social Behavior*, ed. J. K. Asamen and G. L. Berry (Thousand Oaks, CA: Sage Press, 1998), 305–67.
45. M. Rice and others, "Words from *Sesame Street*: Learning Vocabulary While Viewing." *Developmental Psychology* 26 (1990): 421–28.
46. See note 44 above.
47. See note 33 above.
48. G. G. Sparks and J. Cantor, "Developmental Differences in Fright Responses to a Television Program Depicting a Character Transformation," *Journal of Broadcasting and Electronic Media* 30 (1986): 309–23.
49. J. Cantor and A. Nathanson, "Children's Fright Reactions to Television News," *Journal of Communication* 46, no. 4 (1996): 139–52.
50. J. Cantor, *Mommy, I'm Scared: How TV and Movies Frighten Children and What We Can Do to Protect Them* (San Diego: Harcourt Brace, 1998).
51. J. K. Rosemond, *Six-Point Plan for Raising Happy, Healthy Children* (Kansas City, MO: Andrews and McMeel, 1989), 174.
52. C. Koolstra and T. van der Voort, "Longitudinal Effects of Television on Children's Leisure Time Reading," *Human Communication Research* 23 (1997): 4–36.
53. J. K. Rosemond, *Making the Terrible Two's Terrific!* (Kansas City: Andrews and McMeel, 1993), 49.
54. L. R. Naigles and L. Mayeux, "Television as Incidental Language Teacher," in *Handbook of Children and the Media*, ed. D. G. Singer and J. L. Singer (Thousand Oaks, CA: Sage Publications, 2001), 150.
55. K. Felix, "Census Bureau Report on Computers and Children," *Multimedia Schools* 8, no. 6 (2001): 10.
56. S. W. Haugland, "What Role Should Technology Play in Young Children's Learning? Part I," *Young Children* 54, no. 6, (1999): 26–31.
57. M. K. Meyerhoff, "Babies and Computers," *Pediatrics for Parents* 19, no. 6, (2001): 8.
58. C. Johnston, "Interactive Storybook Software and Kindergarten Children: The Effect on Verbal Ability and Emergent Storybook Reading Behaviors," PhD diss., Florida State Univ., 1995 (Abstract in *Dissertation Abstracts International*, publ. nr. A4270, 1995: 56).
59. C. R. Smith, "Click and Turn the Page: An Exploration of Multiple Storybook Literacy," *Reading Research Quarterly* 36, no. 2 (2001): 152.
60. S. W. Haugland, "What Role Should Technology Play in Young Children's Learning? Part II: Early Childhood Classrooms in the 21st Century, Using Computers to Maximize Learning," *Young Children* 55, no. 1, (2000): 12–18.
61. T. M. Heft, and S. Swaminathan, "The Effects of Computers on the Social Behavior of Preschoolers," *Journal of Research in Childhood Education* 16, no. 2 (2002): 162.

62. S. Haugland, "Enhancing Children's Sense of Self and Community through Utilizing Computers," *Early Childhood Education Journal* 23, no. 4 (1996): 227–30.
63. D. H. Clements, and S. Swaminathan, "Technology and School Change," *Childhood Education* 71 (1995): 275–81.
64. "Prolonged Computer Use in Children Can Lead to Vision Problems Due to Eyestrain, Study Finds," *Ophthalmology Times* 27, no. 8 (2002): 18.
65. See note 57 above.
66. National Association for the Education of Young Children, "Technology and Young Children—Ages 3 through 8," NAEYC position statement, 2000, http://www.naeyc.org/resources/position_statements/pstech98.htm (accessed April 23, 2002).

Chapter 3

1. M. W. Casby, "Otitis Media and Language Development: A Meta-analysis," *American Journal of Speech-Language Pathology* 10 (2001): 65–80.
2. Agency for Healthcare Research and Quality, "Management of Acute Otitis Media," Summary, *Evidence Report/Technology Assessment:* Number 15, June 2000, http://www.ahrq.gov/clinic/otitissum.htm (accessed August 24, 2001).
3. R. B. Gillam, T. P. Marquardt, and F. N. Martin, *Communication Sciences and Disorders From Science to Clinical Practice* (San Diego: Singular Publishing Group, 2000), 112.
4. See note 1 above.
5. J. E. Roberts and others, "Otitis Media, the Caregiving Environment, and Language and Cognitive Outcomes at 2 Years," *Pediatrics* 102, no. 2 (1998): 346.
6. M. M. Rovers and others, "The Effect of Ventilation Tubes on Language Development in Infants With Otitis Media with Effusion: A Randomized Trial," *Pediatrics* 106, no. 3 (2000): 593.
7. M. E. Tucker, "Otitis Media in Day Care (Pediatric Briefs)," *Pediatric News* 36, no. 2 (2002): 3.
8. Benton County Health Department. "Poisoning Our Children: The Dangers of Second-hand Smoke," http://www.co.benton.or.us/health/hdp/2ndhand.htm (accessed July 4, 2002).
9. J. Duncan and others, "Exclusive Breast-feeding for at Least 4 months Protects against Otitis Media," *Pediatrics* 91, no. 5 (2003): 867.
10. M. Niemala, M. Uhari, and M. Mottonen, "A Pacifier Increases the Risk of Recurrent Acute Otitis Media in Children in Day Care Centers," *Pediatrics* 96, no. 5 (1995): 884.
11. M. Wilson-Adkins and C. Adkins, "A New Conjugate Vaccine against Pneumococcal Disease," *Nurse Practitioner* 26, no. 5 (2001): 52–59.
12. *Advance for Speech-Language Pathologists and Audiologists* 12, no. 28, (2002): 27.
13. American Speech-Language-Hearing Association, *Newborn Hearing Screening and Your Baby,* 2000.
14. Ibid.
15. S. Friel-Patti, "Auditory Linguistic Processing and Language Learning," in *Language Learning Disabilities in School-age Children and Adolescents,* ed. G. P. Wallach and K. G. Butler (New York: Merrill, 1994), 373–92.
16. J. W. Hall, "CAPD in Y2K: An Introduction to Audiologic Assessment and Management," *The Hearing Journal* 52, no. 10 (1999): 35; M. G. Masters, N. A. Stecker, and J. Katz, *Central Auditory Processing Disorders: Mostly Management* (Needham Heights: Allyn and Bacon, 1998), 36.
17. Fact Sheet: "What Are Central Auditory Processing Problems in Children?" American Speech-Language-Hearing Association, 1990.

18. E. F. Jimenez, "The Pacifier," 2001, http://www.diagnostico.com/Pediatrics/Healthy/Pacifier.stm (accessed April 21, 2002).
19. M. Niemela and others, "Pacifier as a Risk Factor for Acute Otitis Media: A Randomized, Controlled Trial of Parental Counseling," *Pediatrics* 106, no. 3 (2000): 483; M. Niemala and others, "A Pacifier Increases the Risk of Recurrent Acute Otitis Media in Children in Day Care Centers," *Pediatrics* 96, no. 5 (1995): 884.
20. See note 18 above.
21. D. C. Bahr, *Oral Motor Assessment and Treatment: Ages and Stages* (Needham, MA: Allyn and Bacon, 2001), 122.
22. Ibid., 122, 131.
23. Ibid., 127.
24. R. S. Walter, "Issues Surrounding the Development of Feeding and Swallowing," in *Disorders of Feeding and Swallowing in Infants and Children: Pathophysiology Diagnosis and Treatment*, ed. D. N. Tuchman and R. S. Walter (San Diego: Singular Publishing Group, 1994), 27–35.
25. D. C. Bahr, *Oral Motor Assessment and Treatment: Ages and Stages* (Needham, MA: Allyn and Bacon, 2001), 121.
26. Ibid., 74.
27. S. E. Morris and M. D. Klein, *Pre-feeding Skills: A Comprehensive Resource for Mealtime Development*, 2nd ed. (San Antonio: Therapy Skill Builders, 2000).
28. See note 24 above.
29. See note 27 above.
30. D. C. Bahr, *Oral Motor Assessment and Treatment: Ages and Stages* (Needham, MA: Allyn and Bacon, 2001).
31. C. Fernando, *Tongue Tie from Confusion to Clarity: A Guide to the Diagnosis and Treatment of Ankyloglossia* (Sydney: Tandem Publications, 1998).
32. A. H. Messner and M. L. Lalakea, "Ankyloglossia: Controversies in Management," *International Journal of Pediatric Otorhinolaryngology* 54, no. 2-3 (2000): 123–31.
33. M. R. Colyar and C. R. Ehrhardt, "Frenotomy for Ankyloglossia," in *Ambulatory Care Procedures for the Nurse Practitioner* (Philadelphia: F. A. Davis, 1999), 325.
34. J. L. Paradise, "Evaluation and Treatment for Ankyloglossia," *Journal of the American Medical Association (JAMA)* 262 (1990): 2371.
35. C. Bowen, "Tongue-tie," 2000, http://members.tripod.com/~Caroline_Bowen/tonguetie.html (accessed April 29, 2002).
36. A. H. Messner and others, "Ankyloglossia: Incidence and Associated Feeding Difficulties," *Archives of Otolaryngology Head and Neck Surgery* 126, no. 1 (2000): 36–39.
37. Ibid.
38. C. Fernando, *Tongue Tie from Confusion to Clarity: A Guide to the Diagnosis and Treatment of Ankyloglossia* (Sydney: Tandem Publications, 1998), 17.
39. Ibid., 18.
40. Ibid., 11.
41. Ibid., 10.
42. Ibid., 28.
43. See note 32 above.
44. C. Fernando, *Tongue Tie from Confusion to Clarity: A Guide to the Diagnosis and Treatment of Ankyloglossia* (Sydney: Tandem Publications, 1998), 40.
45. N. A. Craighead, P. W. Newman, W. A. Secord, *Assessment and Remediation of Articulatory and Phonological Disorders*, 2nd ed. (Columbus: Merrill Publishing, 1989), 74, 75.

46. C. Bowen, "Lisping," 2001, http://members.tripod.com/Caroline_Bowen/lisping.htm (accessed July 2, 2002).
47. W. O. Haynes, M. J. Moran, and R. H. Pindzola, *Communication Disorders in the Classroom: An Introduction for Professionals in School Settings* (Dubuque, IA: Kendall/Hunt Publishing Company, 1999), 56.
48. Ibid.
49. See note 46 above.
50. A. Smit and L. Hand, *Smit-Hand Articulation and Phonology Evaluation* (Los Angeles: Western Psychological Services, 1997); P. Grunwell, "Natural Phonology," in *The New Phonologies: Developments in Clinical Linguisitics*, ed. M. Ball and R. Kent (San Diego: Singular Publishing Group,) 68; C. Bowen, *Developmental Phonological Disorders: A Practical Guide for Families and Teachers* (Melbourne: ACER Press, 1998).
51. S. McCleod, J. van Doorn, and V. A. Reed, "Normal Acquisition of Consonant Clusters," *American Journal of Speech-Language Pathology* 10 (2001): 99–110.
52. B. Dodd and S. McEvoy, "Twin Language or Phonological Disorder?" *Journal of Child Language* 21 (1994): 273–89.
53. A. Smit and others, "The Iowa Articulation Norms Project and Its Nebraska Replication," *Journal of Speech and Hearing Disorders* 55 (1990): 779–98.
54. H. A. Peterson and T. P. Marquardt, *Appraisal and Diagnosis of Speech and Language Disorders*, 3rd ed. (Englewood Cliffs, NJ: Prentice-Hall, 1994), 242.
55. Ibid., 262.
56. E. G. Conture, *Stuttering: Its Nature, Diagnosis and Treatment* (Needham Heights: Allyn and Bacon, 2001), 138.
57. W. O. Haynes, M. J. Moran, and R. H. Pindzola, *Communication Disorders in the Classroom: An Introduction for Professionals in School Settings* (Dubuque, IA: Kendall/Hunt Publishing Company, 1999), 161.
58. S. Felsenfeld, "Epidemiology and Genetics of Stuttering," in *Nature and Treatment of Stuttering: New Directions*, 2nd ed., ed. R. Curlee and G. Siegel (Boston: Allyn and Bacon, 1997), 3–23.
59. W. O. Haynes, M. J. Moran, and R. H. Pindzola, *Communication Disorders in the Classroom: An Introduction for Professionals in School Settings* (Dubuque, IA: Kendall/Hunt Publishing Company, 1999), 159.
60. F. Yairi and N. Ambrose, "Early Childhood Stuttering I: Persistence and Recovery Rates," *Journal of Speech Language and Hearing Research* 42 (1999): 1097–1112.
61. E. G. Conture, *Stuttering: Its Nature, Diagnosis and Treatment* (Needham Heights: Allyn and Bacon, 2001), 139.
62. W. O. Haynes, M. J. Moran, and R. H. Pindzola, *Communication Disorders in the Classroom: An Introduction for Professionals in School Settings* (Dubuque, IA: Kendall/Hunt Publishing Company, 1999), 156–57.
63. E. Conture and E. Kelly, "Young Stutterer's Non-speech Behaviors During Stuttering," *Journal of Speech and Hearing Research* 34, no. 5 (1991): 1041–56.
64. H. A. Peterson and T. P. Marquardt, *Appraisal and Diagnosis of Speech and Language Disorders*, 3rd ed. (Englewood Cliffs, NJ: Prentice-Hall, 1994), 245.
65. E. G. Conture, *Stuttering: Its Nature, Diagnosis and Treatment* (Needham Heights: Allyn and Bacon, 2001), 139.
66. C. L. Mithers, "Late Bloomers," *Parenting*, November 1998, 104.
67. L. Rescorla, "The Language Development Survey: A Screening Tool for Delayed Language in Toddlers," *Journal of Speech and Hearing Disorders* 54 (1989): 587–99.

68. A. M. Wetherby and others, "First Birthday Report," *Progress Report for Healthcare and Childcare Providers of Infants and Toddlers*, 1999, http://firstwords.fsu.edu/pdf/1birthday.pdf (accessed June 8, 2002).
69. K. S. Berger, *The Developing Person Through the Life Span*, 3rd ed. (New York: Worth Publishers, Inc., 1994).
70. R. Case, and Y. Okamoto, "The Role of Central Conceptual Structures in the Development of Children's Thought," in *Monographs of the Society of Research in Child Development* 61, no. 2, 246, 1996).
71. J. Piaget, *The Origins of Intelligence in Children* (New York: International Universities Press, 1952.)
72. E. Bates. P. Dale, and D. Thal, "Individual Differences and Their Implications for Theories of Language Development," in *The Handbook of Child Language*, ed. P. Fletcher and B. MacWhinney (Oxford: Blackwells, 1995), 114.
73. K. Lifter and L. Bloom. "Intentionality and the Role of Play in the Transition to Language," in *Transitions in Prelinguistic Communication*, ed. A. Wetherby, S. Warren, and J. Reichle (Baltimore, Brookes Publishing, 1998), 161–95.
74. L. B. Leonard, *Children with Specific Language Impairment* (Cambridge, MA: MIT Press, 1998).
75. M. Lahey and J. Edwards, "Specific Language Impairment: Preliminary Investigation of Factors Assessed with Family History and with Patterns of Language Performance," *Journal of Speech and Hearing Research* 38 (1995): 643–57.
76. A. Wetherby, and B. Prizant, *Communication and Symbolic Behavior Scales Developmental Profile: Preliminary Normed Edition* (Baltimore: Brookes Publishing, 2001).
77. U.S. Department of Education. "Eighteenth Annual Report to Congress on the Implementation of the Individuals with Disabilities Education Act," prepared by the Division of Innovation and Development, Office of Special Education Programs (Washington, DC: U.S. Department of Education, 1997).
78. See note 68 above.
79. A. M. Wetherby and others, "Third Birthday Report," *Progress Report for Healthcare and Childcare Providers of Infants and Toddlers*, 2001, http://firstwords.fsu.edu/pdf/3Bday.pdf (accessed June 8, 2002).
80. P. Mundy and others, "Nonverbal Communication and Early Language Acquisition in Children with Down Syndrome and in Normally Developing Children," *Journal of Speech and Hearing Research* 38 (1995): 157–67.
81. R. E. Owens, *Language Disorders: A Functional Approach to Assessment and Intervention*, 3rd ed. (Needham Heights, NJ: Allyn and Bacon, 1999), 262.
82. R. E. Owens, "Language Impairments," in *Language Disorders: A Functional Approach to Assessment and Intervention*, 3rd ed. (see note 82 above), 19–52.
83. H. Scarborough and W. Dobrich, "Development of Children with Early Language Delay," *Journal of Speech and Hearing Research* 33 (1990): 70–83.
84. D. J. Thal and J. Katich, "Predicaments in Early Identification of Specific Language Impairment," in *Assessment of Communication and Language*, ed. S. Warren and J. Reichle (Baltimore, Brookes Publishing, 1996), 9.

Chapter 4

1. R. E. Owens, *Language Development: An Introduction*, 3rd ed. (Columbus, OH: Charles E. Merrill, 1995).
2. L. Fenson and others, "Variability in Early Communicative Development," *Monographs of the Society for Research in Child Development* 59, no. 242 (1994).

3. K. M. Kitchner and others, "Developmental Range of Reflective Judgment: The Effect of Contextual Support and Practice on Developmental Stage," *Developmental Psychology* 29 (1993): 893–906.
4. R. E. Stark, L. E. Bernstein, and M. E. Demorest, "Vocal Communication in the First 18 Months of Life," *Journal of Speech and Hearing Research* 36 (1993): 548–58.
5. R. E. Owens, *Language Development: An Introduction*, 3rd ed. (Columbus, OH: Charles E. Merrill, 1995), 72.
6. K. Michelsson, "Why Do Infants Cry?" *Lancet* 358 (2001): 1376–77.
7. J. E. Roberts and S. A. Zeisel, *Ear Infections and Language Development* (ASHA and U.S. Department of Education, ECI# 2000-9008, 2000).
8. R. M. Golinkoff, and K. Hirsh-Pasek, *How Babies Talk* (New York: Dutton, 1999), 20.
9. American Speech-Language Hearing Association, *How Does Your Child Hear and Talk?* 2002.
10. See note 7 above.
11. C. Stoel-Gammon, "Prelinguistic Vocal Development: Measurement and Predictions," in *Phonological Development: Models, Research, Implications*, ed. C. A. Ferguson, L. Menn, and C. Stoel-Gammon (Timonium, MD: York Press, 1992), 439–56; G. J. Whitehurst and others, "The Continuity of Babble and Speech in Children with Specific Expressive Language Delay," *Journal of Speech and Hearing Research* 34 (1991): 1121–29.
12. M. Vihman, "Early Syllables and the Construction of Phonology," in *Phonological Development: Models, Research, Implications* (see note 11), 393–422.
13. R. E. Owens, *Language Development: An Introduction*, 3rd ed. (Columbus, OH: Charles E. Merrill, 1995), 86.
14. See note 9 above.
15. P. Mitchell and R. Kent, "Phonetic Variation in Multi-syllabic Babbling," *Journal of Child Language* 17 (1990): 247–65.
16. R. E. Owens, *Language Development: An Introduction*, 3rd ed. (Columbus, OH: Charles E. Merrill, 1995), 90.
17. S. Ward, *Baby Talk: Strengthen Your Child's Ability to Listen, Understand, and Communicate* (New York, NY: Ballantine Books, 2001), 46.
18. See note 2 above.
19. See note 4 above.
20. A. Wetherby and others, "Third Birthday Report," *Progress Report for Healthcare and Childcare Providers of Infants and Toddlers*, 2001, http://firstwords.fsu.edu/pdf/3Bday.pdf (accessed June 8, 2002).
21. A. Wetherby and B. Prizant, *Communication and Symbolic Behavior Scales-Normed Edition* (Baltimore: Brookes Publishing, 1993)
22. R. E. Owens, *Language Development: An Introduction*, 3rd ed. (Columbus, OH: Charles E. Merrill, 1995), 94.
23. M. P. Robb, H. R. Bauer, and A. A. Tyler, "A Quantitative Analysis of the Single-Word Stage," *First Language* 14 (1994): 37–48.
24. K. Apel and J. Masterson, *Beyond Baby Talk* (Roseville, CA: Prima Publishing, 2001), 23.
25. See note 20 above.
26. See note 2 above.
27. S. Ward, *Baby Talk: Strengthen Your Child's Ability to Listen, Understand, and Communicate* (New York, NY: Ballantine Books, 2001), 103.
28. L. Rescorla, J. Mirak, and L. Singh, "Vocabulary Growth in Late Talkers: Lexical Development from 2;0 to 3;0," *Journal of Child Language* 27 (2000): 293–311.
29. R. M. Golinkoff, and K. Hirsh-Pasek, *How Babies Talk* (New York: Dutton, 1999), 123–26.

30. See note 2 above.
31. L. Fenson and others, *MacArthur Communicative Development Inventories (CDI)* (San Diego: Singular Publishing Group, 1993).
32. L. Bloom, *The Transition from Infancy to Language* (New York: Cambridge University Press, 1993), 81.
33. J. Coplan and J. Gleason, "Unclear Speech: Recognition and Significance of Unintelligible Speech in Pre-school Children," *Pediatrics* 82 (1988): 447–52.
34. J. Hampton and K. Nelson, "The Relation of Maternal Language to Variation in Rate and Style of Language Acquisition," *Journal of Child Language* 20 (1993): 313–42.
35. K. Nelson, "Structure and Strategy in Learning to Talk," *Monographs of the Society for Research in Child Development* 38, no. 149 (1973).
36. Ibid.
37. See note 34 above.
38. Ibid.
39. Ibid.
40. C. Stoel-Gammon, "Normal and Disordered Phonology in Two-year-olds," *Topics in Language Disorders* 11, no. 4 (1991): 21–32.
41. L. Bloom, *The Transition from Infancy to Language* (New York: Cambridge University Press, 1993), 98.
42. R. E. Owens, *Language Development: An Introduction*, 3rd ed. (Columbus, OH: Charles E. Merrill, 1995), 102.
43. See note 2 above.
44. J. M. Anglin, "Vocabulary Development: A Morphological Analysis," *Monographs for the Society for Research in Child Development*, 58, no. 238 (1993).
45. E. V. Clark, "Later Lexical Development and Word Formation," in *The Handbook of Child Language*, ed. P. Fletcher and B. MacWhinney (Oxford: Blackwells, 1995), 393.
46. S. Pinker, "Language Acquisition," in *Language: An Invitation to Cognitive Science*, 2nd ed, ed. L.R. Gleitman and M. Liberman (Cambridge, MA: MIT Press, 1995), 1:142.
47. See note 33 above.
48. S. McCleod, J. van Doorn, and V. A. Reed, "Normal Acquisition of Consonant Clusters," *American Journal of Speech-Language Pathology* 10 (2001): 99–110.
49. R. E. Owens, *Language Development: An Introduction*, 3rd ed. (Columbus, OH: Charles E. Merrill, 1995), 97.
50. Ibid., 102.
51. E. Bialystok, *Bilingualism in Development: Language, Literacy, and Cognition* (New York: Cambridge University Press, 2001), 28.
52. R. E. Owens, *Language Development: An Introduction*, 3rd ed. (Columbus, OH: Charles E. Merrill, 1995), 103.
53. Ibid., 109.
54. W. O. Haynes and B. B. Shulman, *Communication Development: Foundations, Processes, and Clinical Applications* (Englewood Cliffs, NJ: Prentice Hall, 1994), 75.
55. Ibid., 368.

Chapter 5

1. "General Brain Development," *BrainWonders*, http://www.zerotothree.org/brainwonders/parents-body.html (accessed June 26, 2003).
2. J. L. Elman and others, *Rethinking Innateness: A Connectionist Perspective on Development* (Cambridge, MA: MIT Press, 1996).

3. B. Hart and T. R. Risley, *Meaningful Differences in the Everyday Experience of Young American Children* (Baltimore: Brookes Publishing, 1995), 182.
4. L. M. Hulit, and M. R. Howard, *Born to Talk: An Introduction to Speech and Language Development* (Needham Heights, MA: Macmillan Publishing Company, 1993), 110.
5. M. Krantz, *Child Development: Risk and Opportunity* (Belmont, CA: Wadsworth Publishing Company, 1994), 179.
6. C. Hannaford, *The Dominance Factor* (Atlanta: Great Ocean Publishers, 1997), 121.
7. P. Schiller, *Start Smart! Building Brain Power in the Early Years* (Beltsville, MD: Gryphon House, Inc., 1999), 55.
8. S. Snyder, "Early Childhood Music Lessons from 'Mr. Holland's Opus'," *Early Childhood Education Journal* 24 (1996): 103–105.
9. L. Kleiner and D. Devine, *Babies Make Music* (Redondo Beach, CA: Music Rhapsody, 1996).
10. J. Defty, *Creative Fingerplays and Action Rhymes: An Index and Guide to Their Use* (Phoenix: The Oryx Press, 1992); "Finger Plays and Action Rhymes for Infants and Toddlers," *Texas Child Care* 2, no. 1 (1998): 38–42.
11. C. Stoel-Gammon, "Role of Babbling and Phonology in Early Linguistic Development," in *Transitions in Prelinguistic Communication*, ed. A. Wetherby, and others (Baltimore: Brookes Publishing, 1998), 93.
12. L. Bloom, *The Transition from Infancy to Language* (New York: Cambridge University Press, 1993), 40.
13. Ibid., 41.
14. J. Cooke and D. Williams, *Working with Children's Language: Intervention Strategies for Therapy* (Tucson: Communication Skill Builders, 1985), 20–21.
15. D. Koppenhaver and D. Yoder, "Literacy Issues in Persons with Severe Physical and Speech Impairments," in *Issues and Research in Special Education*, ed. R. Gaylord-Ross (New York: Teachers' College Press, 1992), 156–201.
16. M. Harris and others, "Symmetries and Asymmetries in Early Lexical Comprehension and Production," *Journal of Child Language* 22 (1995): 1–18.
17. L. Bloom, *The Transition from Infancy to Language* (New York: Cambridge University Press, 1993), 96.
18. R. M. Golinkoff and others, "Early Object Labels: The Case for a Developmental Lexical Principles Framework," *Journal of Child Language* 21 (1994): 125–55.
19. M. Tomasello and A. C. Kruger, "Joint Attention on Actions: Acquiring Verbs in Ostensive and Non-ostensive Contexts," *Journal of Child Language* 19 (1992): 311–33.
20. Ibid.
21. Ibid.
22. J. Cooke and D. Williams, *Working with Children's Language: Intervention Strategies for Therapy* (Tucson: Communication Skill Builders, 1985), 111.
23. Ibid., 79.
24. R. E. Owens, *Language Disorders: A Functional Approach to Assessment and Intervention*, 3rd ed. (Needham Heights: Allyn and Bacon, 1999), 268.
25. J. K. Rosemond, *Six-Point Plan for Raising Happy, Healthy Children* (Kansas City, MO: Andrews and McMeel, 1989), 145.
26. See note 24 above.
27. C. Bowen, "Word Retrieval Activities for Children," 2000, http://members.tripod.com/~Caroline_Bowen/wordretrieval.html (accessed October 14, 2001).
28. Ibid.
29. R. E. Owens, *Language Development: An Introduction*, 3rd ed. (Columbus, OH: Charles E. Merrill, 1995).

30. S. Hall and L. Moats, *Straight Talk About Reading: How Parents Can Make a Difference During the Early Years* (Chicago: Contemporary Books, 1999), 216–22.

Chapter 6

1. S. Hall and L. Moats, *Straight Talk About Reading: How Parents Can Make a Difference During the Early Years* (Chicago: Contemporary Books, 1999), 51.
2. M. Senechal and J. Lefevre, "Parental Involvement in the Development of Children's Reading Skill: A Five-year Longitudinal Study," *Child Development* 73, no. 2 (2002): 445.
3. D. T. Allison and J. A. Watson, "The Significance of Adult Storybook Reading Styles on the Development of Young Children's Emergent Reading," *Journal of Reading* 34, no. 1 (1994): 57–72.
4. I. L. Beck and M. G. McKeown, "Text Talk: Capturing the Benefits of Read-aloud Experiences for Young Children," *The Reading Teacher* 55, no. 1 (2001): 10.
5. L. M. Justice and H. K. Ezell, "Use of Storybook Reading to Increase Print Awareness in At-Risk Children," *American Journal of Speech-Language Pathology* 11 (2002): 17–29.
6. S. Hall and L. Moats, *Straight Talk About Reading: How Parents Can Make a Difference During the Early Years* (Chicago: Contemporary Books, 1999), 144.
7. Ibid.
8. Ibid., 61.
9. J. A. Carroll, *Meaningful Print: Creating an Environment with Print-Rich Experiences* (Carthage: Teaching and Learning Company, 1999), iv.
10. See note 6 above.
11. M. Burns and C. Snow, eds., *Starting Out Right: A Guide to Promoting Children's Reading Success* (Washington, DC: National Academy Press, 1999).
12. J. A. Carroll, *Meaningful Print: Creating an Environment with Print-Rich Experiences* (Carthage: Teaching and Learning Company, 1999), 78.
13. M. Daniels, *Dancing With Words: Signing for Hearing Children's Literacy* (Westport, CT: Bergin and Garvey, 2001), 19, 25, 26.
14. S. Hall and L. Moats, *Straight Talk About Reading: How Parents Can Make a Difference During the Early Years* (Chicago: Contemporary Books, 1999), 168.
15. Ibid., 144.
16. Ibid., 176.
17. J. R. Gentry, "A Retrospective on Invented Spelling and a Look Forward," *The Reading Teacher* 54, no. 3, (2000): 318.
18. H. W. Catts and others, "Estimating the Risk of Future Reading Difficulties in Kindergarten Children: A Research-based Model and Its Clinical Instrumentation," *Language, Speech, and Hearing Services in Schools* 32 (2001): 38–50.
19. See note 5 above.
20. S. Hall and L. Moats, *Straight Talk About Reading: How Parents Can Make a Difference During the Early Years* (Chicago: Contemporary Books, 1999), 144.
21. M. Stuart, "Prediction and Qualitative Assessment of Five- and Six-year-old Children's Reading: A Longitudinal Study," *British Journal of Educational Psychology* 65 (1995): 287–96.
22. See note 5 above.
23. S. Hall and L. Moats, *Straight Talk About Reading: How Parents Can Make a Difference During the Early Years* (Chicago: Contemporary Books, 1999), 65.
24. Dolch, E.W. *Methods in Reading*. Champaign,IL: Garrard Publishing Company, 1955.
25. C. Carlilie, *Simply Sight Words: A Program for Beginner Readers K–2*, (Belton, TX, 2001); E. W. Dolch, *Methods in Reading* (Champaign, IL: Garrard Publishing Company, 1955).

26. M. Daniels, *Dancing With Words: Signing for Hearing Children's Literacy* (Westport, CT: Bergin and Garvey, 2001), 154.
27. S. Hall and L. Moats, *Straight Talk About Reading: How Parents Can Make a Difference During the Early Years* (Chicago: Contemporary Books, 1999), 221.
28. L. M. Justice and others, "A Sequential Analysis of Children's Responsiveness to Parental Print References During Shared Book-Reading Interactions," *American Journal of Speech-Language Pathology* 11 (2002): 30–40.
29. S. B. Graves and others, *Young Children: An Introduction to Early Childhood Education* (St. Paul: West Publishing Company, 1996), 306.
30. M. Krantz, *Child Development Risk and Opportunity* (Belmont, CA: Wadsworth Publishing Company, 1994), 423–25.
31. R. Slavin and others, "Every Child Reading: An Action Plan of the Learning First Alliance," 1998, http://www.readbygrade3.com (accessed July 1, 2003).
32. S. B. Neuman, *Put Reading First: The Research Building Blocks for Teaching Children to Read* (Jessup, MD: National Institute for Literacy at ED Pubs., 2001).
33. See note 31 above.
34. S. Hall and L. Moats, *Straight Talk About Reading: How Parents Can Make a Difference During the Early Years* (Chicago: Contemporary Books, 1999), 80.
35. R. Slavin and others, "Every Child Reading: An Action Plan of the Learning First Alliance," 1998, http://www.readbygrade3.com (accessed December 8, 2001)
36. C. E. Snow and others, *Preventing Reading Difficulties in Young Children,* (Washington, DC: National Academy Press, 1998), 80–83, http://www4.nationalacademies.org/webcr.nsf/5c50571a75df494485256a95007a091e/106f9f59b57 85c4c852567dc00169c49?OpenDocument (April 22, 2002).
37. S. G. Blythe, "Early Learning in the Balance: Priming the First ABC," *Support for Learning* 15, no. 4 (2000): 154–58.
38. S. Hall and L. Moats, *Straight Talk About Reading: How Parents Can Make a Difference During the Early Years* (Chicago: Contemporary Books, 1999), 310.
39. E. Shatil and others, "On the Contribution of Kindergarten Writing to Grade One Literacy: A Longitudinal Study in Hebrew," *Applied Psycholinguistics* 21 (2000): 1–21.
40. D. Aram and I. Levin, "Mother-Child Joint Writing and Storybook Reading: Relations with Literacy among Low SES Kindergartners," *Merrill-Palmer Quarterly* 48, no. 2 (2002): 202.
41. L. R. Sipe, "Invention, Convention and Intervention: Invented Spelling and the Teacher's Role," *The Reading Teacher* 55, no. 3 (2001): 264.
42. L. Baker and others, "Home Experiences Related to the Development of Word Recognition," in *Word Recognition in Beginning Literacy*, ed. J. L. Metsala and L. C. Ehri (Hillsdale, NJ: Erlbaum, 1998), 263–88.
43. D. Richgels, "Invented Spelling Ability and Printed Word Learning in Kindergarten," *Reading Research Quarterly* 30, no. 1 (1995): 96–109.
44. See note 35 above.

Chapter 7

1. J. Garcia, *Sign with Your Baby: How to Communicate with Infants before They Can Speak* (Seattle: Northlight Communications, 2000), 5.
2. M. Daniels, *Dancing With Words: Signing for Hearing Children's Literacy* (Westport, CT: Bergin and Garvey, 2001), 79.
3. L. Acredolo, and S. Goodwyn, *Baby Signs: How to Talk with Your Baby before Your Baby Can Talk* (Chicago: Contemporary Books, 1996), 5.
4. M. Daniels, *Dancing With Words: Signing for Hearing Children's Literacy* (Westport, CT: Bergin and Garvey, 2001), 122.

5. N. Charbonneau, "Early Childhood Critical Time to Learn Sign Language," *Health Scout News*, January 8, 2002, http//health.yahoo.com/search/healthnews?lb=sandp=id:7021 (accessed February 10, 2002).
6. L. Acredolo, and S. Goodwyn, "The Long-term Impact of Symbolic Gesturing during Infancy on IQ at Age 8" (paper presented at the meetings of the International Society for Infant Studies, Brighton, UK, July 2000).
7. S. W. Goodwyn and L. Acredolo, "Symbolic Gesture versus Word: Is There a Modality Advantage for Onset of Symbol Use?" *Child Development* 64, no. 3 (1993): 688.
8. J. Schwarz, "Hearing Infants Show Preference for Sign Language over Pantomime," University of Washington Press Release, June 2002, http://www.washington.edu/newsroom/news/2002archive/06-02archive/k060402.html (accessed October 20, 2003).
9. H. A. Schunk, "The Effect of Singing Paired with Signing on Receptive Vocabulary Skills or Elementary ESL Students," *Journal of Music Therapy* 36 (1999): 110–24.
10. S. A. Madsen, "The Effect of Music Paired With and Without Gestures on the Learning and Transfer of New Vocabulary: Experimenter-derived Nonsense words," *Journal of Music Therapy* 28 (1991): 222–30.
11. S. Snyder, "Early Childhood Music Lessons from 'Mr. Holland's Opus'," *Early Childhood Education Journal* 24 (1996): 103–105.
12. Ibid.
13. M. Daniels, *Dancing With Words: Signing for Hearing Children's Literacy* (Westport, CT: Bergin and Garvey, 2001), 21.
14. Ibid., 19, 20.

Chapter 8

1. L. Malave, "Parent Characteristics: Influence in the Development of Bilingualism in Young Children," *NYSABE Journal* 12 (1997): 15–42.
2. E. Bialystok, *Bilingualism in Development: Language, Literacy, and Cognition* (New York: Cambridge University Press, 2001), 9.
3. See note 1 above.
4. Ibid.
5. M. Rosenberg, "Raising Bilingual Children." *The Internet TESL Journal* II, no. 6 (Spring 1996), http://www.aitech.ac.jp/~iteslj/Articles/Rosenberg-Bilingual.html (accessed February 24, 2001).
6. M. Bruck and F. Genesee, "Phonological Awareness in Young Second Language Learners," *Journal of Child Language* 22 (1995): 307–24.
7. E. Bialystok, T. Shenfield, and J. Codd, "Languages, Scripts, and the Environment: Factors in Developing Concepts of Print," *Developmental Psychology* 36 (2000): 66–76.
8. Ibid.
9. N. Segalowitz, and M. Hebert, "Phonological Recoding in the First- and Second-language Reading of Skilled Bilinguals," in *Bilingual Performance in Reading and Writing*, ed. A.H. Cumming (Ann Arbor, MI: John Benjamins, 1994), 103–35.
10. F. Grosjean, "Living with Two Languages and Two Cultures," in *Cultural and Language Diversity and the Deaf Experience*, ed. I. Parasnis (New York: Cambridge University Press. 1996), 22.
11. E. Bialystok, *Bilingualism in Development: Language, Literacy, and Cognition* (New York: Cambridge University Press, 2001), 232.
12. S. Romaine, *Bilingualism*, 2nd ed. (Oxford: Blackwell, 1995).

13. M. Malakoff and K. Hakuta, "Translation Skill and Metalinguistic Awareness in Bilinguals," in *Language Processing in Bilingual Children*, ed. E. Bialystok (Cambridge: Cambridge University Press, 1991), 141–66.
14. B. Z. Pearson and others, "The Relation of Input Factors to Lexical Learning by Bilingual Infants," *Applied Psycholinguistics* 18 (1997): 41–58.
15. E. Bialystok, *Bilingualism in Development: Language, Literacy, and Cognition* (New York: Cambridge University Press, 2001), 241.
16. See note 5 above.
17. P. K. Kuhl and others, "Foreign-Language Experience in Infancy: Effects of Short-term Exposure and Social Interaction on Phonetic Learning," *Proceedings of the National Academy of Sciences of the United States of America* 100, no. 15 (2003): 9096.
18. A. De Houwer, "Bilingual Language Acquisition," in *The Handbook of Child Language*, ed. P. Fletcher and B. MacWhinney (Cambridge, Mass.: Blackwell Publishers Ltd., 1995), 234.
19. D. Birdsong, "Ultimate Attainment in 2nd Language Acquisition," *Language*, 68, no. 4 (1992): 706–55.
20. E. Bialystok, *Bilingualism in Development: Language, Literacy, and Cognition* (New York: Cambridge University Press, 2001), 79–83.
21. D. Battle, *Communication Disorders in Multicultural Populations*, 3rd ed. (Boston: Butterworth-Heinemann, 2002), 207.
22. E. Nicoladis, and F. Genesee, "A Longitudinal Study of Pragmatic Differentiation in Young Bilingual Children," *Language Learning* 46 (1996): 439–64.
23. N. Poulisse, "Language Production in Bilinguals," in *Tutorials in Bilingualism: Psycholinguistic Perspectives*, ed. A. M. B. de Groot. and others (Mahwah, NJ: Lawrence Erlbaum Associates, 1997), 201–24.
24. E. Bialystok, *Bilingualism in Development: Language, Literacy, and Cognition* (New York: Cambridge University Press, 2001), 244.
25. E. Harding, and P. Riley, *The Bilingual Family* (Cambridge, UK: Cambridge University Press, 1986), 51.
26. J. M. Meisel, "The Simultaneous Acquistion of Two First Languages," in *Trends in Bilingual Acquisition*, ed. J. Cenoz and F. Genessee (Philadelphia: John Benjamins, 2001), 26.
27. F. Genessee and others, "Language Differentiation in Early Bilingual Development," *Journal of Child Language* 22 (1995): 611–31.
28. V. F. Gutierrez-Clellen, "Language Choice in Intervention with Bilingual Children," *American Journal of Speech-Language Pathology* 8 (1999): 291–302.
29. See note 27 above.
30. D. Battle, *Communication Disorders in Multicultural Populations*, 3rd ed. (Boston: Butterworth-Heinemann, 2002), 208.
31. S. H. Marinova-Todd and others, "Three Misconceptions about Age and L2 Learning," *TESOL Quarterly* 34, no. 1 (2000): 9–34.
32. See note 5 above.
33. E. Bialystok, *Bilingualism in Development: Language, Literacy, and Cognition* (New York: Cambridge University Press, 2001), 229–30.
34. O. Dunn, *Help Your Child with a Foreign Language* (Princeton: Berlitz Publishing Company, 1994), 42.
35. See note 14 above.
36. See note 5 above.
37. B. Hart and T. R. Risley, *Meaningful Differences in the Everyday Experience of Young American Children* (Baltimore: Brookes Publishing, 1995): 145–46.
38. M. Juan-Garau, and C. Perez-Vidal. "Mixing and Pragmatic Parental Strategies in Early Bilingual Acquisition," *Journal of Child Language* 28 (2001): 59–86.

39. See note 14 above.
40. See note 1 above.
41. H. A. Schunk, "The Effect of Singing Paired with Signing on Receptive Vocabulary Skills or Elementary ESL Students," *Journal of Music Therapy* 36 (1999): 110–24.
42. E. Harding, and P. Riley, *The Bilingual Family* (Cambridge, UK: Cambridge University Press, 1986), 80.
43. S. Quay, "Early Trilingual Development," in *Trends in Bilingual Acquisition* (see note 26 above), 197.
44. Ibid., 196.
45. Ibid., 194.
46. Immigration and Naturalization Service, U.S. Department of Justice, "Immigrant-Orphans Adopted by U.S. Citizens by Sex, Age, and Region and Selected Country of Birth, at 65–66," Table 15, 1998, *Statistical Yearbook of the Immigration and Naturalization Services* (November 2000), http://www.ins.usdoj.gov/ graphics/aboutins/statistics/1998yb.pdf (accessed February 26, 2002).
47. Ibid.
48. Russian Ministery of Education, "Statistics on Orphans in Russia as of December 1, 2000," http://www.ed.gov.ru/obzor.html (accessed August 24, 2002).
49. L. H. Albers and others, "Health of Children Adopted from the Former Soviet Union and Eastern Europe: Comparison with Preadoptive Medical Records," *The Journal of the American Medical Association* 278, no. 11 (1997): 922.
50. T. C. Benoit and others, "Romanian Adoption: The Manitoba Experience," *Archives of Pediatrics and Adolescent Medicine* 150, no. 12 (1996): 1278.
51. D. Johnson, "Adopting an Institutionalized Child: What Are the Risks?" (1996), http://www.theadoptionguide.com/News/AdoptinganInstitutionalizedChild.html (accessed July 19, 2002); B. Gindis, "Language-Related Issues for International Adoptees and Adoptive Families," in *International Adoption: Challenges and Opportunities*, ed. T. Tepper and others (Meadowlands, PA: Parent Network for the Post-Institutionalized Child, 2000), 98–108.
52. G. Steinberg and B. Hall, *Inside Transracial Adoption* (Indianapolis: Perspectives Press, 2000), 206.
53. T. Tepper and L. Hannon, "Introduction: What Is Post-Institutional Response?" (1999), http://www.pnpic.org/bookintro.htm (accessed August 23, 2002).
54. T. Doolittle, "Language Impairments" (1999), http://home.att.net/~Practical Attachment/page14.html (accessed August 22, 2002).
55. B. Gindis, "Language-Related Issues for International Adoptees and Adoptive Families," in *International Adoption: Challenges and Opportunities*, ed. T. Tepper and others (Meadowlands, PA: Parent Network for the Post-Institutionalized Child, 2000), 98–108.
56. Ibid.
57. H. S. Wilkinson, "Psycho-legal Process and Issues in International Adoption," *The American Journal of Family Therapy* 23, no. 2 (1995): 173–83.
58. S. Glennen, "Language Development and Delay in Internationally Adopted Infants and Toddlers: A Review," *American Journal of Speech-Language Pathology* 11 (2002), 333–39.
59. S. Glennen and M. G. Masters, "Typical and Atypical Language Development in Infants and Toddlers Adopted from Eastern Europe," *American Journal of Speech-Language Pathology* 11 (2002), 417–33.
60. Ibid.
61. See note 58 above.

62. R. S. Federici, "Raising the Post-Institutionalized Child: Risks, Challenges and Innovative Treatment" (1999), http://www.drfederici.com/Raising%20the%20P-I%20Child.htm (accessed August 22, 2002).
63. G. Steinberg and B. Hall, *Inside Transracial Adoption* (Indianapolis: Perspectives Press, 2000), 161.
64. M. Freundlich and J. K. Lieberthal, "The Gathering of the First Generation of Adult Korean Adoptees: Adoptee's Perceptions of International Adoption" (2000), http://www.adoptioninstitute.org/ (accessed March 5, 2002).
65. See note 57 above.
66. See note 64 above.
67. Ibid.
68. H. Erichsen and J. Nelson-Erichsen, *How to Adopt Internationally: A Guide for Agency-Directed and Independent Adoptions*, 2000–2002 ed. (Fort Worth, TX: Mesa House Publishing, 2000), 180.
69. See note 64 above.
70. See note 57 above.
71. See note 46 above.
72. H. Van Gulden and L. M. Bartels-Rabb, "Learning Disabilities and Adopted Children," in *Real Parents, Real Children: Parenting the Adopted Child* (New York: Crossroad Publishing, 1993).
73. Ibid.
74. U.S. Census Bureau, "Census 2000, Demographic Profile, Table DP-2" (2002), http://censtats.census.gov/data/US/01000.pdf (accessed August 25, 2002).
75. U.S. Census Bureau, "Census 1999, Demographic Profile, Table CPH-L-96" (1999), http://www.ccnsus.gov/population/www/socdemo/lang_use.html (August 25, 2002).
76. C. Roseberry-McKibbin and A. Brice, "What's 'Normal,' What's Not? Acquiring English as a Second Language" (2002), http://www.asha.org/easl-acquiring-english-as-a-second-language.cfm (accessed February 18, 2002).
77. D. Battle, *Communication Disorders in Multicultural Populations*, 3rd ed. (Boston: Butterworth-Heinemann, 2002), 212–15.
78. See note 10 above.
79. See note 1 above.
80. V. Pacini-Ketchabaw and others, "Struggling to Preserve Home Language: The Experiences of Latino Students and Families in the Canadian School System," *Bilingual Research Journal* 25 (2001): 1–31.
81. D. Battle, *Communication Disorders in Multicultural Populations*, 3rd ed. (Boston: Butterworth-Heinemann, 2002), 216.
82. See note 76 above.
83. E. Bialystok, *Bilingualism in Development: Language, Literacy, and Cognition* (New York: Cambridge University Press, 2001), 79–83.
84. E. Bialystok, *Bilingualism in Development: Language, Literacy, and Cognition* (New York: Cambridge University Press, 2001), 229–30.
85. J. F. Hamers, "Cognitive and Language Development of Bilingual Children," in *Cultural and Language Diversity and the Deaf Experience* (see note 10 above), 51–75.
86. K. Hakuta and others, "How Long Does It Take English Learners to Attain Proficiency?" The University of California Linguistic Minority Research Institute, policy report 2000-1 (2001).
87. See note 1 above.
88. A. DeHouwer, "Two or More Languages in Early Childhood: Some General Points and Practical Recommendations," *ERIC Digest: Clearinghouse on Languages and Linguistics*, July 1999, EDO-FL-99-03, http://www.cal.org/ericcll/digest/earlychild.html (accessed July 12, 2002).

89. A. Notari-Syverson and A. Losardo, "Assessing Children's Language in Meaningful Contexts," in *Assessment of Communication and Language*, ed. K. Cole and others (Baltimore: Brookes Publishing, 1996), 263.
90. R. McCathern and others, "The Role of Directives in Early Language Intervention," *Journal of Early Intervention* 19 (1995): 91–101.
91. A. van Kleeck, "Potential Cultural Bias in Training Parents as Conversational Partners with Their Children Who Have Delays in Language Development," *American Journal of Speech-Language Pathology* 31 (1994): 67–78.
92. See note 90 above.
93. T. Tardif, "Nouns Are Not Always Learned before Verbs: Evidence from Mandarin Speakers' Early Vocabularies," *Developmental Psychology* 32 (1996): 492–504.
94. E. V. M. Lieven, "Cross-linguistic and Cross-cultural Aspects of Language Addressed to Children," in *Input and Interaction in Language Acquisition*, ed. C. Gallaway and B. J. Richards (Cambridge, U.K.: Cambridge University Press, 1994), 56–73.
95. A. Castrogiovanni, "National Strategic Research Plan for Language and Language Disorders, Balance and Balance Disorders, and Voice and Voice Disorders," NIH publication no. 97-3217 (Bethesda, MD: National Institute on Deafness and Other Communication Disorders, 1995).
96. B. Z. Pearson and others, "Lexical Development in Bilingual Infants and Toddlers: Comparison to Monolingual Norms," *Language Learning* 43, no. 1 (1993): 93–120.
97. See note 28 above.
98. Ibid.
99. H. Kayser, "Intervention with Children from Linguistically and Culturally Diverse Backgrounds," in *Language Intervention: Preschool through the Elementary Years*, ed. M. E. Fey and others (Baltimore: Brookes Publishing Co., 1995), 315–32.

Chapter 9

1. N. Temmerman, "A Survey of Childhood Music Education Programs in Australia," *Early Childhood Education Journal* 26, no. 1 (1998): 29–34.
2. N. M. Weinberger, "Music Research: A Broad View," *MuSICA Research Notes* VII, 3 (Fall 2000), http://www.musica.uci.edu/mrn/V7I3F00.html (accessed April 21, 2002).
3. P. L. Bygrave, "Development of Receptive Vocabulary Skills Through Exposure to Music," *Bulletin of the Council for Research in Music Education* 127 (1995–96): 28–34.
4. See note 1 above.
5. S. Snyder, "Early Childhood Music Lessons from 'Mr. Holland's Opus'," *Early Childhood Education Journal* 24 (1996): 103–5.
6. D. T. McDonald and G. M. Simons, *Musical Growth and Development Birth through Six* (New York: Schirmer Books, 1989), 49.
7. N. M. Weinberger, "The Mozart Effect: A Small Part of the Big Picture," *MuSICA Research Notes* VII, 1 (Winter 2000), http://www.musica.uci.edu/mrn/V7I1W00.html#part (accessed April 21, 2002).
8. R. Caulfield, "Mozart Effect: Sound Beginnings?" *Early Childhood Education Journal* 27, no. 2 (1999): 119–21.
9. See note 2 above.
10. L. W. Olsho, "Infant Frequency Discrimination," *Infant Behavior and Development* 7 (1984): 7–35.
11. S. E. Trehub and others, "Infants' Perception of Melodies: The Role of Melodic Contour," *Child Development* 55 (1984): 821–30.

12. P. Schiller, *Start Smart! Building Brain Power in the Early Years* (Beltsville, MD: Gryphon House, Inc., 1999), 71.
13. N. Masataka, "Preference for Infant-Directed Singing in 2-Day-Old Hearing Infants of Deaf Parents," *Developmental Psychology* 35, no. 4 (1999): 1001–5.
14. Ibid.
15. J. Standley, and C. K. Madsen, "Comparison of Infant Preferences and Responses to Auditory Stimuli: Music, Mother, and Other Female Voice," *Journal of Music Therapy* 27, no. 2 (1990): 54–97; R. Baldwin, *You Are Your Child's First Teacher* (Berkeley, CA: Celestial Arts, 1989), 37.
16. J. Whipple, "The Effect of Parent Training in Music and Multimodal Stimulation on Parent-Neonate Interactions in the Neonatal Intensive Care Unit," *Journal of Music Therapy* 37, no. 4 (2000): 250–68.
17. C. H. Hannaford, *Smart Moves: Why Learning Is Not All in Your Head* (Alexandria, VA: Great Ocean Publishers, 1995), 107.
18. D. T. McDonald and G. M. Simons, *Musical Growth and Development Birth through Six* (New York: Schirmer Books, 1989), 42.
19. See note 5 above.
20. L. S. Renegar, "Using Predictable Songs in Beginning Reading Activities," *Reading Horizons* 31, no. 1 (1990): 35–38.
21. P. Schiller, *Start Smart! Building Brain Power in the Early Years* (Beltsville, MD: Gryphon House, Inc., 1999), 55.
22. M. Szabo, "Children's Inaccurate Singing: Selected Contributing Factors," *General Music Today* 14, no. 3 (2001): 4.
23. G. Kolb, "Read with a Beat: Developing Literacy through Music and Song," *The Reading Teacher* 50, no. 1 (1996): 76–79
24. Ibid.
25. D. Register, "The Effects of an Early Intervention Music Curriculum on Prereading/Writing," *Journal of Music Therapy* 38, no. 3 (2001): 239–48; J. Standley and J. Hughes, "Documenting Developmentally Appropriate Objectives and Benefits of a Music Therapy Program for Early Intervention: A Behavior Analysis," *Music Therapy Perspectives* 14, no. 2 (1996): 87–94.
26. D. T. McDonald and G. M. Simons, *Musical Growth and Development Birth through Six* (New York: Schirmer Books, 1989), 48.
27. P. Weikart, *Movement Plus Music: Activities for Children Ages 3 to 7* (Yipsilanti, MI: High/Scope Press, 1985).
28. See note 26 above.
29. L. Kleiner and D. Devine, *Babies Make Music* (Redondo Beach, CA: Music Rhapsody, 1996).
30. S. J. Lamb, and A. H. Gregory, "The Relationship Between Music and Reading in Beginning Readers," *Educational Psychology* 13 (1993): 19–26.
31. U. Frith, "Beneath the Surface of Developmental Dyslexia," in *Surface Dyslexia*, ed. K. E. Patterson and others (Hove, UK: Lawrence, Erlbaum Associates Ltd., 1985), 301–30.
32. See note 22 above.
33. See note 29 above.
34. H. K. Yopp, "Developing Phonemic Awareness in Young Children," *The Reading Teacher* 45 (1992): 696–703.
35. R. D. Friedberg, "Allegorical Lives: Children and Their Imaginary Companions," *Child Study Journal* 25, no. 1 (1995): 1–21.

Index

A

Action rhymes, 202
Activities
    encouraging baby's communication with, 18–9
    musical, 202–5
    pre-writing, 154–5
    See also Games; Play
Acute otis media, 47–8
Adams, Marilyn Jager, 133–4
Adopted children. *See* International adoption
Aichele, Genevieve, 209
Alexander Graham Bell Association for the Deaf and Hard of Hearing (AG Bell), 228
Alphabet
    ideas for learning the letters of, 137–9
    phonetic song on, 213–4
American Academy of Pediatric Dentistry, 55
American Academy of Pediatrics (AAP), 41, 50
American Council on the Teaching of Foreign Languages, 228
American Sign Language (ASL), 138–9
American Speech-Language-Hearing Association (ASHA), 50, 73, 228
Art projects, 120
Associations, 228–30
Attention deficit hyperactivity disorder (ADHD), 52
Auditory brainstorm response (ABR), 50
Auditory processing problems, 52–3

B

Babbling, 82, 83, 105
Babies
    bilingualism and, 171
    Child-Directed Speech used with, 10–2
    communicative acts by, 13–6
    gestures and, 16–7, 157
    hearing screening for, 50–1
    language development in, 68–9
    music and, 200–2
    oral motor development of, 56–8
    providing language stimulation for, 99–112
    sign language used by, 161–2
    stimulating communicative attempts in, 18–9
    voice discovery in, 107–9
    See also Eleven to twelve months old; Five to six months old; Newborns; Nine to ten months old; Seven to eight months old; Three to four months old
Babies Make Music, 102–3
Baby talk, 9, 12
Background knowledge, 132
Behavior regulation, 13–4
Bilingualism
    age at learning second language for, 171–2
    benefits of learning, 169–70
    international adoption and, 186–7, 189
    intervention for speech/language delays and, 196–7
    introducing a second language for, 174–5
    learning English as a Second Language and, 191–5
    providing rich experiences for, 175–8
    resources on, 232, 234
    sign language and, 163
    simultaneous, 172–3
    successive, 173
Birth order, 32–3
Bite reflex, 57
Body parts, 101–2, 113
Boys vs. girls, 31–2
Brain growth, 99–100
Breastfeeding, 49, 59

C

Cause and effect, 119
Centers for Disease Control and Prevention (CDC), 50
Central lisp, 61, 221
Chewing, 57
Child development, 68
Childcare, 36–41
Child-Directed Speech (CDS), 10–2, 42, 100
Cluster reduction/simplification, 64

Color concepts, 119, 216
Computers, 44–6
Conjunctions, 123–5
Consonant clusters, 28–30, 89, 92, 93–4, 216
Consonant harmony, 63
Consonant-like sounds, 77, 78, 79, 87
Context-sensitive voicing, 62
Contrasting concepts, 107
Conventional gestures, 17
Conversational skills
　in five- to six-years-olds, 94, 126
　in four- to five-year-olds, 92
　in six- to seven-year-olds, 95
Cooing, 76, 77
Copulas, 216
Council for Exceptional Children (CEC) and the Division for Learning Disabilities (DLD), 228
Crossover activities, 102, 203, 215
Crying, 5, 76
Culture and language, 195–6

D

Dancing, 202
Daniels, Marilyn, 167
Daycare centers, 36–9, 48
Deictic gestures, 16–7
Developmental delays, 71–2, 180–1
Dialects, 40
Disfluent speech, 65–7
Disordered phonology, 61–2
Dramatic play, 209–10
Dunn, Opal, 175
Dyslexia, 152

E

Ear infections, 47–9, 54–5
Education
　English as a Second Language, 191–5
　international adoption and, 190–1
Educational Resources Information Center (ERIC) Clearinghouse on Disabilities and Gifted Education, 228
Eleven to twelve months old
　communicative expression at, 81–2
　comprehension at, 82
　enhancing language skills at, 110–2
　warning signs at, 82
Emotion words, 226
English as a Second Language (ESL), 190, 191–5
Evan B. Donaldson Adoption Institute, 187, 229

Expansion, 25
Expressive language, 6
Expressive style of learning, 86
Extension, 26
Eye contact, 21, 195
Eye gaze, 13

F

Facial expressions, 101
Fears, 43–4
Fernando, Carmen, 59
Fifteen to eighteen months old
　communicative expression at, 84–5
　comprehension at, 85
　enhancing language skills at, 114–6
　warning signs at, 85
Final consonant deletion, 62
Finger games, 104, 105–6
First grade goals for reading, 150
First words, 82, 111–2
Five to six months old
　comprehension at, 79
　enhancing language skills at, 103–5
　vocal expressions at, 78
　warning signs at, 79
Five to six years old
　communicative expression at, 93–4
　comprehension at, 94
　enhancing language skills at, 126–7
　warning signs at, 95
Four to five years old
　communicative expression at, 92
　comprehension at, 93
　enhancing language skills at, 123–5
　warning signs at, 93
Fronting, 63, 90–1, 222–3

G

Games
　for learning sounds, 119
　memory, 123–4
　rhyming, 122
　sound awareness, 140–2
　word, 124, 127, 142
　See also Activities; Play
Garcia, Joseph, 160, 166
Gender differences, 31–2
Genetic factors, 65–6, 69
Gestures
　baby, 13, 16–7, 80, 81, 157
　learning words and, 110–1
　See also Sign language
Girls vs. boys, 31–2

Giving (gesture), 16
Glennen, Sharon, 182
Gliding, 64
Grammar
  bilingualism and, 173
  correcting, 121–2
  five-year-olds and, 126
  television and, 42
  three-year-olds and, 91

H

Hall, Susan L., 133, 133–4
Health Resources and Services
  Administration (HRSA), 50
Hearing
  ear infections and loss of, 48
  monitoring baby's, 102
Hearing impairment, 49–52
Heller, Lora, 205
Hoarseness, 64
Holiday vocabulary, 223
Home-based childcare, 39–40
Humor, 125

I

Imaginary friends, 208–9
Imaginary play, 90, 115, 121, 207–10
Indirect requests, 96
Individuals with Disabilities Education
  Act (IDEA), 73
Infants. *See* Babies
Instruments, musical, 204
Insurance companies, 73
International adoption
  developmental delays and, 180–1
  exposure to birth culture/language
    and, 187–90
  facilitating communication with
    adopted child after, 185–7
  language development and, 181–5
  older child not speaking adopted
    language and, 190–1
  orphanages and, 180
  resources on, 232, 234
  sign language and, 163, 164
Inter-National Adoption Alliance, 187, 229
International Dyslexia Association, 229
Intersection of gaze, 21
Invented spellings, 153–4

J

Joint attention, 14

Joint Council on International Children's
  Services, 229

K

Kindergarten goals for reading, 149–50
King, Jan, 187, 190
Kinship terms, 125
Kleiner, Lynn, 206

L

Labeling, 110, 113
Language
  components of, 5–6
  cultural differences and, 195–6
Language delays
  developmental delays and, 71–2
  international adoption and, 184–5
  intervention for, 70–1, 72–3, 128, 196–7
  percent of children with, 67–8
  reasons for, 69–70
  statistics on, 7
  warning signs of, 70
Language development
  at 3–4 months old, 77–8
  at 5–6 months old, 78–9
  at 7–8 months old, 79, 79–80
  at 9–10 months old, 80–1
  at 11–12 months old, 81–3
  at 13–14 months old, 83–4
  at 15–18 months old, 84–5
  at 19–24 months old, 86–8
  in 2- to 3-year-olds, 88–90
  in 3- to 4-year-olds, 90–2
  in 4- to 5-year-olds, 92–3
  in 5- to 6-year-olds, 93–5
  in 6- to 7-year-olds, 95–7
  international adoption and, 181–5
  milestones in, 75
  in newborns, 76–7
  perceptual-cognitive skills and, 68–9
  verbal techniques to help, 24–6
Lateral lisp, 61
Learning disabilities, 72
Learning Disabilities Association of
  America (LDA), 229
Learning First Alliance, 149
Lesser, Debbie, 163, 166–7
Letters, 121
  See also Alphabet
Libraries, 114
Limericks, 214–5
Linguistic mapping, 22, 35
Lisps, 60–1, 221–2

Index   259

Literacy
  English as a Second Language and, 195
  language delays and, 72–3
  music and, 199
  resources on, 231–2
  See also Pre-literacy skills; Reading
Little Language Songs for Little Ones (Dyer), 213

M

Make-believe friends, 208–9
Manners vocabulary, 223–4
Masters, M. Gay, 182
Meal vocabulary, 224
Memory games, 123–4
Memory skills, 119
Moats, Louisa C., 133–4
Modeling, 21–2
Movement and music, 201–3
Multilingualism. *See* Bilingualism
Multiple births, 33–4
Music
  activities with, 202–5
  babies and, 102–3, 200–2
  benefits of, 199
  incorporating into child's life, 199–200
  movement and, 201–3
  reading readiness and, 205–7
  resources on, 231
  sign language and, 163–4
  See also Singing; Song(s)
Music lessons, 200
Musical instruments, 204

N

National Academy of Sciences, 147, 154
National Adoption Center, 229
National Adoption Information Clearinghouse, 229
National Association for Family Child Care (NAFCC), 39, 230
National Association for the Education of Young Children (NAEYC), 37, 46, 139, 230
National Association of the Deaf (NAD), 230
National Information Center for Children and Youth with Disabilities (NICHCY), 73, 230
National Institutes of Health (NIH), 50
National Institute of Literacy, 147
National Institute on Deafness and Other Communication Disorders (NIDCD), 50, 230
National Reading Panel, 148
National Research Council, 147
National Resource Center for Special Needs Adoption, 230
Newborns
  comprehension by, 77
  providing verbal stimulation for, 99–100
  vocal expressions by, 76
  warning signs for, 77
  See also Babies
Nine to ten months old
  comprehension at, 81
  enhancing language skills at, 106–9
  vocal expressions at, 80–1
  warning signs at, 81
Nineteen to twenty-four months old
  communicative expressions at, 86–7
  comprehension at, 87–8
  enhancing language skills at, 116–8
  warning signs at, 88
Number concepts, 219

O

On-line resources, 233–4
Open-ended questions, 26
Oral motor development, 56–8
Organizations, 228–30
Otis media with effusion (OME), 47–9
Otoacoustic emissions (OAE), 50

P

Pacifiers, 49, 54–5
Painting, 117
Parallel talk, 24–5
Parentese. *See* Child-Directed Speech (CDS)
Parents
  bilingual experiences provided by, 175–8
  communication encouraged by, 14–5, 18–9, 20–4
  encouraging child's language development, 24–6
  facilitative vs. directive styles used by, 14
  incorporating music into child's life, 199–200
  influence on child's language development, 34–6
  as a language model, 6–10
  role in pre-literacy skills, 131–3, 134–7, 148–9
  television viewing and, 43
Pets, song on, 226–7
Phonemes, international adoption and, 183

Phonemic awareness, 147
Phonetic spelling, 142
Phonics, 147–8
Phonological awareness, 141–3
Phonological processes, 61–4, 90–1, 92
Pitch discrimination, 206
Play
    childcare centers and, 38–9
    creating and constructing things, 121
    enhancing language skills with, 116–7
    finger play, 104
    imaginary, 90, 115, 121, 207–10
    modeling words and, 114
    social games, 113, 115
    See also Activities; Games
Play dough, 116, 120
Pneumoccocal conjugate vaccine (PCV), 49
Pointing (gesture), 16
Post-institutional response, 181
Pragmatics, 95
Pre-literacy skills
    alphabet awareness, 137–9
    bilingualism and, 170
    learning sight words, 144–6
    music and, 205–7
    print awareness, 134–7
    reading and, 131–3
    resources on, 233
    sound awareness, 139–43
    sounding out unfamiliar words, 143–4
    writing activities, 153–5
    See also Literacy; Reading
Premature babies, 69
Pressure equalizing (PE) tubes, 48
Preston, Sarah, 163
Pretend play, 90, 115, 121, 207–10
Prevnar, 49
Print awareness, 134–7
Prompting, 22
Proto-conversations, 101, 103
Proto-words, 82
Puppets, 107, 208
Puzzles, 118–9

Q

Questions
    games with, 123
    open ended, 26
    three-year-olds and, 121

R

Reaching (gesture), 16
Reading
    at 5–6 months old, 104–5
    at 7–8 months old, 106
    at 9–10 months old, 107, 109
    at 11–12 months old, 112
    at 13–14 months old, 113–4
    at 15–18 months old, 116
    at 19–24 months old, 118
    for 2- to 3-year-olds, 120
    for 3- to 4-year-olds, 123
    for 4- to 5-year-olds, 125
    for 5- to 6-year-olds, 127
    for 6- to 7-year-olds, 128–9
    background knowledge acquired with, 132
    bilingualism and, 177
    child participation with, 132–3
    enhancing comprehension and, 148–9
    first grade goals for, 150
    illustrations and, 133
    kindergarten goals for, 149–50
    parental support and, 131
    preverbal communication and, 15–6
    retelling stories after, 133
    second grade goals for, 151
    tips for successful early attempts at, 146–7
    whole language vs. phonics method of teaching, 147–8
    writing vs., 153
    to your baby, 103
    See also Literacy; Pre-literacy skills
Reading problems, 152
Recasting, 25–6
Receptive language, 6
Redundancy, 11–2
Reduplication, 62
Referential style of learning, 86, 117–8
Representational gestures, 16, 17
Rhymes
    action, 202
    games with, 122
    personalized, 202
    pre-literacy skills and, 127, 141, 142–3
    songs with, 213, 217–8
Rhythm sticks, 205
Rosemond, John, 121
R sound, 218–9

S

Scaffolding, 23
Schooling. *See* Education
Scribbling, 153
Second grade goals for reading, 151

Index   *261*

Second language. *See* Bilingualism
Secondhand smoke, 48–9
Self-talk, 24
Semantics, 95
Sentence structure, 128
Service words, 144
Seven to eight months old
　comprehension at, 79–80
　enhancing language skills at, 105–6
　vocal expressions at, 79
　warning signs at, 80
Shapes, 216–7
Showing (gesture), 16
Sight words, 144–6
Sign language
　advantages of, 157–60
　international adoption and, 182, 186
　learning, 160–5
　resources on, 232, 233
　transition to speaking from, 165–7
　using American Sign Language (ASL), 160
Simultaneous bilingualism, 172–3
Singing
　to baby, 100, 106, 201
　libraries and, 114
　signing and, 164
　See also Music, Song(s)
Sippy cups, 55–6
Six to seven years old
　communicative expression at, 95–6
　comprehension at, 96
　enhancing language skills at, 128–9
　warning signs at, 97
Slang, 96
Smoking, 48–9
Social games, 105, 113, 115
Social skills, computers and, 46
Song(s)
　colors, 216
　creating, 126–7
　days of the week, 220
　emotions, 226
　enhancing pre-literacy with, 206–7
　holiday vocabulary, 223
　on imaginary places, 217–8
　interactive motion, 225–6
　limerick, 214–5
　manners, 223–4
　meal vocabulary, 224
　number concepts, 219
　personalized, 202
　pets, 226–7
　phonetic alphabet, 213–4
　seasons, 220–1
　shapes, 216–7
　simple pleasures, 227
　for treatment of lisp, 221–2
　trip to the fair, 224–5
　undersea adventure, 215–6
　using *r* sound, 218–9
　for velar fronting, 222–3
　See also Music; Singing
Sounds
　at 5–6 months old, 103–4
　at 7–8 months old, 105–6
　games for learning, 119
　learning, 26–30, 119
　modeling words and, 119
　phonemic awareness and, 139–41
　phonological awareness and, 141–3
Specific Language Impairment (SLI), 69
Speech
　bilingual testing and intervention for delays in, 196–7
　language vs., 5–6
　modeling sentences for child for, 118
　transition from sign language to, 165–6
Speech-language pathologist
　for bilingual child, 196–7
　lisps and, 61
　seeking, 73–4
　speech/language evaluation by, 72
　stuttering and, 67
Speech problems
　four types of, 60
　lisps, 60–1
　phonological processes, 61–4
　stuttering, 65–7
　vocal abuse, 64–5
Speech sounds. *See* Sounds
Speech therapy, 190
Spelling, 142, 153–4
Stopping, 63, 92
Stories, creating, 126–7
Storytelling, 134–5
Stuttering, 65–7
Stuttering Foundation of America, 230
Surgery, 59–60
Symbolic gestures, 17
Symbolic play, 90
　See also Imaginary play

T

Talking. *See* Speech
Television, 41–4

262　　　　　*Index*

Thirteen to fourteen months old
    communicative expression at, 83
    comprehension at, 83–4
    enhancing language skills at, 112–4
    warning signs at, 84
Three to four months old
    comprehension at, 78
    enhancing language skills at, 101–3
    vocal expression at, 77
    warning signs at, 78
Three to four years old
    communicative expression at, 90–1
    comprehension at, 91
    enhancing language skills at, 120–3
    warning signs at, 91–2
Time concepts, 220–1
Time-delay prompts, 22
Tongue-tie, 58–60
Towson University, 182
Toys, 18–9, 116
Trilingualism, 178–9
Twins, 33–4
Two to three years old
    communicative expression at, 88–9
    comprehension at, 89–90
    enhancing language skills at, 118–20
    warning signs at, 90
Tympanometry, 48

U

University of California at Davis, 158

V

Velar fronting, 222–3
Verbal modeling, 21–2
Verbal prompts, 22
Vocabulary
    at 13–14 months old, 83
    at 15–18 months old, 84
    at 19–24 months old, 86
    of 2- to 3-year-olds, 88
    of 3- to 4-year-olds, 90
    of 4- to 5-year-olds, 92, 93
    emotion, 226
    first words, 82, 111–2
    holiday, 223
    kinship terms, 125
    learning, 110–2, 117–8
    manner, 223–4
    meal, 224
    television and, 42
    time concepts, 220–1
    word comprehension, 80, 83, 85, 91, 94

See also Words
Vocal abuse, 64–5
Vocalizations, 13
Vowel-like sounds, 77, 78

W

Warner, Penny, 38
Water play, 115
Weak syllable deletion, 63
Weinberger, Norman, 199
Whole language method, 147
Wolf Trap Institute, 209–10
Word final-devoicing, 62
Word games, 124, 127, 142
Words
    categorization of, 85
    with multiple meanings, 128
    sight, 144–6
    sounding out familiar, 143–4
    See also Vocabulary
Workbooks, 139
Writing skills, 153–5

Also from Meadowbrook Press

365 Baby Care Tips
If babies came with an owner's manual, *365 Baby Care Tips* would be it. Packed full of the information new parents need to know—from teething, diapers, and feeding to discipline, safety, and staying connected as a couple.

365 Toddler Tips
This book gives parents of toddlers 365 ways to meet everyday challenges. Routines such as "Monster Check" and "Boo-Boo Bunny" are sure to become classics in your home. Along with Warner's help and guidance, you'll also find anecdotes from other parents of toddlers.

Busy Books
The Toddler's Busy Book, *The Preschooler's Busy Book*, *The Children's Busy Book*, and *The Arts and Crafts Busy Book* each contain 365 activities (one for every day of the year) children can do using items found around the home. The books offer parents and caregivers fun ideas that stimulate a child's natural curiosity and creativity and channel a child's energy.

Practical Parenting Tips
This best-selling collection of helpful hints for parents of babies and small children contains 1,500 parent-tested tips for dealing with everything from diaper rash, nighttime crying, and toilet training to temper tantrums and traveling with tots. Parents will save time, trouble, and money.

Discipline without Shouting or Spanking
The most practical guide to discipline available, this newly revised book provides proven methods for handling the 30 most common forms of childhood misbehavior, from temper tantrums to sibling rivalry.

We offer many more titles written to delight, inform, and entertain. To order books with a credit card or browse our full selection of titles, visit our website at:

www.meadowbrookpress.com

or call toll-free to place an order, request a free catalog, or ask a question:

1-800-338-2232

Meadowbrook Press • 5451 Smetana Drive • Minnetonka, MN • 55343